TEXT BOOK OF PRODUCT DEVELOPMENT AND TECHNOLOGY TRANSFER

[According to latest syllabus of M. Pharm of Pharmacy Council of India]

Dr. Manoj Kumar Katual

Head & Associate Professor in Pharmacy

Guru Kashi University

Bhatinda (Punjab)

Dr. Rajeev Kumar

M. Pharm. (Pharmaceutics), Ph.D.

Assistant Professor

Institute of Pharmacy,

V. B. S. Purvanchal University,

Jaunpur (Uttar Pradesh)

Dr. Debashis Purohit

M. Pharm (Industrial Pharmacy), Ph.D.

School of Health and Allied Sciences,

Career Point University,

Kota (Rajasthan)

Dr. Anuj Singhai

Professor

Department of Pharmacy,

Shri Krishna University,

Chattarpur (Madhya Pradesh)

Priya Diwedi

Assistant professor

Rajiv Gandhi institute of technology,

AKS University,

Satna (Madhya Pradesh)

NOTION PRESS

1

TEXT BOOK OF
PRODUCT DEVELOPMENT AND TECHNOLOGY TRANSFER

@Copyright Reserved with Publisher and Authors

All rights reserved. Neither this book nor any part may be reproduced or transmitted in any form or by any mean.

First Edition 2024

Published by:

NOTION PRESS

Publisher and distributor

Head office: Notion press Media Pvt. Ltd.

7, Red cross Road,

Egmore, Chennai,Tamil Nadu 60008

Website: www.notionpress.com

TEXT BOOK OF PRODUCT DEVELOPMENT AND TECHNOLOGY TRANSFER

NOTION PRESS

PREFACE

The authors feel great pleasure in presenting the first edition of the book **"Text Book of Product Development and Technology Transfer"** for graduate and post graduate students. The present book on **Text Book of Product Development and Technology Transfer** has been written according to the syllabus of M. Pharm of Pharmacy Council of India and covers full course of the subject.

THE SALIENT FEATURES OF THE BOOK ARE:-

- *Easy to understand style of writing* which makes the book a self-study material.

- *Each new concept has been introduced through day-today problem of interest* to the students which makes the subject matter interesting.

- *The language of the book, on the whole, is lucid and easy to understand.*

- Wherever needed *neatly labeled figures have been drawn.*

The authors hope that the students, teachers and other readers will find the book interesting and to the point covering the course. We hope that the students will receive the book warmly.

I express a sincere thank you to the Management of Dadasaheb Balpande College of Pharmacy, Gupta College of Technological Sciences, Charak School of Pharmacy, School of Health and Medical Sciences, Department of Pharmaceutical Technology, Adamas University and Hooghly B. C. Roy Institute for their support during the writing of this book.

Every effort is made to keep the book error free. The author will gratefully acknowledge the suggestions to improve the book to make it more useful.

Wishing our readers success in examination and life ahead. The authors feel that their efforts will be fully rewarded if the book serves the purpose for which it is written.

TEXT BOOK OF PRODUCT DEVELOPMENT AND TECHNOLOGY TRANSFER

CONTENT

- Issues facing modern drug packaging
- Selection of Pharmaceutical packaging materials
- Evaluation of Pharmaceutical packaging materials.
- Quality control test of Containers
- Quality control test of closures
- Quality control test of secondary packing materials.

- Development of technology by R & D
- Technology transfer from R & D to production
- Optimization of Technology transfer
- Production of Technology transfer
- Qualitative and quantitative technology models.
- Documentation in technology transfer
  - Development report
  - technology transfer plan and Exhibit

CHAPTER – 1

PRINCIPLES OF DRUG DISCOVERY AND DEVELOPMENT

INTRODUCTION:

Drug Discovery:

Drug discovery is a complex and multifaceted process that involves the identification, development, and optimization of novel therapeutic compounds to address unmet medical needs and improve patient outcomes. It encompasses a wide range of scientific disciplines, technologies, and methodologies aimed at discovering new drugs and advancing them through preclinical and clinical development stages. Here's a detailed overview of the drug discovery process:

1. Target Identification and Validation:

1. **Disease Understanding:** Drug discovery begins with a deep understanding of the pathophysiology of the disease or condition targeted for treatment. This involves studying disease mechanisms, identifying molecular targets, and exploring underlying biological pathways.

2. **Target Selection**: Potential molecular targets, such as proteins, enzymes, receptors, or nucleic acids, that play a key role in disease pathogenesis are identified and validated as viable candidates for therapeutic intervention.

3. **Genomics and Proteomics**: Advances in genomics and proteomics enable the identification of disease-related genes, proteins, and biomarkers, providing valuable insights into potential drug targets and personalized medicine approaches.

2. Hit Generation and Lead Optimization:

1. **High-Throughput Screening (HTS)**: Large compound libraries are screened using automated assays and robotics to identify "hits" – compounds that show activity against the target of interest. HTS allows for the rapid testing of thousands to millions of compounds.

2. **Hit-to-Lead Optimization**: Promising hits are further optimized through medicinal chemistry, structure-activity relationship (SAR) studies, and computational modeling to enhance potency, selectivity, pharmacokinetic properties, and safety profiles.

3. **Chemical Libraries and Design**: Chemists design and synthesize diverse chemical libraries or use computational methods, such as virtual screening and molecular docking, to design novel compounds with optimized drug-like properties.

3. Preclinical Development:

1. **In vitro Studies**: Lead compounds undergo extensive in vitro testing to assess their pharmacological activity, mechanism of action, toxicity, and metabolic stability using cell-based assays and biochemical techniques.

2. **In vivo Studies**: Promising lead candidates are evaluated in animal models to assess their efficacy, pharmacokinetics, safety, and potential adverse effects in living organisms.

3. **ADME-Tox Profiling**: Lead compounds undergo absorption, distribution, metabolism, excretion, and toxicity (ADME-Tox) profiling to predict their pharmacokinetic properties, bioavailability, and potential safety concerns in humans.

4. Clinical Development:

1. **Phase I Clinical Trials**: Initial clinical trials in healthy volunteers assess the safety, tolerability, pharmacokinetics, and pharmacodynamics of the investigational drug candidate.

2. **Phase II Clinical Trials**: Efficacy and safety are evaluated in small patient populations to determine the optimal dose, treatment regimen, and preliminary evidence of therapeutic efficacy.

3. **Phase III Clinical Trials**: Large-scale trials are conducted in diverse patient populations to confirm safety, efficacy, and optimal dosing, providing pivotal data for regulatory approval.

5. Regulatory Approval and Market Access:

1. **New Drug Application (NDA)**: The pharmaceutical company submits a comprehensive NDA to regulatory agencies, such as the FDA, providing data from preclinical and clinical studies to support the safety and efficacy of the drug candidate.

2. **Regulatory Review**: Regulatory agencies review the NDA submission to assess the quality, safety, and efficacy of the drug candidate, determining whether it meets the criteria for marketing approval.

3. **Post-Marketing Surveillance**: Approved drugs undergo post-marketing surveillance to monitor for adverse events, safety concerns, and long-term efficacy in real-world clinical settings.

Drug Development:

Drug development is a comprehensive and systematic process that follows drug discovery, focusing on advancing promising drug candidates through preclinical and clinical development stages toward regulatory approval and commercialization. It involves rigorous testing, evaluation, and optimization of drug candidates to ensure safety, efficacy, and quality before they can be marketed and made available to patients. Here's a detailed overview of the drug development process:

1. Preclinical Development:

1. **Safety Assessment**: Preclinical studies assess the safety profile of drug candidates using in vitro and in vivo models to evaluate potential toxicities, including acute, subchronic, and chronic toxicity, genotoxicity, carcinogenicity, and reproductive toxicity.

2. **Pharmacokinetics and Pharmacodynamics (PK/PD):** Preclinical studies investigate the absorption, distribution, metabolism, and excretion (ADME) of drug candidates, as well as their pharmacological effects and mechanisms of action in animal models.

3. **Dose Selection**: Based on preclinical data, the appropriate dose range and administration route are determined for subsequent clinical trials, considering factors such as efficacy, safety, and target engagement.

2. Clinical Development:

1. **Phase I Clinical Trials**: Phase I trials evaluate the safety, tolerability, pharmacokinetics, and pharmacodynamics of the investigational drug candidate in healthy volunteers to establish the maximum tolerated dose (MTD) and initial safety profile.

2. **Phase II Clinical Trials**: Phase II trials assess the preliminary efficacy, dose-response relationship, and safety of the drug candidate in small patient populations with the target disease or condition, informing dose selection and study design for subsequent trials.

3. **Phase III Clinical Trials**: Phase III trials are large-scale, randomized, controlled studies conducted in diverse patient populations to confirm the efficacy, safety, and optimal dosing of the drug candidate, providing pivotal data for regulatory approval.

3. Regulatory Submission:

1. **New Drug Application (NDA):** The pharmaceutical company submits a comprehensive NDA to regulatory agencies, such as the US Food and Drug Administration (FDA), including data from preclinical and clinical studies to support the safety and efficacy of the drug candidate.

2. **Regulatory Review**: Regulatory agencies review the NDA submission to assess the quality, safety, and efficacy of the drug candidate, determining whether it meets the criteria for marketing approval based on scientific evidence and regulatory standards.

3. **Regulatory Approval**: If the NDA is approved, regulatory agencies grant marketing authorization for the drug candidate, allowing it to be marketed and sold for the approved indications, dosages, and patient populations.

4. Post-Marketing Surveillance:

1. **Phase IV Clinical Trials**: Post-marketing studies, also known as Phase IV trials, continue to evaluate the safety, efficacy, and long-term effects of the approved drug candidate in real-world clinical settings, monitoring for adverse events and rare side effects.

2. **Pharmacovigilance**: Pharmaceutical companies and regulatory agencies conduct ongoing pharmacovigilance activities to monitor the safety profile of the marketed drug, including adverse event reporting, risk assessment, and risk management strategies.

Principles and Considerations:

In drug discovery and development, various principles and considerations guide the process to ensure the successful identification, development, and commercialization of safe and effective therapeutics. These principles encompass scientific, ethical, regulatory, and commercial aspects that are critical for advancing drug candidates from initial discovery to market approval. Here's a detailed overview of the key principles and considerations in drug discovery and development:

1. Scientific Principles:

1. **Target Identification and Validation**: Rigorous scientific research is conducted to identify and validate molecular targets involved in disease pathogenesis, ensuring that drug development efforts are based on a solid understanding of the underlying biology.

2. **Mechanism of Action**: Drug candidates should be designed to interact with specific molecular targets or biological pathways implicated in the disease, with a clear understanding of their mechanism of action and therapeutic rationale.

3. **Efficacy and Safety**: Candidate compounds undergo comprehensive preclinical studies to assess their efficacy and safety profiles, ensuring that they have the desired therapeutic effects while minimizing adverse effects and toxicity.

2. Ethical Considerations:

1. **Patient Safety and Welfare**: Ethical principles dictate that patient safety and welfare are paramount throughout the drug development process, with rigorous adherence to ethical guidelines and regulatory standards for human subject research.

2. **Informed Consent**: Participants in clinical trials must provide informed consent, fully understanding the risks, benefits, and alternatives of participating in the study, and ensuring respect for individual autonomy and decision-making.

3. **Protection of Vulnerable Populations**: Special considerations are given to vulnerable populations, such as children, pregnant women, and individuals with cognitive impairments, to ensure their rights, safety, and well-being are protected in clinical research.

3. Regulatory Compliance:

1. **Regulatory Requirements**: Drug development efforts must comply with stringent regulatory requirements set forth by regulatory agencies, such as the FDA, EMA, and other health authorities, ensuring that data quality, safety, and efficacy standards are met.

2. **Good Laboratory Practice (GLP):** Preclinical studies are conducted in accordance with GLP regulations to ensure the integrity, reliability, and reproducibility of study data, providing a solid scientific foundation for advancing drug candidates into clinical trials.

3. **Good Clinical Practice (GCP)**: Clinical trials adhere to GCP guidelines to ensure the ethical conduct, safety, and integrity of human subject research, with rigorous monitoring, data collection, and reporting procedures in place.

4. Commercial Considerations:

1. **Market Demand and Unmet Needs:** Drug discovery efforts should be aligned with market demand and unmet medical needs, targeting diseases

and conditions where there is a significant clinical need and commercial opportunity.

2. **Intellectual Property Protection**: Intellectual property rights, including patents, trademarks, and proprietary know-how, are essential for protecting the innovative aspects of drug candidates and securing market exclusivity and competitive advantage.

3. **Market Access and Pricing**: Considerations for market access, reimbursement, and pricing strategies are essential for ensuring that innovative therapies are accessible and affordable to patients, healthcare providers, and payers.

5. Lifecycle Management:

1. **Continuous Innovation**: Drug development is an iterative process that involves continuous innovation, optimization, and adaptation based on evolving scientific insights, clinical data, and market dynamics throughout the product lifecycle.

2. **Post-Marketing Surveillance**: Post-marketing surveillance activities, including pharmacovigilance, risk management, and real-world evidence generation, are critical for monitoring the safety, effectiveness, and long-term outcomes of marketed drugs.

3. **Lifecycle Extension Strategies**: Companies may employ lifecycle extension strategies, such as line extensions, reformulations, or indications expansions, to maximize the commercial value and longevity of approved drug products.

CLINICAL RESEARCH PROCESS IN DRUG DISCOVERY AND DEVELOPMENT

The clinical research process is a crucial stage in drug discovery and development, where the safety and efficacy of a potential drug candidate are evaluated in human subjects. Let's delve into the details:

Clinical Research Process:

1. **Phase 0 Trials (Exploratory Phase):**

   a. These are exploratory trials that involve administering very small doses of the investigational drug to a small number of subjects, typically healthy volunteers.

   b. The primary aim is to gather preliminary data on the drug's pharmacokinetics (how the drug moves in the body) and pharmacodynamics (how the drug affects the body).

2. **Phase I Trials (Safety Phase):**

   a. Phase I trials are conducted in a small group of healthy volunteers or individuals with the target disease.

   b. The primary goals are to assess the safety, tolerability, pharmacokinetics, and pharmacodynamics of the drug.

   c. These trials typically involve escalating doses of the drug to determine the maximum tolerated dose (MTD) and any dose-limiting toxicities.

3. **Phase II Trials (Efficacy and Safety Phase):**

   a. Phase II trials enroll a larger group of patients with the target disease.

   b. The primary objectives are to further evaluate the safety and efficacy of the drug and to determine the optimal dosage regimen.

   c. These trials may also provide preliminary data on the drug's effectiveness compared to standard treatments or placebo.

4. **Phase III Trials (Confirmatory Phase):**

   a. Phase III trials are large-scale, randomized, controlled trials that enroll hundreds to thousands of patients.

   b. The primary goal is to confirm the efficacy and safety of the drug in a diverse patient population.

c. These trials provide the most robust evidence of a drug's effectiveness and are often used to support regulatory approval.

5. Phase IV Trials (Post-Marketing Surveillance):

a. Phase IV trials are conducted after regulatory approval and involve monitoring the drug's safety and effectiveness in real-world clinical settings.

b. These trials may identify rare or long-term adverse effects that were not detected during earlier phases of development.

Key Considerations:

1. **Informed Consent**: Participants in clinical trials must provide informed consent after receiving detailed information about the study objectives, procedures, potential risks, and benefits.

2. **Ethical Oversight**: Clinical trials must adhere to ethical principles outlined in guidelines such as the Declaration of Helsinki and be approved by Institutional Review Boards (IRBs) or Ethics Committees.

3. **Regulatory Compliance**: Clinical trials are subject to regulatory oversight by government agencies such as the FDA (in the United States) or the EMA (in Europe). Trials must comply with regulatory requirements for study conduct, data integrity, and participant safety.

4. **Data Collection and Analysis**: Rigorous data collection and analysis are essential to ensure the reliability and validity of trial results. This includes standardized endpoints, statistical analysis plans, and independent data monitoring committees.

5. **Patient Recruitment and Retention**: Recruiting and retaining participants in clinical trials can be challenging. Strategies to enhance recruitment and retention include effective communication, community engagement, and patient support services.

6. **Interdisciplinary Collaboration**: Clinical trials require collaboration among researchers, clinicians, regulatory agencies, sponsors, and study

participants to ensure the successful conduct of the trial and the integrity of the data.

DEVELOPMENT AND INFORMATIONAL CONTENT FOR INVESTIGATIONAL NEW DRUGS APPLICATION (IND), NEW DRUG APPLICATION (NDA)

Investigational New Drug (IND) Application:

1. **Purpose:**
   a. An IND application is submitted to regulatory agencies such as the FDA in the United States or the EMA in Europe.
   b. It allows the sponsor (typically a pharmaceutical company or research institution) to initiate clinical trials of an investigational drug in humans.

2. **Contents of the IND Application:**
   a. **Preclinical Data**: Detailed information on the results of preclinical studies, including pharmacology, toxicology, and pharmacokinetics, conducted in laboratory and animal models.
   b. **Clinical Protocols**: Detailed protocols for proposed clinical trials, including study objectives, design, patient population, dosing regimens, and endpoints.
   c. **Investigator Information**: Qualifications and credentials of the clinical investigators who will conduct the trials.
   d. **Manufacturing Information**: Description of the manufacturing process, quality control measures, and stability data for the investigational drug.
   e. **Regulatory Commitments**: Assurance that the sponsor will comply with regulatory requirements, including reporting adverse events and maintaining data integrity.

3. **FDA Review Process:**

a. The FDA reviews the IND application to ensure that the proposed clinical trials are safe for human subjects and scientifically sound.

b. The review process typically takes 30 days, after which the sponsor can proceed with clinical trials unless the FDA requests additional information or places the IND on clinical hold.

4. Clinical Trials Under the IND:

a. Once the IND is active, the sponsor can initiate Phase I clinical trials to evaluate the safety, pharmacokinetics, and pharmacodynamics of the investigational drug.

b. Subsequent phases of clinical trials (Phase II and Phase III) can be conducted under the same IND, with ongoing reporting of safety and efficacy data to the FDA.

New Drug Application (NDA):

1. Purpose:

a. An NDA is submitted to regulatory agencies to seek approval for marketing a new drug.

b. It contains comprehensive data from preclinical and clinical studies demonstrating the safety and efficacy of the drug.

2. Contents of the NDA:

a. **Preclinical Data**: Detailed summaries of preclinical studies, including pharmacology, toxicology, and pharmacokinetics, conducted to support the safety of the drug.

b. **Clinical Data**: Comprehensive data from Phase I, II, and III clinical trials, including study results, adverse event reports, and statistical analyses.

c. **Manufacturing Information**: Detailed information on the manufacturing process, quality control measures, and stability data to ensure consistent product quality.

d. **Labeling**: Proposed labeling for the drug, including prescribing information, dosage regimens, contraindications, warnings, and precautions.

e. **Post-Marketing Commitments**: Proposed plans for post-marketing surveillance, including additional studies or monitoring to assess long-term safety and effectiveness.

3. **FDA Review Process:**

a. The FDA reviews the NDA to evaluate the safety, efficacy, and quality of the proposed drug.

b. The review process involves a thorough examination of all submitted data, including clinical trial results, manufacturing processes, and proposed labeling.

c. If the FDA determines that the benefits of the drug outweigh its risks and that the data support approval, the NDA is granted marketing authorization.

4. **Post-Approval Responsibilities:**

a. After approval, the sponsor is responsible for complying with post-marketing requirements, including continued monitoring of the drug's safety and effectiveness.

b. The FDA may require additional post-marketing studies or impose risk mitigation measures to ensure the safe use of the drug in real-world settings.

ABBREVIATED NEW DRUG APPLICATION (ANDA):

1. **Purpose:**

a. An Abbreviated New Drug Application (ANDA) is a regulatory submission to the FDA in the United States for the approval of generic drugs.

b. Unlike New Drug Applications (NDAs), which require extensive preclinical and clinical data, ANDAs rely on demonstrating bioequivalence to a reference listed drug (RLD) to obtain approval.

2. **Contents of the ANDA:**

   a. **Chemical Composition**: Detailed information on the active pharmaceutical ingredient (API) and its formulation, including manufacturing processes and specifications.

   b. **Pharmaceutical Equivalents**: Documentation showing that the generic drug product is pharmaceutically equivalent to the reference listed drug (RLD) in terms of dosage form, strength, route of administration, and labeling.

   c. **Bioequivalence Studies**: Data from bioequivalence studies demonstrating that the generic drug product achieves similar systemic exposure to the RLD, typically through comparative pharmacokinetic studies in healthy volunteers.

   d. **Stability Studies**: Evidence of the generic drug product's stability under specified storage conditions, ensuring that it remains safe and effective throughout its shelf life.

   e. **Labeling**: Proposed labeling for the generic drug product, including prescribing information, dosage regimens, warnings, precautions, and other information required by FDA regulations.

   f. **Post-Approval Commitments**: Agreements to comply with post-marketing requirements, such as ongoing monitoring of adverse events and submission of annual reports to the FDA.

3. **Bioequivalence Studies:**

   a. Bioequivalence studies are a critical component of ANDAs and involve comparing the pharmacokinetic profiles of the generic drug product and the reference listed drug (RLD).

b. These studies typically measure parameters such as maximum plasma concentration (Cmax) and area under the plasma concentration-time curve (AUC) to assess systemic exposure.

c. The FDA requires that the 90% confidence intervals for the ratio of geometric means of Cmax and AUC fall within predefined bioequivalence acceptance criteria (usually 80-125%).

4. **FDA Review Process:**

a. The FDA reviews the ANDA to ensure that the generic drug product meets all regulatory requirements for safety, efficacy, and quality.

b. The review process involves evaluating data from bioequivalence studies, chemistry, manufacturing, and controls (CMC), labeling, and other relevant information.

c. If the FDA determines that the generic drug product is bioequivalent to the RLD and meets all regulatory standards, it grants approval for marketing.

5. **Market Approval and Post-Marketing Responsibilities:**

a. Once approved, the generic drug product can be marketed and sold in the United States as a therapeutically equivalent and interchangeable alternative to the RLD.

b. The sponsor is responsible for complying with post-marketing requirements, including monitoring and reporting adverse events, updating labeling as needed, and maintaining product quality and consistency.

Supplemental New Drug Application (SNDA):

Purpose:

A Supplemental New Drug Application (SNDA) serves a critical role in the lifecycle of a pharmaceutical product by allowing manufacturers to propose changes or additions to an already approved New Drug Application (NDA). The purpose of an SNDA within the principles of drug discovery and development is multifaceted and includes the following:

1. Introduction of Changes or Additions:

1. **New Indications**: An SNDA may seek approval for new indications, dosages, or patient populations not initially included in the original NDA. This allows for the expansion of the therapeutic use of the drug based on additional clinical data or scientific evidence.

2. **Dosage Forms or Strengths**: Manufacturers may propose changes to the dosage forms (e.g., tablets, capsules, injections) or strengths of the drug to accommodate patient needs or optimize treatment regimens.

3. **Manufacturing Process Changes**: SNDA may include proposals for modifications to the manufacturing process, such as changes in equipment, facilities, or procedures, to improve efficiency, scalability, or cost-effectiveness.

2. Lifecycle Management:

1. **Patent Extension**: Introducing new indications, dosage forms, or strengths through an SNDA can extend the patent life of the drug, providing manufacturers with additional market exclusivity and revenue-generating opportunities.

2. **Market Expansion**: SNDA approvals enable manufacturers to penetrate new markets, reach different patient populations, or address unmet medical needs, thereby expanding the commercial potential of the drug.

3. Regulatory Compliance:

1. **Continued Compliance**: Manufacturers are required to submit an SNDA to regulatory authorities to ensure ongoing compliance with regulatory requirements, including safety, efficacy, and quality standards.

2. **Risk Management**: SNDA submissions may include updated risk assessments, safety data, and risk mitigation strategies to address any new safety concerns or risks identified during post-marketing surveillance.

4. Clinical Development:

1. **Clinical Studies**: SNDA submissions often include data from additional clinical studies or post-marketing surveillance activities to support the proposed changes or additions, demonstrating the safety and efficacy of the drug in the new context.

2. **Real-World Evidence**: Manufacturers may leverage real-world evidence, such as observational studies or patient registries, to provide supplementary data supporting the proposed changes or new indications.

5. Patient Access and Public Health:

1. **Improved Patient Access**: Approvals obtained through SNDA allow patients to access new treatment options, expanded indications, or alternative dosage forms, potentially improving treatment outcomes and quality of life.

2. **Public Health Impact**: SNDA approvals may have broader public health implications by addressing unmet medical needs, reducing disease burden, or providing therapeutic alternatives for specific patient populations.

Types of Changes:

Supplemental New Drug Applications (SNDAs) allow pharmaceutical companies to propose various types of changes or additions to an already approved New Drug Application (NDA). These changes are categorized into different types based on their nature and impact on the drug product. Here are the types of changes typically included in an SNDA within the principles of drug discovery and development:

1. New Indications:

1. **Expansion of Indications**: Manufacturers may seek approval for new therapeutic indications or uses of the drug that were not included in the original NDA. This could involve demonstrating the efficacy and safety

of the drug for treating additional diseases, conditions, or patient populations.

2. **Pediatric Indications**: SNDA submissions may include data from pediatric studies to support the approval of the drug for use in pediatric patients, addressing unmet medical needs in this population.

2. Dosage Form Changes:

1. **New Dosage Forms**: Manufacturers may propose the introduction of new dosage forms (e.g., tablets, capsules, injections, patches) to provide patients with alternative administration options or to improve compliance.

2. **Modified Release Formulations**: SNDA submissions may include modified-release formulations to extend the duration of drug action, enhance patient convenience, or improve therapeutic outcomes.

3. Dosage Strength Changes:

1. **Higher or Lower Strengths**: Manufacturers may seek approval for higher or lower strengths of the drug to accommodate individual patient needs, optimize dosing regimens, or address specific therapeutic requirements.

2. **Fixed-Dose Combinations**: SNDAs may include proposals for fixed-dose combinations of the drug with other active ingredients to improve treatment outcomes, simplify dosing regimens, or address combination therapy needs.

4. Manufacturing Process Changes:

1. **Process Optimization**: Manufacturers may propose modifications to the manufacturing process, such as changes in equipment, facilities, or procedures, to improve efficiency, scalability, or cost-effectiveness.

2. **Quality Control Measures**: SNDAs may include updates to quality control measures, specifications, or testing methods to ensure the consistent quality and purity of the drug product.

5. Labeling Changes:

1. **New Labeling Claims**: SNDAs may seek approval for new labeling claims, including updates to indications, dosage recommendations, contraindications, warnings, precautions, and adverse reactions based on additional clinical data or post-marketing experience.
2. **Patient Information Updates**: Manufacturers may propose revisions to patient information leaflets or package inserts to provide updated information on drug use, safety, storage, and handling to healthcare professionals and patients.

6. Stability Studies and Data:

a. Stability Updates: SNDAs may include additional stability data to support proposed changes, ensuring that the drug product remains stable and maintains its quality attributes throughout its shelf life under various storage conditions.

b. Compatibility Studies: Manufacturers may conduct compatibility studies to assess the compatibility of the drug with packaging materials, delivery devices, or other components, especially for new dosage forms or packaging configurations.

Contents of the SNDA:

The contents of a Supplemental New Drug Application (SNDA) are crucial for providing comprehensive information to regulatory agencies, such as the US Food and Drug Administration (FDA), to support proposed changes or additions to an already approved New Drug Application (NDA). The contents of an SNDA typically include the following components:

1. Cover Letter:

a. **Introduction**: A brief overview of the purpose of the SNDA submission, including a summary of the proposed changes or additions and their significance.

2. Table of Contents:

a. **Outline**: A detailed list of all sections and subsections included in the SNDA submission, providing easy navigation for regulatory reviewers.

3. Executive Summary:

a. **Summary of Changes**: A concise summary of the proposed changes or additions outlined in the SNDA submission, including their rationale and significance.

b. **Key Findings**: Highlights of the supporting data, clinical studies, and other relevant information that substantiate the proposed changes.

4. Introduction:

a. **Background**: An overview of the drug product, including its indication(s), dosage form(s), strengths, and current approved labeling.

b. **Purpose of the SNDA**: Clear statement of the objectives and goals of the SNDA submission, outlining the specific changes or additions being proposed.

5. Supporting Data and Studies:

a. **Clinical Data**: Results from clinical studies supporting the proposed changes, including efficacy and safety data, pharmacokinetic/pharmacodynamic (PK/PD) studies, and patient outcomes.

b. **Nonclinical Data**: Preclinical studies, such as pharmacology, toxicology, and pharmacokinetic studies, demonstrating the safety and efficacy of the proposed changes.

c. **Analytical Data**: Analytical data confirming the quality, purity, and stability of the drug product following the proposed changes, including chemistry, manufacturing, and controls (CMC) data.

d. **Stability Data**: Stability studies demonstrating the shelf-life and storage conditions of the drug product under the proposed changes.

e. **Comparative Data**: Comparative data comparing the proposed changes with the previously approved formulation, dosage form, or manufacturing process.

6. Manufacturing Information:

a. **Manufacturing Process Description**: Detailed description of the proposed changes to the manufacturing process, including equipment, facilities, procedures, and controls.

b. **Quality Control Measures**: Specifications, testing methods, and quality control measures ensuring the consistent quality and purity of the drug product following the proposed changes.

7. Labeling:

a. **Proposed Labeling Changes**: Drafts of proposed labeling changes, including updates to indications, dosage recommendations, warnings, precautions, adverse reactions, and patient information leaflets.

b. **Rationale for Labeling Changes**: Justification and rationale for the proposed labeling changes based on supporting data and clinical evidence.

8. Regulatory Documentation:

a. **Regulatory History**: Summary of the regulatory history of the drug product, including previous approvals, labeling changes, and post-marketing commitments.

b. **Regulatory Compliance**: Declaration of compliance with regulatory requirements and standards for the proposed changes, including Good Manufacturing Practices (GMP) and Good Clinical Practices (GCP).

9. Conclusion:

a. **Summary of Findings**: Recapitulation of the key findings and conclusions supporting the proposed changes outlined in the SNDA submission.

b. **Request for Approval**: Clear request for regulatory approval of the proposed changes or additions to the drug product.

10. Appendices:

a. Additional Data: Supplementary data, tables, figures, or supporting documents referenced in the main body of the SNDA submission.

FDA Review Process:

The FDA review process of a Supplemental New Drug Application (SNDA) is a critical step in evaluating proposed changes or additions to an already approved New Drug Application (NDA). The process involves comprehensive review by FDA regulatory reviewers to assess the safety, efficacy, quality, and regulatory compliance of the proposed changes. Here's a detailed overview of the FDA review process for an SNDA:

1. Submission and Acceptance:

1. **SNDA Submission**: The pharmaceutical company submits the SNDA to the FDA, including all required documentation and supporting data outlining the proposed changes or additions to the approved drug product.
2. **Application Review**: FDA regulatory staff review the submitted SNDA to ensure it is complete, accurate, and meets regulatory requirements for acceptance.

2. Division Assignment and Preliminary Review:

1. **Division Assignment:** The FDA assigns the SNDA to a specific review division within the Center for Drug Evaluation and Research (CDER) or the Center for Biologics Evaluation and Research (CBER) based on the therapeutic area and nature of the proposed changes.
2. **Preliminary Review**: Regulatory reviewers conduct an initial assessment of the SNDA submission to identify key issues, review the completeness of the data, and determine the scope of the review process.

3. Comprehensive Review:

1. **Clinical Review**: Clinical reviewers evaluate the efficacy and safety data submitted in support of the proposed changes, including clinical trial results, pharmacokinetic/pharmacodynamic (PK/PD) studies, and patient outcomes.

2. **Nonclinical Review**: Nonclinical reviewers assess preclinical data, including pharmacology, toxicology, and pharmacokinetic studies, to evaluate the potential risks associated with the proposed changes.

3. **Chemistry, Manufacturing, and Controls (CMC) Review**: CMC reviewers examine the manufacturing process changes, quality control measures, analytical data, and stability studies to ensure the consistent quality, purity, and stability of the drug product.

4. **Labeling Review**: Labeling reviewers assess proposed labeling changes, including updates to indications, dosing recommendations, warnings, precautions, adverse reactions, and patient information leaflets, for accuracy, clarity, and regulatory compliance.

4. Consultation and Communication:

1. **Interactions with Sponsor:** FDA regulatory reviewers may engage in ongoing communication and consultations with the pharmaceutical company to address questions, clarify issues, or request additional information as needed throughout the review process.

2. **Advisory Committees**: In some cases, the FDA may convene advisory committees, comprised of external experts, to provide independent evaluation and recommendations on specific issues related to the SNDA submission, such as safety or efficacy concerns.

5. Review Team Decision:

1. **Integrated Review**: Following a thorough evaluation of all relevant data and information, the review team prepares an integrated review document summarizing the findings, conclusions, and recommendations regarding the SNDA submission.

2. **Decision Making:** The FDA review team discusses the SNDA submission and presents their recommendations to senior management for a final decision on whether to approve or reject the proposed changes or additions to the drug product.

6. Regulatory Action:

1. **Approval or Complete Response**: Based on the review findings, the FDA issues a regulatory action letter to the pharmaceutical company, either approving the SNDA with or without conditions, or issuing a Complete Response Letter (CRL) outlining deficiencies or concerns that must be addressed before approval.
2. **Post-Approval Requirements**: If approved, the FDA may impose post-approval requirements, such as post-marketing studies, labeling updates, or risk mitigation measures, to ensure ongoing safety monitoring and regulatory compliance.

Post-Approval Responsibilities:

Following the approval of a Supplemental New Drug Application (SNDA), pharmaceutical companies have specific post-approval responsibilities outlined by regulatory agencies such as the US Food and Drug Administration (FDA). These responsibilities are crucial for ensuring ongoing compliance with regulatory requirements and maintaining the safety, efficacy, and quality of the approved drug product. Here are the post-approval responsibilities associated with an SNDA:

1. Compliance with Regulatory Commitments:

1. **Adherence to Approval Conditions**: Pharmaceutical companies must comply with any conditions or requirements outlined in the approval letter, including the implementation of post-approval studies, labeling updates, risk management strategies, or other regulatory commitments.

2. **Timely Completion of Post-Approval Studies**: Companies are responsible for conducting post-approval studies or trials as required by the FDA to address specific safety, efficacy, or risk mitigation concerns identified during the review process.

2. Labeling Updates and Reporting:

1. **Timely Labeling Revisions**: Manufacturers must promptly update the drug product labeling to reflect any approved changes resulting from the SNDA, including updates to indications, dosing recommendations, warnings, precautions, adverse reactions, and patient information leaflets.

2. **Submission of Supplemental Changes**: Manufacturers are required to submit Changes Being Effected (CBE) supplements or Prior Approval Supplements (PAS) to the FDA to notify the agency of any proposed labeling changes resulting from the SNDA approval.

3. Pharmacovigilance and Safety Monitoring:

1. **Post-Marketing Surveillance**: Pharmaceutical companies must continue to monitor the safety and efficacy of the approved drug product through post-marketing surveillance activities, including adverse event reporting, pharmacovigilance studies, and periodic safety updates.

2. **Adverse Event Reporting**: Companies are responsible for collecting, evaluating, and reporting adverse event data to regulatory agencies, healthcare professionals, and the public in accordance with pharmacovigilance requirements and timelines.

4. Manufacturing and Quality Assurance:

1. **Maintaining Manufacturing Standards**: Manufacturers must continue to adhere to Good Manufacturing Practices (GMP) and ensure the consistent quality, purity, and stability of the drug product through robust manufacturing processes, quality control measures, and ongoing monitoring.

2. **Reporting Manufacturing Changes**: Companies are required to report any significant changes to the manufacturing process, facilities, or controls to the FDA through supplements or variations to the marketing application, as per regulatory requirements.

5. Risk Management and Communication:

1. **Risk Mitigation Strategies**: Manufacturers must implement and maintain risk management strategies to minimize known and potential risks associated with the drug product, including monitoring, assessment, and mitigation of identified safety concerns.

2. **Risk Communication**: Pharmaceutical companies are responsible for communicating relevant safety information, updates, and warnings to healthcare professionals, patients, and the public through appropriate channels to ensure informed decision-making and patient safety.

6. Post-Approval Inspections and Audits:

1. **Regulatory Inspections**: Pharmaceutical companies may undergo periodic inspections and audits by regulatory agencies to assess compliance with post-approval requirements, including manufacturing standards, labeling regulations, and pharmacovigilance obligations.

2. **Corrective Actions**: Companies must address any deficiencies or non-compliance identified during regulatory inspections promptly, implementing corrective and preventive actions to mitigate risks and ensure ongoing compliance.

SCALE UP POST APPROVAL CHANGES (SUPAC) AND BULK ACTIVE CHEMICAL POST APPROVAL CHANGES (BACPAC)

Scale-Up and Post-Approval Changes (SUPAC) and Bulk Active Chemical Post-Approval Changes (BACPAC) are regulatory frameworks established to guide pharmaceutical companies in making certain changes to drug products after they have received approval. Let's explore each in detail:

Scale-Up and Post-Approval Changes (SUPAC):

Scale-Up and Post-Approval Changes (SUPAC) is a regulatory framework established by regulatory agencies, such as the US Food and Drug Administration (FDA), to guide pharmaceutical manufacturers in managing changes to drug manufacturing processes and formulations after a drug has been approved for marketing. Let's delve into SUPAC in detail:

1. Purpose of SUPAC:

1. **Ensuring Consistency**: The primary goal of SUPAC is to ensure that changes made to manufacturing processes or formulations do not adversely affect the safety, efficacy, or quality of the drug product.

2. **Regulatory Compliance**: SUPAC provides guidelines for manufacturers to comply with regulatory requirements regarding post-approval changes while maintaining product quality and patient safety.

2. Types of Changes Covered:

1. **Scale-Up Changes**: These changes involve increasing production scale, such as transitioning from laboratory-scale to pilot-scale or commercial-scale manufacturing. Scale-up changes may impact factors like mixing, blending, and equipment configuration.

2. **Post-Approval Changes**: These encompass modifications to drug formulation, manufacturing processes, equipment, facilities, or labeling after regulatory approval has been obtained. Examples include changes in raw materials, manufacturing sites, or manufacturing methods.

3. SUPAC Guidelines:

1. **SUPAC for Immediate Release Solid Oral Dosage Forms**: This guidance document provides recommendations for changes to immediate-release solid oral dosage forms, such as tablets and capsules. It includes recommendations for scale-up and post-approval changes affecting formulation, manufacturing process, and specifications.

2. **SUPAC for Modified Release Solid Oral Dosage Forms**: This guidance document addresses changes to modified-release solid oral dosage forms, including extended-release tablets and capsules. It outlines considerations for changes to formulation, manufacturing process, and specifications to maintain product performance and safety.

3. **SUPAC for Sterile Products**: This guidance document focuses on changes to sterile drug products, including injectables and ophthalmic preparations. It provides recommendations for changes related to formulation, manufacturing process, container closure systems, and microbiological aspects.

4. Regulatory Considerations:

1. **Prior Approval Requirement**: Certain changes covered under SUPAC may require prior approval from regulatory agencies before implementation to ensure adequate assessment of potential risks and impacts on product quality and patient safety.

2. **Reporting Requirements**: Manufacturers are often required to submit supplements or variations to their marketing applications, such as Changes Being Effected (CBE) supplements or Prior Approval Supplements (PAS), to notify regulatory agencies of proposed changes and obtain approval.

5. Documentation and Reporting:

1. **Change Control Procedures**: Manufacturers should establish robust change control procedures to systematically document and assess proposed changes, including their rationale, potential impact on product quality, and risk mitigation measures.

2. **Submission of Documentation**: Manufacturers are responsible for preparing and submitting appropriate documentation, such as chemistry, manufacturing, and controls (CMC) data, to support proposed changes and demonstrate their impact on product quality and safety.

Bulk Active Chemical Post-Approval Changes (BACPAC):

Bulk Active Chemical Post-Approval Changes (BACPAC) is a regulatory framework that focuses specifically on changes related to the bulk active pharmaceutical ingredient (API) in a drug product. BACPAC is part of the broader Scale-Up and Post-Approval Changes (SUPAC) guidance established by regulatory agencies like the US Food and Drug Administration (FDA). Here's an in-depth look at BACPAC within the context of drug discovery and development:

1. Purpose of BACPAC:

1. **Focused on API Changes**: BACPAC guidelines are designed to provide recommendations for managing post-approval changes related specifically to the bulk active chemical ingredient in a drug product.

2. **Ensuring Product Quality and Safety**: The primary goal of BACPAC is to ensure that changes made to the bulk API, such as sourcing, manufacturing process, or specifications, do not compromise the quality, efficacy, or safety of the finished drug product.

2. **Types of Changes Covered**:

1. **Changes to API Source**: This includes changes in the source of the bulk active ingredient, such as sourcing from a different supplier or manufacturing facility.

2. **Changes in Manufacturing Process**: BACPAC also addresses modifications to the manufacturing process of the bulk API, such as changes in equipment, process parameters, or synthesis route.

3. **Changes in Specifications**: Any changes to the specifications of the bulk API, including physical and chemical properties, impurity profiles, particle size distribution, or stability characteristics, fall under BACPAC.

3. Regulatory Considerations:

1. **Prior Approval Requirement**: Depending on the nature and significance of the change, BACPAC changes may require prior approval from

regulatory agencies before implementation to ensure patient safety and product quality.

2. **Reporting Requirements**: Manufacturers are typically required to submit supplements or variations to their marketing applications, such as Changes Being Effected (CBE) supplements or Prior Approval Supplements (PAS), to notify regulatory agencies of proposed BACPAC changes and obtain approval.

4. Documentation and Reporting:

1. **Change Control Procedures**: Manufacturers should establish robust change control procedures to systematically document and assess proposed BACPAC changes, including their rationale, potential impact on product quality, and risk mitigation measures.

2. **Submission of Documentation**: Adequate documentation, including chemistry, manufacturing, and controls (CMC) data, should be prepared and submitted to regulatory agencies to support proposed BACPAC changes and demonstrate their impact on product quality and safety.

5. Evaluation of Impact:

1. **Assessment of Quality Attributes**: Manufacturers must evaluate the impact of BACPAC changes on critical quality attributes (CQAs) of the drug product, such as potency, purity, stability, and bioavailability.

2. **Comparability Studies**: Comparability studies may be necessary to demonstrate that the drug product remains comparable in quality, safety, and efficacy following BACPAC changes, especially for significant modifications to the bulk API or manufacturing process.

POST MARKETING SURVEILLANCE

Post-marketing surveillance, also known as pharmacovigilance, is a critical component of drug discovery and development. It involves the ongoing monitoring of pharmaceutical products after they have been approved and marketed to ensure their safety, efficacy, and quality in real-world clinical practice. Let's delve into the details:

Purpose of Post-Marketing Surveillance:

Post-marketing surveillance, also known as pharmacovigilance, plays a crucial role in the principles of drug discovery and development by monitoring the safety, efficacy, and quality of pharmaceutical products after they have been approved and marketed. Let's explore the purposes of post-marketing surveillance in detail:

1. Detecting Adverse Events:

1. **Identification of Adverse Events (AEs):** Post-marketing surveillance aims to detect and monitor adverse events or side effects associated with the use of a drug in a larger and more diverse population than was studied during clinical trials.

2. **Rare and Long-Term Effects**: Clinical trials may not capture rare or long-term adverse events due to their limited duration and sample size. Post-marketing surveillance helps identify any safety concerns that may emerge over time with prolonged use of the drug.

2. Assessing Real-World Effectiveness:

1. **Monitoring Effectiveness:** Post-marketing surveillance involves monitoring the effectiveness of the drug in real-world clinical practice to ensure that it achieves the desired therapeutic outcomes in patients as expected based on clinical trial data.

2. **Comparative Effectiveness**: Surveillance activities may compare the effectiveness of the drug with other available treatments or assess its effectiveness in specific patient populations not adequately represented in clinical trials.

3. Identifying Drug Interactions:

1. **Detection of Drug-Drug Interactions**: Post-marketing surveillance helps identify potential drug-drug interactions or interactions with other substances that may impact the safety or effectiveness of the drug.

2. **Assessment of Comorbid Conditions**: Surveillance activities may evaluate how the drug interacts with common comorbid conditions or concomitant medications used by patients in real-world settings.

4. Evaluating Real-World Safety Profiles:

1. **Long-Term Safety Monitoring**: Post-marketing surveillance is essential for evaluating the long-term safety profile of the drug, including the identification of rare or delayed adverse events that may not have been evident during clinical trials.

2. **Risk-Benefit Assessment**: Continuous monitoring of the safety and effectiveness of a drug allows for ongoing assessment of its risk-benefit profile, ensuring that the benefits of the drug outweigh any potential risks.

5. Regulatory Compliance and Reporting:

1. **Regulatory Obligations**: Pharmaceutical companies are required to conduct post-marketing surveillance as part of their regulatory obligations to ensure ongoing compliance with regulatory requirements.

2. **Adverse Event Reporting**: Surveillance activities involve the collection, analysis, and reporting of adverse event data to regulatory agencies, healthcare professionals, and the public to facilitate timely regulatory action and risk communication.

Components of Post-Marketing Surveillance:

Post-marketing surveillance, a crucial aspect of drug discovery and development, involves several components aimed at monitoring the safety, efficacy, and quality of pharmaceutical products after they have been approved and marketed. Let's explore these components in detail:

1. Adverse Event Reporting:

1. **Spontaneous Reporting**: Healthcare professionals, patients, and pharmaceutical companies are encouraged to report any suspected adverse reactions associated with the use of a drug to regulatory authorities, such as the FDA's Adverse Event Reporting System (FAERS) in the United States or the Indian Pharmacovigilance Program in India.

2. **Timely Reporting**: Adverse events should be reported promptly to ensure timely detection and assessment of potential safety concerns.

2. Pharmacovigilance Studies:

1. **Retrospective Analysis**: Pharmacovigilance studies involve the retrospective analysis of real-world data sources, such as electronic health records, insurance claims databases, or patient registries, to assess the safety and effectiveness of drugs in clinical practice.

2. **Signal Detection**: These studies aim to detect signals of potential safety concerns from spontaneous adverse event reports, pharmacovigilance databases, and other sources of real-world data.

3. Risk Management Plans (RMPs):

1. **Risk Identification**: Pharmaceutical companies are required to develop risk management plans outlining strategies for monitoring and minimizing known and potential risks associated with the use of their products.

2. **Risk Minimization Strategies**: RMPs may include risk minimization strategies such as additional monitoring, restricted distribution, or patient education programs aimed at mitigating identified risks.

4. Post-Marketing Clinical Trials:

1. **Phase IV Trials**: In some cases, post-marketing surveillance may involve conducting additional clinical trials, known as Phase IV trials, to further evaluate the safety, efficacy, or effectiveness of a drug in specific patient populations or to address unresolved safety concerns.

2. **Real-World Data Collection**: These trials may utilize real-world data sources and pragmatic trial designs to assess how the drug performs in routine clinical practice.

5. Labeling Updates and Risk Communication:

1. **Labeling Revisions**: Based on the findings of post-marketing surveillance activities, regulatory agencies may require updates to product labeling to reflect new safety information, dosage adjustments, contraindications, warnings, precautions, or other relevant updates.

2. **Risk Communication**: Healthcare professionals, patients, and regulatory agencies should be informed of any significant safety concerns identified through post-marketing surveillance activities through appropriate risk communication channels.

6. Periodic Safety Reports:

1. **Periodic Safety Update Reports (PSURs)**: Pharmaceutical companies are required to submit periodic safety reports summarizing the safety data collected during post-marketing surveillance activities to regulatory agencies.

2. **Ongoing Safety Monitoring**: PSURs provide regulatory agencies with a comprehensive overview of the safety profile of the drug over time, allowing for ongoing safety monitoring and assessment.

Regulatory Oversight:

Regulatory oversight is a critical aspect of post-marketing surveillance in drug discovery and development, ensuring that pharmaceutical products remain safe, effective, and of high quality throughout their lifecycle after approval and commercialization. Let's explore regulatory oversight in post-marketing surveillance in detail:

1. Regulatory Agencies:

1. **FDA (United States)**: In the United States, the Food and Drug Administration (FDA) oversees post-marketing surveillance activities to monitor the safety and effectiveness of pharmaceutical products.

2. **EMA (European Union)**: In the European Union, the European Medicines Agency (EMA) plays a similar role, overseeing pharmacovigilance activities and monitoring the safety of medicinal products.

3. **CDSCO (India):** In India, the Central Drugs Standard Control Organization (CDSCO) is responsible for regulating pharmaceutical products and overseeing post-marketing surveillance activities to ensure their safety and efficacy.

2. Regulatory Requirements:

1. **Post-Marketing Requirements**: Regulatory agencies may impose post-marketing requirements on pharmaceutical companies, such as conducting post-marketing surveillance studies, submitting periodic safety reports, or implementing risk management plans.

2. **Labeling Updates**: Regulatory agencies may require pharmaceutical companies to update product labeling to reflect new safety information or changes in dosage, warnings, or precautions identified through post-marketing surveillance activities.

3. **Risk Communication**: Regulatory agencies facilitate risk communication by disseminating safety alerts, advisories, and public health warnings to healthcare professionals and the public based on findings from post-marketing surveillance activities.

3. Pharmacovigilance Systems:

1. **Adverse Event Reporting**: Regulatory agencies establish pharmacovigilance systems to collect, analyze, and evaluate adverse event reports submitted by healthcare professionals, patients, and pharmaceutical companies.

2. **Signal Detection**: Regulatory agencies use sophisticated data mining and signal detection techniques to identify potential safety concerns or emerging risks from adverse event reports and other sources of real-world data.

4. Inspections and Audits:

1. **Compliance Inspections**: Regulatory agencies conduct inspections and audits of pharmaceutical companies' pharmacovigilance systems and post-marketing surveillance activities to ensure compliance with regulatory requirements.

2. **Good Pharmacovigilance Practices (GVP)**: Regulatory agencies provide guidelines and standards for good pharmacovigilance practices (GVP) to ensure the quality, consistency, and integrity of post-marketing surveillance activities.

5. Enforcement Actions:

1. **Warning Letters**: Regulatory agencies may issue warning letters or enforcement actions to pharmaceutical companies found to be non-compliant with post-marketing surveillance requirements or failing to adequately address identified safety concerns.

2. **Product Withdrawal or Recall**: In severe cases where significant safety risks are identified, regulatory agencies may require the withdrawal or recall of pharmaceutical products from the market to protect public health.

PRODUCT REGISTRATION GUIDELINES OF CDSCO

The Central Drugs Standard Control Organization (CDSCO) in India is responsible for regulating the import, manufacture, distribution, and sale of drugs, cosmetics, medical devices, and diagnostics. Let's explore the product registration guidelines set forth by the CDSCO in detail:

Purpose of Product Registration:

In the context of the Central Drugs Standard Control Organization (CDSCO) in India, the purpose of product registration is multifaceted, serving regulatory, public health, and commercial objectives. Let's delve into the detailed purposes of product registration within the guidelines of CDSCO:

Regulatory Compliance:

1. **Safety and Efficacy Assurance**: Product registration ensures that pharmaceuticals, medical devices, cosmetics, and other healthcare products meet established standards of safety, efficacy, and quality before they can be marketed and sold in India.

2. **Quality Control**: Registration processes involve evaluating manufacturing processes, quality control measures, and product specifications to ensure consistency, purity, and potency of healthcare products.

3. **Compliance with Regulatory Standards**: Product registration ensures compliance with regulatory standards and guidelines set forth by CDSCO, including requirements related to manufacturing practices, labeling, packaging, and product specifications.

Public Health Protection:

1. **Prevention of Harm**: Product registration aims to prevent the entry of substandard, counterfeit, or unsafe products into the market, thereby protecting consumers from potential harm and adverse health effects.

2. **Ensuring Access to Safe Products**: Registration ensures that consumers have access to safe and effective healthcare products that have undergone thorough evaluation and regulatory oversight, thereby promoting public health and safety.

3. **Risk Mitigation:** By identifying and mitigating potential risks associated with healthcare products, product registration helps minimize the occurrence of adverse events and ensures the safe use of products by healthcare professionals and patients.

Commercial Considerations:

1. **Market Access:** Product registration is a prerequisite for market access, allowing manufacturers and distributors to legally market and sell their products in India. Compliance with registration requirements facilitates market entry and ensures fair competition in the healthcare industry.

2. **Building Trust**: Registration builds trust among healthcare professionals, patients, and regulatory agencies by demonstrating that products have undergone rigorous evaluation and meet established standards of quality, safety, and efficacy. This fosters confidence in the healthcare system and encourages informed decision-making by stakeholders.

Product Registration Process:

The product registration process within the guidelines of the Central Drugs Standard Control Organization (CDSCO) in India is a crucial step for ensuring the safety, efficacy, and quality of pharmaceuticals, medical devices, cosmetics, and other healthcare products before they can be marketed and sold in the country. Let's explore the detailed steps involved in the product registration process with CDSCO:

1. Preparing the Application:

1. **Identify the Product**: Determine the specific product to be registered, whether it's a new drug, generic drug, medical device, cosmetic, or other regulated healthcare product.

2. **Compile Documentation**: Gather all necessary documentation and data required for the registration application, including:
   a. Product composition and formulation
   b. Manufacturing process and facilities details
   c. Preclinical and clinical study data (for drugs)
   d. Device specifications and testing data (for medical devices)
   e. Safety assessment data (for cosmetics)

2. Submission of Application:

1. **Application Form**: Complete the appropriate application form prescribed by CDSCO for the specific type of product being registered, such as Form 44 for new drugs or Form MD-16 for medical devices.

2. **Online Submission**: Submit the application electronically through the online portal of CDSCO, commonly known as SUGAM.

3. **Application Fee**: Pay the applicable registration fee as specified by CDSCO. The fee amount may vary depending on the type of product and the complexity of the application.

3. Review and Evaluation:

1. **Administrative Review**: CDSCO conducts an administrative review to ensure that the submitted application is complete and meets all regulatory requirements. Incomplete applications may be rejected or returned for additional information.

2. **Technical Evaluation**: Subject matter experts within CDSCO review the submitted data and documentation to assess the safety, efficacy, and quality of the product. This evaluation may involve assessment of manufacturing processes, clinical trial data (for drugs), and compliance with relevant standards and guidelines.

3. **Communication with Applicant**: CDSCO may request additional information or clarification from the applicant during the review process through formal queries or correspondence.

4. Inspection of Manufacturing Facilities:

1. **Inspection Requirement**: For certain products, such as drugs and medical devices, CDSCO may conduct inspections of manufacturing facilities to ensure compliance with Good Manufacturing Practices (GMP) and other regulatory requirements.

2. **Facility Compliance**: Manufacturing facilities must adhere to GMP standards to ensure the quality, purity, and consistency of the products manufactured.

5. Labeling and Packaging Review:

1. **Labeling Compliance**: CDSCO reviews the labeling and packaging materials to ensure compliance with regulatory requirements, including proper labeling of active ingredients, dosage instructions, warnings, precautions, and storage conditions.

2. **Promotional Material Review**: For drugs, CDSCO also reviews promotional materials, such as advertisements and marketing brochures, to ensure they are accurate, balanced, and not misleading.

6. Regulatory Decision:

1. **Approval**: If the product meets all regulatory requirements and is deemed safe, effective, and of high quality, CDSCO grants approval for marketing and sale in India.

2. **Conditional Approval or Rejection**: If deficiencies or concerns are identified during the review process, CDSCO may grant conditional approval, request additional data, or reject the application.

7. Post-Approval Obligations:

1. **Post-Market Surveillance**: After approval, manufacturers are required to conduct post-market surveillance to monitor the safety and effectiveness of the product in real-world clinical practice.

2. **Adverse Event Reporting**: Manufacturers must report any adverse events or incidents related to the use of the product to CDSCO.

3. **Labeling Updates**: Manufacturers are responsible for updating product labeling as needed to reflect new safety information, dosage adjustments, or other relevant updates.

Post-Registration Responsibilities:

After obtaining product registration approval from the Central Drugs Standard Control Organization (CDSCO) in India, manufacturers and sponsors have several post-registration responsibilities to ensure ongoing compliance with regulatory requirements and to uphold the safety, efficacy, and quality of their products. Here are the key post-registration responsibilities within the product registration guidelines of CDSCO:

1. Manufacturing and Quality Control:

1. **Adherence to Good Manufacturing Practices (GMP)**: Manufacturers must continue to comply with GMP regulations to ensure the quality, purity, and consistency of their products throughout the manufacturing process.

2. **Quality Control Measures**: Implement robust quality control measures to monitor the quality attributes of the product and ensure compliance with approved specifications.

3. **Routine Inspections and Audits**: Prepare for and undergo routine inspections and audits conducted by CDSCO to verify continued compliance with regulatory standards and requirements.

2. Adverse Event Monitoring and Reporting:

1. **Adverse Event Reporting**: Manufacturers are required to promptly report any adverse events or adverse drug reactions associated with their products to CDSCO.

2. **Timely Reporting**: Adverse events must be reported in a timely manner as per CDSCO regulations, with serious and unexpected events requiring expedited reporting within specified timeframes.

3. **Continuous Surveillance**: Implement systems for continuous monitoring of adverse events, including post-marketing surveillance studies and ongoing review of safety data.

3. Labeling Compliance and Updates:

1. **Labeling Revisions**: Manufacturers are responsible for updating product labeling as needed to reflect new safety information, dosage adjustments, contraindications, warnings, precautions, and other relevant updates.

2. **Compliance with Labeling Regulations**: Ensure continued compliance with CDSCO regulations regarding product labeling, including requirements for content, format, clarity, and readability.

4. Post-Market Surveillance Studies:

1. **Post-Market Surveillance**: Conduct post-market surveillance studies to monitor the safety, effectiveness, and long-term outcomes of the product in real-world clinical practice.

2. **Risk Evaluation and Mitigation Strategies (REMS)**: Implement risk evaluation and mitigation strategies as necessary to manage known or potential risks associated with the product.

5. Compliance with Regulatory Commitments:

1. **Fulfillment of Regulatory Obligations**: Fulfill any regulatory commitments made during the product registration process, including post-approval studies, labeling updates, and other regulatory requirements.

2. **Communication with CDSCO**: Maintain open communication with CDSCO and promptly address any inquiries, requests for information, or regulatory actions related to the product.

6. Periodic Renewals and Reviews:

1. **Renewal of Registration**: Ensure timely renewal of product registration as per CDSCO guidelines to maintain market authorization and compliance with regulatory requirements.

2. **Periodic Reviews**: Conduct periodic reviews of product safety and efficacy data to identify any emerging risks or trends and take appropriate corrective actions as needed.

PRODUCT REGISTRATION GUIDELINES OF USFDA

The Central Drugs Standard Control Organization (CDSCO) in India is responsible for regulating the import, manufacture, distribution, and sale of drugs, cosmetics, medical devices, and diagnostics. Let's explore the product registration guidelines set forth by the CDSCO in detail:

Purpose of Product Registration:

The purpose of product registration in the guidelines of the US Food and Drug Administration (FDA) is to ensure the safety, efficacy, and quality of pharmaceuticals, medical devices, cosmetics, and other healthcare products available in the United States. Let's explore this purpose in detail:

Regulatory Compliance:

1. **Safety Assurance:** Product registration ensures that healthcare products undergo rigorous evaluation by the FDA to determine their safety profiles. This evaluation involves assessing potential risks and benefits associated with the use of the product.

2. **Efficacy Assessment**: The FDA evaluates clinical data submitted by manufacturers to determine the effectiveness of pharmaceuticals, medical devices, and other healthcare products. This ensures that products meet the intended therapeutic goals and provide meaningful benefits to patients.

3. **Quality Standards**: Product registration requires manufacturers to adhere to established quality standards, such as Good Manufacturing Practices (GMP) and Quality System Regulations (QSR), to ensure the consistency, purity, and potency of healthcare products.

Public Health Protection:

1. **Preventing Harm**: By requiring product registration, the FDA aims to prevent the entry of substandard, counterfeit, or unsafe products into the US market. This protects consumers from potential harm and adverse

health effects associated with the use of unregulated or poorly manufactured products.

2. **Ensuring Access to Safe Products**: Product registration ensures that consumers have access to safe and effective healthcare products that have undergone thorough evaluation and regulatory oversight. This promotes public confidence in the healthcare system and protects patients' rights to access quality healthcare products.

3. **Risk Mitigation**: Through product registration, the FDA identifies and mitigates potential risks associated with healthcare products. This may involve implementing risk management strategies, such as labeling requirements, post-market surveillance, and risk evaluation and mitigation strategies (REMS), to minimize the occurrence of adverse events.

Commercial Considerations:

1. **Market Access**: Product registration is a prerequisite for market access, allowing manufacturers and distributors to legally market and sell their products in the United States. This ensures fair competition and promotes innovation in the healthcare industry.

2. **Building Trust**: Product registration builds trust among healthcare professionals, patients, and regulatory agencies by demonstrating that products have undergone rigorous evaluation and meet established standards of quality, safety, and efficacy. This fosters confidence in the healthcare system and encourages informed decision-making by stakeholders.

Product Registration Process:

The product registration process with the US Food and Drug Administration (FDA) is critical for ensuring the safety, efficacy, and quality of pharmaceuticals, medical devices, cosmetics, and other healthcare products sold in the United States. Let's explore the detailed steps involved in the product registration process with the USFDA:

1. Preparing the Application:

1. **Identify the Product**: Determine the specific product to be registered, whether it's a new drug, generic drug, biologic, medical device, cosmetic, or other regulated healthcare product.

2. **Compile Documentation**: Gather all necessary documentation and data required for the registration application, including:
   a. Manufacturing information
   b. Product formulation
   c. Analytical methods
   d. Preclinical and clinical study data (for drugs and biologics)
   e. Device specifications and testing data (for medical devices)

2. Submission of Application:

1. **Electronic Submission**: Submit the registration application electronically through the FDA's electronic submission gateway (ESG) or other designated electronic submission portals.

2. **Form FDA 356h**: For drugs and biologics, submit Form FDA 356h, also known as the "Application to Market a New Drug, Biologic, or an Antibiotic Drug for Human Use."

3. **User Fees**: Pay applicable user fees, such as the Prescription Drug User Fee Act (PDUFA) fees for new drug applications (NDAs) or abbreviated new drug applications (ANDAs).

3. Review and Evaluation:

1. **Administrative Review**: FDA conducts an administrative review to ensure that the submitted application is complete and meets all regulatory requirements.

2. **Scientific Review**: Subject matter experts within the FDA review the submitted data and documentation to assess the safety, efficacy, and quality of the product.

3. **Communication with Applicant**: FDA may request additional information or clarification from the applicant during the review process through formal requests or information letters.

4. Inspection of Manufacturing Facilities:

1. **Pre-Approval Inspection (PAI):** For drugs, biologics, and medical devices, FDA may conduct a pre-approval inspection of manufacturing facilities to assess compliance with Good Manufacturing Practices (GMP).

2. **Facility Compliance**: Manufacturing facilities must comply with GMP regulations to ensure the quality, purity, and consistency of the products manufactured.

5. Labeling and Packaging Review:

1. **Labeling Compliance:** FDA reviews the labeling and packaging materials to ensure compliance with regulatory requirements, including proper labeling of active ingredients, dosage instructions, warnings, and precautions.

2. **Promotional Material Review**: For drugs, FDA also reviews promotional materials, such as advertisements and marketing brochures, to ensure they are truthful, balanced, and not misleading.

6. Regulatory Decision:

1. **Approval**: If the product meets all regulatory requirements and is deemed safe, effective, and of high quality, FDA grants approval for marketing and sale in the United States.

2. **Complete Response Letter (CRL)**: If deficiencies or concerns are identified during the review process, FDA may issue a complete response

letter outlining the specific issues that need to be addressed before approval can be granted.

7. Post-Approval Obligations:

1. **Post-Marketing Surveillance**: After approval, manufacturers are required to conduct post-marketing surveillance to monitor the safety and effectiveness of the product in real-world clinical practice.

2. **Adverse Event Reporting**: Manufacturers must report any adverse events or incidents related to the use of the product to FDA through the FDA Adverse Event Reporting System (FAERS).

3. **Labeling Updates**: Manufacturers are responsible for updating product labeling as needed to reflect new safety information, dosage adjustments, or other relevant updates.

Post-Registration Responsibilities:

After obtaining product registration approval from the US Food and Drug Administration (FDA), manufacturers and sponsors have various post-registration responsibilities to ensure ongoing compliance with regulatory requirements and to promote the continued safety, efficacy, and quality of their products. Let's delve into the details of these post-registration responsibilities:

1. Adverse Event Monitoring and Reporting:

1. **Adverse Event Reporting**: Manufacturers are required to promptly report any adverse events or adverse drug reactions associated with their products to the FDA through the FDA Adverse Event Reporting System (FAERS).

2. **Timely Reporting**: Adverse events must be reported in a timely manner according to FDA regulations, with serious and unexpected events requiring expedited reporting within specified timeframes.

3. **Continuous Monitoring**: Manufacturers must implement systems for continuous monitoring of adverse events, including post-marketing surveillance studies and ongoing review of safety data.

2. Labeling Updates and Compliance:

1. **Labeling Revisions**: Manufacturers are responsible for updating product labeling as needed to reflect new safety information, dosage adjustments, contraindications, warnings, precautions, and other relevant updates.

2. **Compliance with Labeling Regulations**: Product labeling must comply with FDA regulations, including requirements for content, format, clarity, and readability to ensure that consumers and healthcare professionals have access to accurate and up-to-date information.

3. Manufacturing Quality and Compliance:

1. **Continued Compliance with GMP**: Manufacturers must maintain compliance with Good Manufacturing Practices (GMP) regulations to ensure the quality, purity, and consistency of their products throughout the manufacturing process.

2. **Inspections and Audits:** FDA may conduct periodic inspections and audits of manufacturing facilities to assess compliance with regulatory requirements and identify any deviations or deficiencies that need to be addressed.

4. Post-Marketing Studies and Surveillance:

1. **Post-Marketing Surveillance Studies**: Manufacturers may be required to conduct post-marketing surveillance studies to monitor the safety, effectiveness, and long-term outcomes of their products in real-world clinical practice.

2. **Risk Evaluation and Mitigation Strategies (REMS)**: Manufacturers may need to implement REMS programs to manage known or potential risks associated with their products, including additional monitoring, education, and distribution restrictions.

5. Compliance with Regulatory Commitments:

1. **Fulfillment of Regulatory Obligations**: Manufacturers must fulfill any regulatory commitments made during the product registration process,

including post-approval studies, labeling updates, and other regulatory requirements.

2. **Communication with FDA**: Manufacturers should maintain open communication with the FDA and promptly address any inquiries, requests for information, or regulatory actions related to their products.

Multiple Choice Questions (MCQs)

Q1. What is the primary purpose of an Investigational New Drug (IND) application?

A) To market a new drug immediately

B) To initiate clinical trials of an investigational drug in humans

C) To approve packaging of new drugs

D) To analyze the commercial success of new drugs

Q2. Which phase of clinical trials focuses primarily on evaluating the drug's safety in healthy volunteers?

A) Phase I

B) Phase II

C) Phase III

D) Phase IV

Q3. During which phase are drug's efficacy and dosage regimen primarily determined?

A) Phase I

B) Phase II

C) Phase III

D) Phase IV

Q4. What is the focus of Phase III clinical trials?

A) Safety and dosage

B) Long-term adverse effects

C) Efficacy and safety in diverse populations

D) Initial human testing

Q5. Which regulatory document must be submitted to obtain marketing approval for a new drug?

A) IND

B) NDA

C) SNDA

D) ANDA

Q6. Post-marketing surveillance is also known as:

A) Phase II trial

B) Phase IV trial

C) IND

D) NDA

Q7. Which of the following is NOT a component of the New Drug Application (NDA)?

A) Preclinical data

B) Marketing strategy

C) Clinical data

D) Manufacturing information

Q8. What type of drug application is used for generic drugs to demonstrate bioequivalence?

A) IND

B) NDA

C) SNDA

D) ANDA

Q9. The FDA review process for a new drug application typically involves:

A) Inspection of manufacturing facilities only

B) Review of promotional materials only

C) Both clinical and nonclinical data review

D) Examination of financial forecasts

Q10. A Supplemental New Drug Application (SNDA) is used for:

A) First-time drug approval

B) Changes or additions to an already approved drug

C) Approving a generic drug

D) Initial clinical trials

Q11. Which of the following studies would NOT be included in an Abbreviated New Drug Application (ANDA)?

A) Bioequivalence studies

B) Large-scale clinical efficacy trials

C) Pharmaceutical equivalence documentation

D) Stability studies

Q12. In the context of drug development, "Phase 0" trials are described as:

A) Large-scale efficacy tests

B) Early exploratory trials involving very small doses

C) Post-marketing surveillance

D) Trials for secondary indications

Q13. Which phase of clinical development is critical for determining the optimal dosing regimen?

A) Phase I

B) Phase II

C) Phase III

D) Phase IV

Q14. What does pharmacokinetics study in drug trials?

A) Long-term safety

B) The drug's movement within the body

C) Immediate adverse reactions

D) The drug's effectiveness compared to other drugs

Q15. Which guideline is specifically designed for managing post-approval changes in drug manufacturing or formulation?

A) BACPAC

B) SUPAC

C) NDA

D) IND

Q16. What is the purpose of the FDA's "Complete Response Letter"?

A) To approve a drug with no further requirements

B) To request further information or studies before approval

C) To notify the sponsor of full compliance

D) To indicate immediate marketing approval

Q17. An ANDA submission primarily requires which of the following?

A) New clinical safety and efficacy data

B) Bioequivalence studies data

C) A full report of patient reactions

D) Long-term safety data

Q18. Post-approval changes to a drug that are significant enough to impact its quality must be reported through:

A) Periodic Safety Update Reports

B) An Abbreviated New Drug Application

C) A Supplemental New Drug Application

D) A New Drug Application

Q19. Which of the following is NOT typically a focus of preclinical studies?

A) Pharmacokinetics

B) Bioequivalence

C) Toxicology

D) Pharmacodynamics

Q20. In drug development, what is the main goal of Phase IV clinical trials?

A) To determine the initial safety profile of the drug

B) To monitor long-term effects and safety in a larger population

C) To assess the bioequivalence with other drugs

D) To establish pharmacokinetic properties

Short Answer Type Questions (Subjective)

1. What is the main objective of drug discovery?
2. Define the term "hit generation" in drug discovery.
3. What is the purpose of pharmacokinetic studies during preclinical development?
4. Describe the role of Phase I clinical trials in drug development.
5. What is an IND, and why is it important?
6. Outline the significance of Phase III clinical trials.
7. Explain the concept of "bioequivalence" as it pertains to ANDAs.
8. What is the primary aim of post-marketing surveillance?
9. How do Phase IV trials contribute to drug safety?
10. What is the purpose of a Supplemental New Drug Application (SNDA)?
11. Describe the role of pharmacovigilance in drug safety.
12. What are the key components of a New Drug Application (NDA)?
13. How does the FDA review process for an NDA work?
14. Explain the concept of "risk-benefit assessment" in pharmacovigilance.
15. What are the key considerations for patient recruitment in clinical trials?
16. Define the purpose of a Scale-Up and Post-Approval Changes (SUPAC) framework.
17. What are the regulatory requirements for a drug to be approved by the CDSCO in India?
18. Describe the "Good Manufacturing Practices" (GMP) requirements.
19. How is the effectiveness of a drug monitored in real-world settings after approval?
20. What is the importance of adverse event reporting in post-marketing surveillance?

Long Answer Type Questions (Subjective)

1. Discuss the stages of drug discovery and development, emphasizing the transition from preclinical to clinical phases.
2. Elaborate on the critical role of target identification and validation in the success of drug development programs.
3. Describe the process and regulatory requirements for submitting a New Drug Application (NDA) to the FDA.
4. Analyze the impact of pharmacokinetics and pharmacodynamics studies on dose selection and drug efficacy evaluation during clinical trials.
5. Explain the process and significance of obtaining an Abbreviated New Drug Application (ANDA) for generic drugs, including the necessary studies to prove bioequivalence.
6. Discuss the ethical considerations and challenges faced in recruiting participants for clinical trials, particularly in vulnerable populations.
7. Outline the regulatory review process for a Supplemental New Drug Application (SNDA) and the types of changes it can encompass.
8. Describe the procedures and importance of post-marketing surveillance in maintaining drug safety and efficacy in the general population.
9. Explain how regulatory agencies like the FDA and CDSCO ensure the compliance of drug manufacturers with post-approval commitments and regulations.
10. Discuss the challenges and strategies in drug lifecycle management, focusing on patent extensions, market expansion, and post-approval changes.

Answer Key for the MCQs

1. (B) To initiate clinical trials of an investigational drug in humans
2. (A) Phase I

3. (B) Phase II

4. (C) Efficacy and safety in diverse populations

5. (B) NDA

6. (B) Phase IV trial

7. (B) Marketing strategy

8. (D) ANDA

9. (C) Both clinical and nonclinical data review

10.(B) Changes or additions to an already approved drug

11.(B) Large-scale clinical efficacy trials

12.(B) Early exploratory trials involving very small doses

13.(B) Phase II

14.(B) The drug's movement within the body

15.(B) SUPAC

16.(B) To request further information or studies before approval

17.(B) Bioequivalence studies data

18.(C) A Supplemental New Drug Application

19.(B) Bioequivalence

20.(B) To monitor long-term effects and safety in a larger population

CHAPTER – 2

PRE-FORMULATION STUDIES

INTRODUCTION:

Pre-formulation studies are a crucial aspect of pharmaceutical development, laying the groundwork for the formulation of safe, effective, and stable drug products. These studies involve a series of comprehensive investigations aimed at understanding the physicochemical properties of a drug substance prior to formulation. Here's a detailed introduction to pre-formulation studies:

1. **Objective**: The primary goal of pre-formulation studies is to gather essential information about the drug substance to aid in the development of a stable and bioavailable dosage form. These studies provide critical insights into the behavior of the drug substance under various conditions, enabling formulation scientists to design appropriate dosage forms and manufacturing processes.

2. **Physicochemical Characterization**: Pre-formulation studies involve the thorough characterization of the physical and chemical properties of the drug substance. This includes assessing parameters such as solubility, partition coefficient, polymorphism, crystal habit, hygroscopicity, melting point, and pH solubility profile. By understanding these properties, formulation scientists can make informed decisions regarding formulation strategies and excipient selection.

3. **Compatibility Studies**: Compatibility studies are conducted to evaluate the compatibility of the drug substance with various excipients, packaging materials, and manufacturing processes. These studies help identify potential interactions that may affect the stability, efficacy, or safety of the final dosage form. Techniques such as differential scanning

calorimetry (DSC), Fourier-transform infrared spectroscopy (FTIR), and stability studies are commonly used to assess compatibility.

4. **Solid-State Characterization**: For solid dosage forms, it's essential to understand the solid-state properties of the drug substance, including its crystalline form, polymorphism, and particle size distribution. Techniques such as X-ray diffraction (XRD), microscopy, and particle size analysis are employed to characterize the solid-state properties and optimize formulation parameters such as particle size and morphology.

5. **Solubility and Dissolution Studies**: Solubility and dissolution behavior significantly influence the bioavailability and therapeutic efficacy of a drug. Pre-formulation studies involve determining the intrinsic solubility of the drug substance and investigating factors that may impact its dissolution rate, such as pH, temperature, and presence of excipients. These studies guide formulation development efforts aimed at improving drug solubility and dissolution kinetics.

6. **Stability Studies**: Assessing the stability of the drug substance is critical for ensuring the quality and shelf-life of the final dosage form. Pre-formulation studies include stability testing under various environmental conditions (e.g., temperature, humidity, light) to identify degradation pathways and establish appropriate storage conditions. Accelerated stability studies are often conducted to predict long-term stability and guide formulation optimization.

7. **Formulation Development Strategy**: Based on the insights gained from pre-formulation studies, formulation scientists develop a formulation strategy tailored to the specific characteristics of the drug substance. This may involve selecting suitable excipients, dosage forms (e.g., tablets, capsules, suspensions), and manufacturing processes to achieve the desired drug delivery profile and stability.

CONCEPT OF PRE-FORMULATION STUDIES

The concept of pre-formulation studies revolves around conducting a series of systematic investigations on a drug substance before it is formulated into a dosage form. These studies are fundamental to the pharmaceutical development process, providing essential insights into the physicochemical properties, stability, and compatibility of the drug substance. Here's a detailed breakdown of the concept of pre-formulation studies:

1. **Understanding the Drug Substance**: Pre-formulation studies aim to comprehensively understand the characteristics of the drug substance. This includes its chemical structure, molecular weight, pKa (dissociation constant), and pharmacological properties. By gaining insights into the fundamental properties of the drug molecule, scientists can anticipate its behavior in different formulations and physiological conditions.

2. **Physicochemical Characterization**: One of the primary objectives of pre-formulation studies is to characterize the physicochemical properties of the drug substance. This involves assessing parameters such as solubility, partition coefficient, crystallinity, polymorphism, hygroscopicity, and thermal behavior. Through techniques like spectroscopy, chromatography, microscopy, and thermal analysis, scientists gain a detailed understanding of how the drug interacts with its environment.

3. **Compatibility Assessment**: Pre-formulation studies include compatibility assessments to identify potential interactions between the drug substance and excipients, packaging materials, or manufacturing processes. Compatibility studies aim to ensure that the final dosage form remains stable, safe, and effective throughout its shelf-life. Techniques such as Fourier-transform infrared spectroscopy (FTIR), differential scanning calorimetry (DSC), and stability testing are employed to evaluate compatibility.

4. **Solid-State Characterization**: For drugs intended for solid dosage forms, understanding the solid-state properties is crucial. Pre-formulation studies involve characterizing the drug substance's crystal structure, particle size distribution, surface area, and polymorphic forms. Techniques such as X-ray diffraction (XRD), scanning electron microscopy (SEM), and particle size analysis help in assessing the physical properties of the drug substance.

5. **Solubility and Dissolution Studies**: Pre-formulation studies encompass solubility and dissolution studies to evaluate the drug substance's ability to dissolve in various media and its dissolution rate. These studies provide insights into factors affecting drug bioavailability and guide formulation strategies aimed at improving solubility and dissolution kinetics. Methods like shake-flask method, HPLC (High-Performance Liquid Chromatography), and dissolution apparatus are commonly employed in solubility and dissolution studies.

6. **Stability Evaluation**: Assessing the stability of the drug substance is essential to ensure the quality and efficacy of the final product. Pre-formulation studies include stability evaluations under different storage conditions (e.g., temperature, humidity, light) to identify degradation pathways and establish appropriate storage conditions. Accelerated stability studies are conducted to predict long-term stability and guide formulation optimization.

7. **Formulation Strategy Development**: Based on the insights gained from pre-formulation studies, formulation scientists develop a formulation strategy tailored to the specific characteristics of the drug substance. This may involve selecting suitable excipients, dosage forms, and manufacturing processes to achieve the desired drug delivery profile and stability.

ORGANOLEPTIC PROPERTIES OF PRE-FORMULATION STUDIES

Organoleptic properties refer to the sensory characteristics of a substance as perceived by the human senses, particularly taste, odor, appearance, and texture. While often considered in later stages of formulation and during quality control, organoleptic properties can also be relevant in pre-formulation studies. Here's how they fit into pre-formulation studies in detail:

1. **Taste and Odor**: The taste and odor of a drug substance can significantly impact patient acceptability and compliance with medication. In pre-formulation studies, evaluating the taste and odor of the drug substance provides important insights into its palatability and potential challenges in formulation development. For example, if a drug has a bitter taste, strategies such as taste masking may be required to improve patient acceptance. Similarly, unpleasant odors may necessitate the inclusion of odor-masking agents or formulation techniques to mitigate odor issues.

2. **Appearance**: The appearance of a drug substance, including its color, clarity, and physical form, can influence formulation decisions and patient acceptance. Pre-formulation studies often include visual inspection and characterization of the appearance of the drug substance. Changes in appearance, such as discoloration or formation of particles, may indicate degradation or instability of the substance, which can impact formulation development and shelf-life considerations.

3. **Texture**: While less commonly assessed in pre-formulation studies compared to taste, odor, and appearance, the texture of a drug substance can be relevant in certain cases, particularly for topical or orally disintegrating dosage forms. Texture analysis may involve evaluating properties such as hardness, friability, or compressibility for solid dosage forms, or viscosity and rheological properties for semi-solid or liquid formulations. Understanding the texture of the drug substance can inform

formulation strategies aimed at achieving desired characteristics in the final dosage form.

4. **Impact on Formulation Development**: Organoleptic properties identified during pre-formulation studies can guide formulation development efforts to address sensory issues and optimize the final dosage form. For example, if a drug has a bitter taste, formulation scientists may explore taste-masking techniques such as encapsulation or the use of sweetening agents. Similarly, if the appearance of the drug substance changes upon exposure to light or moisture, formulation strategies to enhance stability and prevent degradation may be necessary.

5. **Patient Acceptance and Compliance**: Ultimately, consideration of organoleptic properties is crucial for ensuring patient acceptance and compliance with medication. Pre-formulation studies that assess taste, odor, appearance, and texture lay the groundwork for developing dosage forms that are not only safe and effective but also palatable and convenient for patients to use. By addressing organoleptic issues early in the formulation process, pharmaceutical companies can improve the overall patient experience and medication adherence.

PURITY OF PRE-FORMULATION STUDIES

Purity is a critical aspect of pre-formulation studies, ensuring that the drug substance used as the active ingredient in pharmaceutical formulations is of high quality and free from impurities that could affect its safety, efficacy, or stability. Here's a detailed exploration of the role of purity in pre-formulation studies:

1. **Definition of Purity**: Purity refers to the degree to which a substance is free from impurities, including other chemicals, by-products, or contaminants. In the context of pre-formulation studies, assessing the purity of the drug substance involves identifying and quantifying any

impurities present and ensuring that they are within acceptable limits as per regulatory guidelines and pharmacopeial standards.

2. **Impurities**: Drug substances can be prone to various types of impurities, including organic impurities (e.g., related substances, degradation products), inorganic impurities (e.g., heavy metals, salts), residual solvents, and process-related impurities. Pre-formulation studies aim to identify and quantify these impurities to understand their potential impact on the quality and safety of the final dosage form.

3. **Characterization Techniques**: Characterizing impurities requires the use of analytical techniques capable of detecting and quantifying low levels of impurities in the drug substance. Common analytical methods employed in pre-formulation studies include chromatography techniques such as high-performance liquid chromatography (HPLC), gas chromatography (GC), and mass spectrometry (MS), as well as spectroscopic techniques like infrared (IR) and ultraviolet-visible (UV-Vis) spectroscopy.

4. **Limit Setting**: Regulatory authorities, such as the International Council for Harmonisation of Technical Requirements for Pharmaceuticals for Human Use (ICH), provide guidelines on acceptable limits for impurities in drug substances and products. These guidelines help establish appropriate specifications for purity during pre-formulation studies. Setting limits involves considering factors such as the toxicological significance of impurities, the intended route of administration, and the duration of use.

5. **Impact on Formulation Development**: The presence of impurities in the drug substance can impact formulation development in several ways. For example, certain impurities may affect the stability of the drug substance or interact with excipients, leading to formulation challenges or decreased shelf-life. By understanding the purity profile of the drug substance,

formulation scientists can make informed decisions regarding formulation strategies and excipient selection to mitigate potential risks.

6. **Stability Considerations**: Impurities can also influence the stability of the drug substance and the final dosage form. Pre-formulation studies include stability testing to evaluate the degradation kinetics of both the drug substance and its impurities under various storage conditions. This information helps establish appropriate storage conditions and shelf-life specifications for the formulated product.

7. **Quality Control**: Ensuring the purity of the drug substance is an integral part of quality control throughout the pharmaceutical development process. Analytical methods developed during pre-formulation studies for impurity characterization are transferred to quality control laboratories for routine testing of raw materials, intermediates, and finished products to maintain product quality and compliance with regulatory requirements.

IMPURITY PROFILES OF PRE-FORMULATION STUDIES

Impurity profiling is a crucial aspect of pre-formulation studies, aiming to identify, characterize, and quantify impurities present in the drug substance. These impurities can arise from various sources, including synthesis, degradation, or environmental factors, and can impact the safety, efficacy, and stability of the final pharmaceutical product. Here's a detailed exploration of impurity profiles in pre-formulation studies:

1. **Definition of Impurity Profiles**: Impurity profiles refer to the comprehensive characterization of impurities present in the drug substance, including identification of impurity types, levels, and potential sources. Impurity profiles provide critical information about the purity of the drug substance and help guide formulation development, process optimization, and quality control strategies.

2. **Types of Impurities**: Impurities in drug substances can be categorized into different types based on their origin and chemical nature. These include:

   a. **Related Substances**: Impurities that are structurally related to the drug substance, such as intermediates, by-products, or degradation products formed during synthesis or storage.

   b. **Inorganic Impurities**: Impurities of inorganic origin, such as heavy metals, metal salts, or residual catalysts from synthesis processes.

   c. **Organic Volatile Impurities (OVIs)**: Residual solvents used during synthesis or purification processes, which may pose risks to patient safety if present above acceptable limits.

   d. **Chiral Impurities**: Enantiomeric impurities that arise from the presence of stereoisomers or chiral intermediates during synthesis.

   e. **Isomeric Impurities**: Impurities that differ in the arrangement of atoms within the molecule, such as geometric or positional isomers.

3. **Characterization Techniques**: Characterizing impurity profiles requires the use of sensitive and selective analytical techniques capable of detecting and quantifying impurities at trace levels. Common analytical methods employed in pre-formulation studies for impurity profiling include:

   a. **High-Performance Liquid Chromatography (HPLC):** Separation and quantification of impurities based on their chromatographic behavior.

   b. **Gas Chromatography (GC):** Analysis of volatile impurities, such as residual solvents, using gas-phase separation.

   c. **Mass Spectrometry (MS)**: Identification of impurities based on their mass-to-charge ratio, often coupled with chromatographic techniques for enhanced selectivity.

   d. **Nuclear Magnetic Resonance (NMR) Spectroscopy**: Structural elucidation of impurities based on their proton or carbon chemical shifts.

4. **Quantification and Limit Setting**: Once identified, impurities must be quantified to assess their levels relative to acceptable limits defined by regulatory authorities and pharmacopeial standards. Setting appropriate limits involves considering factors such as the toxicological significance of impurities, the intended route of administration, and the duration of use.

5. **Stability Studies**: Impurity profiles can change over time due to degradation processes, environmental factors, or interactions with excipients. Pre-formulation studies include stability testing to evaluate the stability of both the drug substance and its impurities under various storage conditions. This information helps establish shelf-life specifications and storage conditions for the formulated product.

6. **Impact on Formulation Development**: Impurity profiles play a significant role in formulation development by informing decisions regarding excipient selection, formulation strategies, and manufacturing processes. For example, the presence of certain impurities may necessitate the use of specific excipients to enhance stability or mitigate degradation pathways.

7. **Quality Control**: Impurity profiling is essential for quality control throughout the pharmaceutical development process. Analytical methods developed during pre-formulation studies are transferred to quality control laboratories for routine testing of raw materials, intermediates,

and finished products to ensure compliance with regulatory requirements and maintain product quality and safety.

PARTICLE SIZE IN PRE-FORMULATION STUDIES

Particle size analysis is a fundamental aspect of pre-formulation studies, especially for drug substances intended for solid dosage forms. The size of particles can significantly influence various properties of pharmaceutical formulations, including dissolution rate, bioavailability, stability, and manufacturability. Here's a detailed exploration of particle size in pre-formulation studies:

1. **Definition and Importance**: Particle size refers to the dimensions of individual particles within a sample, typically measured in terms of diameter or equivalent spherical diameter. In pre-formulation studies, analyzing particle size is crucial for understanding the physical characteristics of the drug substance and optimizing formulation parameters to achieve desired performance attributes in the final dosage form.

2. **Particle Size Distribution**: Particle size analysis involves determining the distribution of particle sizes within a sample, rather than focusing solely on average particle size. Particle size distribution provides insights into the range of particle sizes present, including the presence of fine particles, aggregates, or oversized particles that may impact formulation performance or pose challenges during manufacturing.

3. **Characterization Techniques**: Various analytical techniques are available for particle size analysis in pre-formulation studies, each offering unique advantages and limitations:

    a. **Laser Diffraction**: Measures particle size distribution based on the scattering pattern of laser light passing through a sample.

b. **Dynamic Light Scattering (DLS):** Determines particle size by analyzing fluctuations in the intensity of light scattered by particles in suspension.

c. **Microscopy**: Direct observation and measurement of particle size using optical or electron microscopy techniques.

d. **Sieve Analysis:** Separation of particles based on size using a series of mesh screens with defined openings.

e. **Coulter Counter**: Electrical sensing zone method for counting and sizing particles suspended in an electrolyte solution.

f. **Image Analysis**: Digital image processing techniques for quantifying particle size and shape characteristics from microscopic images.

4. **Influence on Formulation Development:**

   a. **Dissolution Rate:** Particle size significantly affects the dissolution rate of drug substances, with smaller particles generally exhibiting faster dissolution kinetics due to increased surface area available for interaction with dissolution media.

   b. **Bioavailability**: The particle size of the drug substance can impact its bioavailability, particularly for poorly soluble compounds where particle size reduction techniques may improve solubility and absorption.

   c. **Content Uniformity**: Uniform particle size distribution is essential for ensuring content uniformity in solid dosage forms, preventing segregation or uneven distribution of drug particles within the formulation.

   d. **Manufacturability**: Particle size influences the flow properties, compressibility, and blend homogeneity of powders, affecting the manufacturability of solid dosage forms such as tablets and capsules.

5. **Stability Considerations**: Particle size stability is critical for maintaining the quality and performance of pharmaceutical formulations over time. Changes in particle size distribution due to aggregation, Ostwald ripening, or polymorphic transformations can impact stability and shelf-life specifications, requiring careful monitoring during pre-formulation studies and stability testing.

6. **Regulatory Considerations**: Regulatory authorities may require documentation of particle size distribution data as part of the drug development process, especially for generic drug products seeking regulatory approval through the Abbreviated New Drug Application (ANDA) pathway in the United States or similar processes in other regions.

SHAPE IN PRE-FORMULATION STUDIES

In pre-formulation studies, the assessment of particle shape is as crucial as analyzing particle size. Particle shape influences various aspects of pharmaceutical formulations, including flow properties, compaction behavior, dissolution rate, and stability. Here's a detailed exploration of the role of particle shape in pre-formulation studies:

1. **Definition and Importance**: Particle shape refers to the physical form or morphology of individual particles within a sample. It can vary widely, ranging from spherical to irregular, and can have a significant impact on the performance and processing of pharmaceutical formulations. Understanding particle shape is essential for optimizing formulation parameters and predicting the behavior of drug substances in dosage forms.

2. **Characterization Techniques**: Several techniques are available for the characterization of particle shape in pre-formulation studies, each offering unique advantages and limitations:

a. **Microscopy**: Optical microscopy, scanning electron microscopy (SEM), and transmission electron microscopy (TEM) are commonly used to visualize and analyze particle morphology at various magnifications.

b. **Image Analysis**: Digital image processing techniques allow for quantitative analysis of particle shape parameters, such as aspect ratio, roundness, and surface roughness, from microscopic images.

c. **Dynamic Image Analysis**: Dynamic image analysis systems capture real-time images of particles in motion and analyze shape characteristics based on changes in particle orientation over time.

3. **Influence on Formulation Development:**

a. **Flow Properties**: Particle shape significantly affects the flowability of powders, with irregularly shaped particles often exhibiting poorer flow properties compared to spherical particles. Understanding the shape characteristics of drug substances is essential for predicting powder flow behavior during manufacturing processes such as blending, tableting, and capsule filling.

b. **Compaction Behavior**: The shape of particles can influence their compaction behavior during tablet manufacturing, affecting tablet weight uniformity, hardness, and disintegration properties. Irregularly shaped particles may exhibit higher interparticle friction and require additional lubricants or compression modifiers to achieve desired tablet properties.

c. **Dissolution Rate**: Particle shape can impact the dissolution rate of drug substances, with factors such as surface area, surface roughness, and particle orientation influencing the rate and extent of drug release from solid dosage forms. Spherical particles generally exhibit more uniform dissolution behavior compared to irregularly shaped particles.

    d. **Stability Considerations**: Particle shape stability is essential for maintaining the quality and performance of pharmaceutical formulations over time. Changes in particle shape due to mechanical stress, attrition, or polymorphic transformations can impact stability, dissolution kinetics, and bioavailability, necessitating careful monitoring during pre-formulation studies and stability testing.

4. **Regulatory Considerations**: Regulatory authorities may require documentation of particle shape characteristics as part of the drug development process, especially for generic drug products seeking regulatory approval through the Abbreviated New Drug Application (ANDA) pathway in the United States or similar processes in other regions.

SURFACE AREA IN PRE-FORMULATION STUDIES

Surface area analysis is a vital aspect of pre-formulation studies, especially for solid-state drug substances. The surface area of particles directly impacts various pharmaceutical properties such as dissolution rate, stability, reactivity, and bioavailability. Here's a detailed exploration of the role of surface area in pre-formulation studies:

1. **Definition and Importance**: Surface area refers to the total area of all exposed surfaces of particles within a sample. In pre-formulation studies, surface area analysis provides critical information about the physical characteristics of the drug substance and its interaction with formulation components. Surface area is particularly relevant for solid-state drug substances, where it influences dissolution kinetics, stability, and processing properties.

2. **Characterization Techniques**: Several techniques are available for the measurement of surface area in pre-formulation studies, each offering unique advantages and limitations:

    a. **BET (Brunauer-Emmett-Teller) Method**: Gas adsorption technique based on the principles of physical adsorption, commonly used for measuring specific surface area and pore size distribution of porous materials.

    b. **Gas Permeation Method**: Measurement of gas permeability through a porous membrane or film, which correlates with the surface area of the sample.

    c. **Mercury Intrusion Porosimetry**: Determination of pore size distribution and total pore volume by measuring the intrusion of mercury into the sample under pressure.

    d. **Dynamic Vapor Sorption (DVS):** Measurement of water vapor sorption and desorption kinetics, which can provide insights into the surface area and porosity of hygroscopic materials.

3. **Influence on Formulation Development:**

    a. **Dissolution Rate:** Surface area plays a crucial role in determining the dissolution rate of solid dosage forms. Higher surface area generally leads to faster dissolution kinetics due to increased contact between the drug substance and dissolution medium. Surface area analysis helps identify particle size distribution and morphology factors that influence dissolution behavior.

    b. **Stability Considerations**: Surface area affects the exposure of drug molecules to environmental factors such as light, moisture, and oxidative species, which can impact stability and shelf-life. High surface area materials are often more susceptible to degradation reactions, necessitating careful monitoring and control during formulation development and stability testing.

c. **Reactivity**: Surface area influences the reactivity of drug substances in solid-state reactions, such as polymorphic transformations, chemical degradation, and physical interactions with excipients. Surface area analysis helps assess the potential for these reactions and optimize formulation strategies to mitigate stability risks.

d. **Bioavailability:** Surface area can impact the bioavailability of orally administered drugs by influencing dissolution and absorption rates in the gastrointestinal tract. Pre-formulation studies aim to optimize particle size and surface area to enhance drug solubility and bioavailability, especially for poorly water-soluble compounds.

4. **Manufacturability:** Surface area analysis helps predict the flow properties, compressibility, and blend homogeneity of powders, which are critical considerations for tabletting, encapsulation, and other solid dosage form manufacturing processes. Understanding surface area facilitates the selection of suitable excipients and processing conditions to ensure uniformity and consistency in the final product.

5. **Regulatory Considerations**: Regulatory authorities may require documentation of surface area data as part of the drug development process, especially for generic drug products seeking regulatory approval through the Abbreviated New Drug Application (ANDA) pathway in the United States or similar processes in other regions.

SOLUBILITY OF PRE-FORMULATION STUDIES

Solubility assessment is a critical component of pre-formulation studies, particularly for drug substances intended for oral administration. Solubility determines the amount of drug that can dissolve in a given solvent or physiological fluid, influencing crucial aspects such as bioavailability, formulation design, and dosage form selection. Here's a detailed exploration of the role of solubility in pre-formulation studies:

1. **Definition and Importance**: Solubility refers to the ability of a substance to dissolve in a solvent to form a homogeneous solution. In pre-formulation studies, assessing the solubility of drug substances provides essential information about their physicochemical properties and behavior in biological fluids. Solubility impacts various aspects of drug development, including formulation design, dosage form selection, and bioavailability optimization.

2. **Characterization Techniques**: Several techniques are available for the measurement of solubility in pre-formulation studies, each offering unique advantages and limitations:

    a. **Shake Flask Method**: Manual or automated shaking of drug substance in a series of solvents followed by filtration and analysis to determine solubility equilibrium.

    b. **Saturation Solubility Method**: Preparation of saturated solutions of drug substance in various solvents at equilibrium conditions, followed by quantification of dissolved drug concentration using analytical techniques such as UV-Vis spectroscopy or HPLC.

    c. **Thermodynamic Methods**: Measurement of solubility as a function of temperature using techniques such as turbidimetry, conductometry, or isothermal titration calorimetry.

    d. **pH Solubility Profile**: Determination of solubility as a function of pH to assess ionization behavior and identify optimal pH conditions for drug solubilization.

3. **Influence on Formulation Development:**

    a. **Bioavailability:** Solubility is a critical determinant of drug bioavailability, particularly for orally administered drugs. Poorly soluble compounds may exhibit low bioavailability due to limited dissolution and absorption rates in the gastrointestinal tract. Pre-formulation studies aim to optimize solubility to enhance drug absorption and systemic exposure.

b. **Formulation Design**: Solubility data guide the selection of appropriate formulation strategies to improve drug solubilization and bioavailability. Techniques such as particle size reduction, solid dispersion, complexation, and lipid-based formulations are employed to enhance solubility and dissolution kinetics.

c. **Dosage Form Selection**: Solubility influences the selection of dosage forms suitable for drug administration. Highly soluble drugs may be formulated as immediate-release tablets, solutions, or suspensions, while poorly soluble drugs may require modified-release formulations or alternative delivery approaches to achieve desired therapeutic outcomes.

4. **Stability Considerations**: Solubility can impact the stability of drug substances and formulated products by affecting chemical degradation, physical stability, and polymorphic transformations. Pre-formulation studies include stability testing to evaluate the influence of solubility on degradation kinetics and shelf-life specifications under various storage conditions.

5. **Regulatory Considerations**: Regulatory authorities may require documentation of solubility data as part of the drug development process, especially for generic drug products seeking regulatory approval through the Abbreviated New Drug Application (ANDA) pathway in the United States or similar processes in other regions. Solubility data are essential for establishing bioequivalence and demonstrating therapeutic equivalence with reference products.

METHODS TO IMPROVE SOLUBILITY OF DRUGS:

Surfactants & its importance

Surfactants play a crucial role in improving the solubility of poorly water-soluble drugs, making them an important consideration in pre-formulation studies. Surfactants can enhance drug solubility by reducing surface tension, increasing wetting properties, promoting micelle formation, and improving dispensability in aqueous media. Here's a detailed exploration of the importance of surfactants and methods to improve drug solubility in pre-formulation studies:

1. **Role of Surfactants:**

    a. **Reduction of Surface Tension**: Surfactants lower the interfacial tension between solid drug particles and the dissolution medium, facilitating the wetting and dispersion of drug particles and enhancing the rate and extent of dissolution.

    b. **Micelle Formation**: Surfactants can form micelles in solution, where hydrophobic drug molecules are solubilized within the hydrophobic core of the micelle, increasing their apparent solubility in aqueous media.

    c. **Emulsification**: Surfactants stabilize emulsions by reducing the interfacial tension between immiscible phases (e.g., oil and water), enabling the dispersion of hydrophobic drug molecules in aqueous vehicles.

    d. **Complexation**: Certain surfactants can form complexes with poorly soluble drugs through non-covalent interactions, such as hydrogen bonding or hydrophobic interactions, leading to improved solubility and dissolution characteristics.

2. **Methods to Improve Solubility using Surfactants:**

    a. **Solid Dispersions**: Surfactants are commonly used in solid dispersion formulations to enhance the solubility and dissolution rate of poorly water-soluble drugs. In solid dispersions, the drug is dispersed as fine particles within a hydrophilic matrix, often composed of surfactants or polymers, to increase drug surface area and promote dissolution.

b. **Microemulsion**s: Microemulsions are thermodynamically stable colloidal dispersions of oil, water, surfactants, and cosurfactants. Surfactants in microemulsions help solubilize hydrophobic drugs in the oil phase, improving their apparent solubility and bioavailability.

c. **Self-emulsifying Drug Delivery Systems (SEDDS)**: SEDDS formulations contain surfactants and cosurfactants that spontaneously form oil-in-water emulsions upon dilution with aqueous media. Surfactants in SEDDS enhance drug solubilization in the oil phase, facilitating absorption and improving oral bioavailability.

d. **Nano emulsions:** Nanoemulsions are colloidal dispersions of nanoscale droplets stabilized by surfactants. Nanoemulsions can improve the solubility and bioavailability of hydrophobic drugs by increasing drug surface area and promoting rapid dissolution and absorption.

e. **Co-solvent Systems**: Surfactants can be used in co-solvent systems to enhance drug solubility by increasing the solubilizing capacity of the solvent and promoting drug dissolution. Surfactants help maintain drug solubility by preventing drug precipitation upon dilution with aqueous media.

f. **Spray Drying**: Surfactants can be incorporated into spray-dried formulations to improve the solubility and dispersibility of poorly water-soluble drugs. Surfactants aid in the formation of stable amorphous drug nanoparticles during the spray drying process, leading to increased drug surface area and enhanced dissolution properties.

3. **Importance in Pre-formulation Studies:**
    a. **Formulation Optimization**: Surfactants are essential components in pre-formulation studies aimed at optimizing drug formulations for improved solubility and bioavailability. Evaluating the impact of different surfactants on drug solubility and dissolution behavior helps identify suitable formulation strategies for further development.
    b. **Compatibility Studies**: Pre-formulation studies include compatibility assessments to ensure the compatibility of surfactants with other formulation components, excipients, and packaging materials. Surfactants should be selected based on their compatibility with the drug substance and other formulation ingredients to minimize potential interactions and stability issues.
    c. **Stability Testing**: Surfactants can influence the physical and chemical stability of drug formulations. Pre-formulation studies involve stability testing to assess the long-term stability of surfactant-containing formulations under various storage conditions, including temperature, humidity, and light exposure.

CO-SOLVENCY

Co-solvency is a technique used in pre-formulation studies to improve the solubility of poorly water-soluble drugs. It involves the addition of co-solvents, which are water-miscible organic solvents, to aqueous media to increase the solubilization capacity and enhance drug dissolution. Co-solvency is a versatile method that can be applied to various dosage forms, including oral solutions, suspensions, and parenteral formulations. Here's a detailed exploration of co-solvency and its importance in methods to improve drug solubility:

1. **Definition and Importance**: Co-solvency refers to the use of water-miscible organic solvents, known as co-solvents, to enhance the solubility of poorly water-soluble drugs in aqueous media. Co-solvency is a widely

used technique in pharmaceutical formulation to overcome solubility limitations and improve drug bioavailability. By increasing the solubilization capacity of the solvent system, co-solvency facilitates the dissolution of hydrophobic drugs and enhances their absorption and therapeutic efficacy.

2. **Selection of Co-solvents:**
   a. **Water Miscibility**: Co-solvents should be miscible with water to ensure homogeneity and uniform distribution in the final formulation.
   b. **Solubilizing Capacity**: Co-solvents should have high solubilizing capacity for the drug substance to achieve the desired solubility enhancement.
   c. **Safety and Toxicity**: Co-solvents should be pharmaceutically acceptable, non-toxic, and compatible with the intended route of administration.
   d. **Regulatory Considerations**: Co-solvents should comply with regulatory guidelines and pharmacopeial standards regarding purity, safety, and permissible levels in pharmaceutical formulations.

3. **Methods to Improve Solubility using Co-solvency:**
   a. **Oral Solutions**: Co-solvency is commonly used to formulate oral solutions of poorly water-soluble drugs. Co-solvents such as ethanol, propylene glycol, polyethylene glycol, and glycerin are added to aqueous vehicles to increase drug solubility and enhance oral bioavailability.
   b. **Parenteral Formulations**: Co-solvency is also employed in parenteral formulations to improve drug solubility and facilitate administration. Co-solvents are added to aqueous injection vehicles

to increase drug solubility and ensure compatibility with physiological fluids.

c. **Suspensions**: Co-solvency can be used to formulate drug suspensions with improved solubility and dispersion characteristics. Co-solvents aid in wetting and dispersing poorly water-soluble drugs in aqueous suspending vehicles, enhancing drug solubilization and uniformity.

4. **Formulation Optimization:**

a. **Solvent Selection**: Co-solvents are selected based on their solubilizing capacity, safety profile, and compatibility with other formulation components. Pre-formulation studies involve screening and optimization of co-solvent systems to achieve maximum solubility enhancement while ensuring formulation stability and safety.

b. **Solvent Ratio Optimization**: The ratio of co-solvent to water is optimized to achieve the desired solubility enhancement without compromising formulation stability, viscosity, or patient acceptability. Pre-formulation studies include evaluating the effect of different co-solvent ratios on drug solubility and formulation properties to identify the optimal formulation composition.

5. **Stability Considerations:**

a. **Chemical Stability**: Co-solvency can influence the chemical stability of drug substances by altering their physical state, solvation environment, and susceptibility to degradation reactions. Pre-formulation studies include stability testing to assess the long-term chemical stability of co-solvent-containing formulations under various storage conditions.

b. **Physical Stability**: Co-solvency can affect the physical stability of formulations by influencing phase separation, precipitation, or crystallization phenomena. Pre-formulation studies involve evaluating the physical stability of co-solvent-containing formulations through visual inspection, particle size analysis, and microscopy techniques.

6. **Regulatory Considerations:**

    a. **Documentation and Compliance**: Co-solvency formulations must comply with regulatory requirements regarding solvent selection, purity, safety, and permissible levels in pharmaceutical products. Pre-formulation studies include documentation of co-solvency data and compliance with regulatory guidelines and pharmacopeial standards.

TECHNIQUES FOR THE STUDY OF CRYSTAL PROPERTIES

Studying crystal properties is crucial in pre-formulation studies aimed at improving the solubility of drugs, especially poorly water-soluble compounds. Understanding crystal properties such as polymorphism, particle size, morphology, and surface area provides valuable insights into the physical characteristics and behavior of drug substances, guiding formulation strategies to enhance solubility and dissolution rate. Here's a detailed exploration of techniques for the study of crystal properties in pre-formulation studies:

1. **X-ray Powder Diffraction (XRPD):**

    a. **Principle:** XRPD is a widely used technique for identifying crystalline phases and characterizing crystal structures based on their diffraction patterns. Crystalline materials exhibit unique diffraction patterns that can be used to determine crystal form, polymorphism, and crystal purity.

    b. **Application**: XRPD is used in pre-formulation studies to identify polymorphic forms, assess crystallinity, and monitor changes in crystal structure during formulation development and processing.

2. **Differential Scanning Calorimetry (DSC):**

a. **Principle:** DSC measures the heat flow associated with thermal transitions, including melting, crystallization, and phase transitions, providing information about the thermal behavior of drug substances and their solid-state forms.

b. **Application:** DSC is used to study crystal properties such as melting point, melting enthalpy, heat of fusion, and thermal stability. Changes in thermal behavior can indicate polymorphic transitions, amorphous content, or interactions with excipients.

3. **Scanning Electron Microscopy (SEM):**

   a. **Principle:** SEM is a high-resolution imaging technique that provides detailed morphological information about the surface characteristics, particle size, and shape of crystalline materials.

   b. **Application:** SEM is used to study crystal properties such as particle morphology, surface roughness, and agglomeration behavior. Understanding crystal morphology helps optimize particle size distribution and surface area for improved solubility.

4. **Optical Microscopy:**

   a. **Principle:** Optical microscopy involves the visual observation and imaging of crystalline materials under magnification, providing qualitative and quantitative information about particle size, shape, and crystal habit.

   b. **Application:** Optical microscopy is used to study crystal properties such as particle morphology, habit, and size distribution. Polarized light microscopy can also be used to identify crystal forms and assess crystal purity.

5. **Laser Diffraction Particle Sizing:**

   a. **Principle:** Laser diffraction measures the scattering pattern of laser light passing through a dispersed particle sample, providing information about particle size distribution.

b. **Application:** Laser diffraction is used to study crystal properties such as particle size distribution and size-related parameters. Understanding particle size distribution helps optimize formulations for improved solubility and dissolution kinetics.

6. **BET Surface Area Analysis:**

   a. **Principle**: BET analysis measures the adsorption of gas molecules onto the surface of solid materials to determine specific surface area, pore size distribution, and surface characteristics.

   b. **Application**: BET analysis is used to study crystal properties such as surface area, porosity, and surface energy. Surface area measurements provide insights into the physical state, surface reactivity, and solubility behavior of crystalline materials.

7. **Raman Spectroscopy:**

   a. **Principle**: Raman spectroscopy measures the vibrational modes of molecules in crystalline materials, providing information about molecular structure, chemical composition, and crystallographic orientation.

   b. **Application**: Raman spectroscopy is used to study crystal properties such as molecular conformation, polymorphism, and crystallinity. Changes in Raman spectra can indicate polymorphic transitions or crystal form modifications.

TECHNIQUES FOR THE STUDY OF POLYMORPHISM

Studying polymorphism is crucial in pre-formulation studies aimed at improving the solubility of drugs, particularly for poorly water-soluble compounds. Polymorphism refers to the ability of a molecule to exist in different crystalline forms with distinct molecular arrangements and physical properties. Understanding polymorphism helps identify the most stable and soluble crystal form of a drug substance, guiding formulation strategies to enhance solubility and dissolution rate. Here's a detailed exploration of techniques for the study of polymorphism in pre-formulation studies:

1. **X-ray Powder Diffraction (XRPD):**
   a. **Principle:** XRPD is a powerful technique for identifying and characterizing polymorphic forms based on their unique diffraction patterns. Each polymorph exhibits characteristic diffraction peaks that can be used to distinguish between different crystal forms.
   b. **Application:** XRPD is widely used in pre-formulation studies to identify polymorphic forms, assess polymorphic purity, and monitor polymorphic transitions during formulation development and processing.

2. **Differential Scanning Calorimetry (DSC):**
   a. **Principle**: DSC measures the heat flow associated with thermal transitions, including melting, crystallization, and polymorphic transitions. Polymorphic forms often exhibit distinct thermal behavior, including differences in melting points, enthalpies, and transition temperatures.
   b. **Application**: DSC is used to study polymorphism by analyzing thermal transitions associated with polymorphic transformations. Changes in melting behavior or heat of fusion can indicate the presence of different polymorphic forms and their relative stability.

3. **Raman Spectroscopy:**
   a. **Principle**: Raman spectroscopy measures the vibrational modes of molecules in crystalline materials, providing information about molecular structure, chemical composition, and crystallographic orientation. Different polymorphic forms exhibit unique Raman spectra due to differences in molecular arrangements.
   b. **Application**: Raman spectroscopy is used to study polymorphism by analyzing characteristic peaks and spectral features associated

with specific polymorphic forms. Changes in Raman spectra can indicate polymorphic transitions or differences in crystal packing arrangements.

4. **Solid-State Nuclear Magnetic Resonance (NMR) Spectroscopy:**
    a. **Principle:** Solid-state NMR spectroscopy measures the interactions between atomic nuclei in crystalline materials, providing information about molecular structure, chemical environment, and crystal lattice parameters. Different polymorphic forms exhibit distinct NMR spectra due to variations in molecular packing and conformation.
    b. **Application**: Solid-state NMR spectroscopy is used to study polymorphism by analyzing chemical shifts, spin-spin coupling constants, and relaxation times associated with specific polymorphic forms. Changes in NMR spectra can indicate polymorphic transitions or differences in crystal packing arrangements.

5. **Single Crystal X-ray Diffraction (SCXRD):**
    a. **Principle**: SCXRD is a technique used to determine the precise atomic arrangement and crystal structure of a single crystal sample. SCXRD provides detailed information about the three-dimensional packing of molecules within the crystal lattice.
    b. **Application**: SCXRD is used to study polymorphism by solving and refining crystal structures of different polymorphic forms. Comparing crystal structures allows for the identification of polymorphic differences and understanding of structure-property relationships.

6. **Hot-Stage Microscopy:**
    a. **Principle**: Hot-stage microscopy involves visual observation and imaging of crystalline materials under controlled temperature

conditions. Polymorphic forms exhibit characteristic melting behavior and morphological changes at specific temperatures.

b. **Application**: Hot-stage microscopy is used to study polymorphism by observing and recording changes in crystal morphology, melting behavior, and phase transitions as a function of temperature. Differences in melting points and thermal behavior indicate the presence of different polymorphic forms.

7. **Computational Modeling and Simulation:**

a. **Principle:** Computational modeling and simulation techniques, such as molecular modeling and crystal structure prediction, can predict and analyze the energetics and stability of different polymorphic forms based on molecular interactions and crystal packing arrangements.

b. **Application:** Computational modeling is used to study polymorphism by predicting the relative stability of different crystal forms, identifying potential polymorphs, and understanding the factors governing polymorphic transformations.

PRE-FORMULATION PROTOCOL

Developing a comprehensive pre-formulation protocol is essential in methods aimed at improving the solubility of drugs. This protocol serves as a systematic approach to gathering essential information about the physicochemical properties of the drug substance and identifying formulation strategies to enhance solubility and dissolution rate. Here's a detailed exploration of the pre-formulation protocol in methods to improve drug solubility:

Characterization of Drug Substance:

In pre-formulation studies, the characterization of the drug substance is a critical step that involves understanding its physical, chemical, and mechanical properties. This characterization provides essential data for the development of a stable and effective pharmaceutical formulation. Here's an outline of what this process typically involves:

1. **Physical Description**: This includes the visual examination of the drug substance, noting its color, odor, texture, and any other observable physical properties. This initial description provides basic information about the substance.

2. **Chemical Structure**: Determining the molecular structure of the drug substance is fundamental. Techniques such as spectroscopy (e.g., NMR, IR, UV-Vis), chromatography (e.g., HPLC), and mass spectrometry are commonly used to elucidate the chemical structure and confirm the identity of the compound.

3. **Purity and Impurities**: Assessing the purity of the drug substance is crucial for ensuring safety and efficacy. Various analytical techniques are employed to quantify impurities, including chromatography and spectroscopy methods. Regulatory agencies often have specific guidelines regarding acceptable levels of impurities.

4. **Solid-State Characterization**: Understanding the solid-state properties of the drug substance is essential for formulation development. Techniques such as X-ray diffraction (XRD), differential scanning calorimetry (DSC), and microscopy (e.g., SEM, TEM) are used to analyze crystallinity, polymorphism, particle size, and morphology.

5. **Hygroscopicity and Stability**: Determining the hygroscopicity and stability of the drug substance is critical for formulation development and shelf-life prediction. Techniques such as moisture sorption analysis and accelerated stability studies are commonly employed to assess these properties.

6. **Solubility and Dissolution Rate**: Assessing the solubility and dissolution rate of the drug substance provides valuable information for formulation design. Various techniques, including shake-flask method, HPLC, and

dissolution testing, are used to determine these parameters under different conditions.

7. **Compatibility Studies:** Investigating the compatibility of the drug substance with excipients and packaging materials is essential to avoid any interactions that may affect product stability or efficacy. Compatibility studies involve mixing the drug substance with excipients and analyzing any physical or chemical changes that occur.

8. **Particle Size and Morphology:** Characterizing the particle size distribution and morphology of the drug substance is crucial for formulation development, particularly for solid dosage forms. Techniques such as laser diffraction, microscopy, and image analysis are used to assess these properties.

9. **Rheological Properties**: Understanding the rheological behavior of the drug substance can help optimize the formulation process, especially for liquid and semi-solid dosage forms. Techniques such as rheometry are used to measure viscosity, flow behavior, and other rheological parameters.

10. **Biopharmaceutical Properties**: Evaluating the biopharmaceutical properties of the drug substance, such as permeability and metabolism, provides insights into its potential bioavailability and pharmacokinetic profile. In vitro and in vivo studies may be conducted to assess these properties.

Solubility Studies:

Solubility studies in pre-formulation protocols are essential for understanding how a drug substance behaves in different solvents and conditions. The solubility of a drug substance can significantly impact its formulation design, bioavailability, and therapeutic efficacy. Here's how solubility studies are typically conducted in pre-formulation studies:

1. **Selection of Solvents**: Different solvents with varying polarity and pH are chosen to cover a wide range of potential formulation conditions. Common solvents include water, organic solvents (e.g., ethanol, methanol, acetone), and aqueous buffers with different pH values.

2. **Equilibrium Solubility Determination**: The drug substance is added to each selected solvent under controlled conditions (e.g., temperature, agitation) until equilibrium is reached. The concentration of the dissolved drug substance is then measured using analytical techniques such as UV-Vis spectrophotometry, HPLC, or dissolution testing.

3. **pH-Solubility Profile**: The solubility of the drug substance is evaluated across a range of pH values to assess its pH-dependent solubility behavior. This information is crucial for formulating drugs that exhibit pH-dependent solubility or stability.

4. **Temperature Dependence**: Solubility studies are often conducted at different temperatures to evaluate the effect of temperature on drug solubility. This data helps in predicting the solubility behavior of the drug substance under different storage and manufacturing conditions.

5. **Kinetic Solubility Studies**: Kinetic solubility studies involve monitoring the rate at which the drug substance dissolves in a solvent over time. This information can be valuable for understanding the dissolution kinetics and designing appropriate dosage forms with desired release profiles.

6. **Salt and Co-solvent Screening**: In some cases, modifying the drug substance's chemical form (e.g., salt formation) or using co-solvents can enhance its solubility. Solubility studies may include screening different salt forms or co-solvents to identify formulations with improved solubility characteristics.

7. **Particle Size Influence**: The particle size of the drug substance can also affect its solubility. Studies may involve assessing the solubility of drug

substance particles with different particle sizes to understand this relationship.

8. **Polymorph Screening**: Polymorphism, where a drug substance can exist in different crystal forms, can significantly impact its solubility. Solubility studies may include screening for different polymorphic forms to identify the most soluble form for formulation development.

9. **Solubility Enhancement Techniques**: Various solubility enhancement techniques, such as complexation, micronization, solid dispersion, and nanosizing, may be evaluated during pre-formulation studies to improve the drug substance's solubility.

10. **Data Analysis and Interpretation**: The solubility data obtained from these studies are analyzed to understand the factors influencing solubility and to identify optimal formulation conditions. This analysis guides the formulation development process towards selecting appropriate excipients and formulation strategies to achieve desired solubility and bioavailability of the drug substance.

Solid-State Characterization:

Solid-state characterization is a crucial aspect of pre-formulation studies, especially for drug substances intended for solid dosage forms. It involves the analysis of the physical properties of the drug substance in its solid state. Here's how solid-state characterization is typically conducted in pre-formulation protocols:

1. **Crystallinity Analysis**: Determining the crystallinity of the drug substance is essential because it affects properties such as solubility, stability, and bioavailability. Techniques like X-ray diffraction (XRD) are used to analyze the crystal structure and identify different crystalline forms of the drug substance.

2. **Polymorphism Screening**: Polymorphism refers to the ability of a substance to exist in multiple crystalline forms. Polymorphic forms may

have different physicochemical properties, including solubility and stability. Solid-state characterization involves screening for polymorphic forms using techniques like XRD, differential scanning calorimetry (DSC), and Raman spectroscopy.

3. **Amorphous Content Determination**: Amorphous forms of a drug substance lack long-range order in their molecular arrangement. Amorphous forms often exhibit higher solubility but lower stability compared to crystalline forms. Techniques like DSC, XRD, and infrared spectroscopy (IR) are used to quantify the amorphous content in the drug substance.

4. **Particle Size and Morphology Analysis**: The particle size and morphology of the drug substance can significantly influence its properties, including dissolution rate and compaction behavior. Techniques like microscopy (e.g., scanning electron microscopy, SEM) and laser diffraction are used to analyze particle size distribution and morphology.

5. **Surface Area Measurement**: The specific surface area of the drug substance affects processes such as dissolution and adsorption. Techniques like Brunauer-Emmett-Teller (BET) analysis using gas adsorption are employed to measure surface area.

6. **Hygroscopicity Studies**: Hygroscopicity refers to the ability of a substance to absorb moisture from the surrounding environment. Understanding the hygroscopic behavior of the drug substance is essential for formulating stable dosage forms. Techniques like dynamic vapor sorption (DVS) are used to study moisture sorption behavior.

7. **Thermal Analysis**: Thermal analysis techniques such as DSC and thermogravimetric analysis (TGA) are used to study the thermal properties of the drug substance, including melting point, glass transition temperature, and thermal stability.

8. **Mechanical Properties Evaluation**: For solid dosage forms, the mechanical properties of the drug substance, such as hardness and compressibility, are important for tablet manufacturing. Techniques like hardness testing and compression studies are used to evaluate these properties.

9. **Compatibility Studies**: Solid-state characterization also involves assessing the compatibility of the drug substance with excipients and packaging materials. Compatibility studies help identify potential interactions that may affect formulation stability. Techniques like DSC and FTIR are often used for this purpose.

10. **Data Analysis and Interpretation**: The data obtained from solid-state characterization studies are analyzed to understand the physicochemical properties of the drug substance and their implications for formulation development. This analysis guides the selection of appropriate formulation strategies and excipients to optimize the performance and stability of the final dosage form.

Formulation Screening:

Formulation screening in pre-formulation studies involves evaluating various formulation prototypes to identify the most promising candidates for further development. The goal is to optimize the formulation parameters and select the most suitable formulation for further optimization and testing. Here's how formulation screening is typically conducted in pre-formulation protocols:

1. **Formulation Design**: Based on the physicochemical properties of the drug substance and the desired dosage form, several formulation prototypes are designed. These prototypes may vary in excipient composition, concentration, pH, viscosity, and other formulation parameters.

2. **Experimental Design**: A systematic approach is employed to generate a matrix of formulation prototypes, typically using a design of experiments

(DoE) approach. This allows for the efficient screening of a wide range of formulation variables while minimizing the number of experiments required.

3. **Prototype Preparation**: Each formulation prototype is prepared according to the predetermined formulation design, using appropriate methods such as blending, granulation, or solvent casting. Care is taken to ensure reproducibility and consistency in preparation.

4. **Physicochemical Characterization**: Each formulation prototype undergoes thorough physicochemical characterization to assess its key attributes, such as appearance, pH, viscosity, density, moisture content, and content uniformity. Analytical techniques such as spectroscopy, chromatography, and microscopy may be employed for characterization.

5. **Stability Assessment**: The stability of each formulation prototype is evaluated under accelerated and long-term storage conditions to assess its physical and chemical stability over time. Stability testing helps identify formulations prone to degradation, phase separation, or other stability issues.

6. **Solubility and Dissolution Studies**: The solubility and dissolution behavior of each formulation prototype are evaluated using appropriate in vitro dissolution tests. This helps assess the formulation's ability to release the drug substance efficiently and predict its in vivo performance.

7. **Compatibility Studies**: Compatibility studies are conducted to assess the compatibility of the drug substance with excipients and packaging materials used in each formulation prototype. Techniques such as differential scanning calorimetry (DSC) and Fourier-transform infrared spectroscopy (FTIR) may be employed to detect any potential interactions.

8. **Particle Size Analysis**: For formulations containing solid particles, particle size distribution analysis is performed to assess the impact of

formulation parameters on particle size and distribution. Techniques such as laser diffraction or microscopy may be used for particle size analysis.

9. **Rheological Characterization**: The rheological behavior of formulations intended for liquid or semi-solid dosage forms is evaluated to assess flow properties, viscosity, and thixotropy. Rheological characterization helps optimize formulation consistency and processability.

10. **Data Analysis and Selection**: The data obtained from physicochemical characterization, stability testing, solubility, and other studies are analyzed to identify formulation prototypes with desirable attributes. Based on predefined criteria and objectives, the most promising formulations are selected for further optimization and testing in subsequent stages of formulation development.

Stability Testing:

Stability testing in pre-formulation studies is essential for assessing the physical and chemical stability of drug substances under various storage conditions. The goal is to identify potential degradation pathways and stability issues early in the formulation development process. Here's how stability testing is typically conducted in pre-formulation protocols:

1. **Selection of Storage Conditions**: Different storage conditions are selected to assess the stability of the drug substance under various environmental factors, including temperature, humidity, light, and oxygen exposure. Common conditions include accelerated (elevated temperature and humidity), long-term (ambient temperature and humidity), and photostability (exposure to light) studies.

2. **Sample Preparation**: Representative samples of the drug substance or formulation prototypes are prepared according to standardized procedures and placed into appropriate containers for storage. Care is taken to ensure uniformity and reproducibility in sample preparation.

3. **Storage Conditions Monitoring**: The storage conditions for each stability study are carefully monitored and controlled to ensure consistency and compliance with regulatory guidelines. Temperature and humidity levels are monitored using calibrated instruments, and light exposure is controlled using appropriate light sources.

4. **Sampling Protocol**: At predetermined time intervals, samples are withdrawn from each stability study and analyzed to assess changes in the drug substance's physical and chemical properties. The sampling frequency and duration of the stability study are determined based on regulatory requirements and the expected stability profile of the drug substance.

5. **Physicochemical Analysis**: Various analytical techniques are employed to assess the stability of the drug substance during storage. This may include visual inspection for changes in appearance, pH measurement, moisture content determination, and content uniformity testing. Analytical methods such as chromatography, spectroscopy, and microscopy may be used to detect and quantify degradation products.

6. **Forced Degradation Studies**: In addition to stability testing under normal storage conditions, forced degradation studies may be conducted to accelerate degradation pathways and assess the drug substance's susceptibility to degradation under stress conditions such as heat, light, pH extremes, and oxidative stress.

7. **Data Analysis and Interpretation**: The data obtained from stability testing are analyzed to evaluate the drug substance's stability profile and identify any degradation trends or stability issues. Statistical analysis may be employed to assess the significance of observed changes and predict shelf-life.

8. **Stability Indicating Assays**: Stability indicating assays are developed to detect and quantify degradation products accurately. These assays are

essential for assessing the drug substance's stability and establishing appropriate specifications for quality control purposes.

9. **Stability Report**: A comprehensive stability report is prepared summarizing the results of stability testing, including any observed degradation pathways, changes in physical and chemical properties, and recommendations for storage conditions and shelf-life determination.

10. **Regulatory Compliance**: All stability testing protocols and procedures are designed to comply with regulatory guidelines, such as those outlined by the International Council for Harmonisation (ICH) and relevant regulatory agencies. Stability data generated during pre-formulation studies are submitted as part of the drug development dossier for regulatory approval.

Regulatory Considerations:

Regulatory considerations play a significant role in pre-formulation studies, as they lay the groundwork for the development of pharmaceutical products that meet regulatory requirements for safety, efficacy, and quality. Here are some key regulatory considerations in pre-formulation protocols:

1. **Compliance with Regulatory Guidelines**: Pre-formulation studies should be conducted in accordance with relevant regulatory guidelines, such as those provided by the International Council for Harmonisation of Technical Requirements for Pharmaceuticals for Human Use (ICH). Guidelines such as ICH Q6A (Specifications: Test Procedures and Acceptance Criteria for New Drug Substances and New Drug Products) and Q6B (Specifications: Test Procedures and Acceptance Criteria for Biotechnological/Biological Products) provide guidance on pre-formulation studies and stability testing requirements.

2. **Quality-by-Design (QbD) Principles**: QbD principles emphasize the importance of understanding the impact of formulation and process variables on product quality and performance. Pre-formulation studies

should be designed to identify critical quality attributes (CQAs) and critical material attributes (CMAs) early in the development process. This proactive approach helps ensure that the final product meets quality specifications and regulatory expectations.

3. **Analytical Method Validation**: Analytical methods used in pre-formulation studies, such as those for characterization, stability testing, and impurity profiling, must be validated to demonstrate their accuracy, precision, specificity, and robustness. Validation protocols should adhere to regulatory guidelines, such as those outlined in ICH Q2 (Validation of Analytical Procedures).

4. **Stability Testing Requirements**: Stability testing is a critical aspect of pre-formulation studies, and regulatory guidelines provide specific requirements for stability testing protocols, including storage conditions, sampling frequency, and analytical methods. Stability data generated during pre-formulation studies are used to establish shelf-life and storage conditions for the final product.

5. **Safety Assessment:** Pre-formulation studies should include an assessment of the drug substance's safety profile, including toxicity, genotoxicity, and potential impurities. Regulatory agencies require comprehensive safety data to evaluate the risk-benefit profile of pharmaceutical products and ensure patient safety.

6. **Regulatory Submissions**: Data generated from pre-formulation studies are included in regulatory submissions, such as investigational new drug (IND) applications, new drug applications (NDAs), or marketing authorization applications (MAAs). These submissions provide regulators with comprehensive information about the drug substance's quality, safety, and efficacy.

7. **Regulatory Interaction**: Pharmaceutical companies may engage in regulatory interactions throughout the pre-formulation and development

process to seek guidance from regulatory agencies and ensure compliance with regulatory requirements. These interactions help address regulatory concerns early in the development process and facilitate the timely approval of pharmaceutical products.

8. **Good Manufacturing Practice (GMP) Compliance**: Pre-formulation studies should be conducted in facilities that comply with GMP regulations to ensure the quality and integrity of data generated. GMP guidelines outline requirements for facilities, equipment, personnel, documentation, and quality control measures to ensure that pharmaceutical products are consistently manufactured to high quality standards.

Stability testing during product development

Stability testing is an integral part of product development, especially in methods aimed at improving the solubility of drugs during pre-formulation studies. Stability testing evaluates the physical, chemical, and microbiological properties of drug formulations under various storage conditions to assess their long-term stability, shelf-life, and suitability for commercialization. Here's a detailed exploration of stability testing during product development in methods to improve drug solubility:

Stability Study Design:

Stability study design in stability testing during product development, particularly in pre-formulation studies, involves careful planning to assess the physical and chemical stability of drug substances or formulations under various storage conditions. Here's how stability study design is typically approached:

1. **Selection of Storage Conditions**: Determine the relevant storage conditions based on regulatory guidelines (e.g., ICH guidelines) and the intended market. This includes considering factors such as temperature, humidity, light exposure, and oxygen levels. Common conditions include long-term, accelerated, and photostability testing.

2. **Container Closure System:** Select appropriate container closure systems to simulate intended packaging. Consider factors such as compatibility, permeability, and protection from environmental factors like moisture and light.

3. **Sample Size and Number**: Determine the number of samples needed for each stability condition to ensure statistical significance. Sample size should consider factors such as variability, sampling frequency, and the desired level of confidence in stability results.

4. **Sampling Time Points**: Establish a sampling schedule based on the expected degradation profile of the drug substance or formulation. Sampling time points should be sufficient to capture any degradation trends over the study duration.

5. **Analytical Methods**: Select validated analytical methods to assess stability parameters such as potency, impurities, and physical characteristics. Ensure that the methods are sensitive, specific, and suitable for quantifying degradation products and changes in quality attributes.

6. **Sample Handling and Storage**: Define procedures for sample handling, storage, and analysis to ensure sample integrity throughout the study. This includes considerations for temperature control, light protection, and minimizing exposure to air and moisture.

7. **Stress Testing**: Conduct forced degradation studies under exaggerated conditions (e.g., high temperature, high humidity, acidic or basic pH) to identify potential degradation pathways and degradation products. This helps establish the specificity of stability-indicating assays.

8. **Data Analysis and Interpretation:** Analyze stability data to assess the degradation kinetics, determine shelf-life, and establish storage conditions. Use statistical methods to evaluate trends, calculate degradation rates, and predict stability under different conditions.

9. **Documentation and Reporting**: Document all aspects of the stability study, including study protocol, sample handling procedures, analytical methods, and stability data. Prepare a comprehensive stability report summarizing the study design, results, conclusions, and recommendations for storage conditions and shelf-life.

10. **Regulatory Compliance**: Ensure that stability study design and execution comply with regulatory requirements and guidelines, such as those outlined in ICH Q1A (Stability Testing of New Drug Substances and Products) and Q1B (Photostability Testing of New Drug Substances and Products). Include stability data in regulatory submissions to support product approval.

Physical Stability Testing:

Physical stability testing in stability testing during product development, particularly in pre-formulation studies, focuses on evaluating the physical attributes and characteristics of drug substances or formulations under various storage conditions. This type of testing helps assess factors such as appearance, phase separation, and physical integrity. Here's how physical stability testing is typically conducted:

1. **Appearance Examination**: Visual inspection is conducted regularly to assess changes in the appearance of the drug substance or formulation. Changes such as color alteration, presence of particulates, phase separation, and formation of crystals or precipitates are noted.

2. **Physical State Assessment**: The physical state of the drug substance or formulation is evaluated, including its form (e.g., solid, liquid, semi-solid), consistency (e.g., viscosity, texture), and homogeneity. Any changes in physical state over time are documented.

3. **Phase Separation**: For liquid or semi-solid formulations, phase separation between immiscible components may occur during storage.

Stability testing involves monitoring for signs of phase separation, such as layering, creaming, or coalescence.

4. **Particle Size and Distribution**: Changes in particle size and distribution of solid particles within the formulation are assessed using techniques such as microscopy, laser diffraction, or sedimentation analysis. Any alterations in particle size or distribution are recorded.

5. **Reconstitution Studies**: For lyophilized or powder formulations intended for reconstitution before administration, reconstitution studies are conducted to evaluate the ease and completeness of reconstitution. Any issues such as incomplete dissolution or formation of aggregates are noted.

6. **Resuspendability Testing**: For suspensions or emulsions, resuspendability testing is performed to assess the ability of the formulation to redisperse uniformly after agitation or storage. The ease of resuspension and any settling or caking tendencies are evaluated.

7. **Container Closure Integrity**: The integrity of the container closure system is evaluated to ensure that it maintains the physical stability of the formulation during storage. Leakage, seal integrity, and compatibility with the formulation are assessed.

8. **Mechanical Stability**: Mechanical stability testing involves subjecting the formulation to physical stresses such as agitation, vibration, or centrifugation to simulate handling and transportation conditions. Any changes in physical appearance or integrity after exposure to mechanical stress are noted.

9. **Temperature Cycling**: Temperature cycling studies involve subjecting the formulation to repeated cycles of temperature variation to assess its physical stability under temperature stress. This helps identify potential issues such as phase separation, crystallization, or physical degradation.

10.**Packaging Compatibility**: Compatibility studies are conducted to evaluate the interaction between the formulation and its packaging materials. Changes in physical appearance, integrity, or performance of the packaging system are monitored over time.

Chemical Stability Testing:

Chemical stability testing in stability testing during product development, particularly in pre-formulation studies, focuses on evaluating the chemical integrity and stability of drug substances or formulations under various storage conditions. This type of testing helps assess factors such as degradation, impurity formation, and chemical reactions that may occur over time. Here's how chemical stability testing is typically conducted:

1. **Forced Degradation Studies**: Forced degradation studies involve subjecting the drug substance or formulation to harsh conditions, such as elevated temperature, humidity, light exposure, and acidic or basic pH, to accelerate degradation pathways. These studies help identify potential degradation products and degradation pathways.

2. **Long-Term Stability Testing**: Long-term stability testing involves storing the drug substance or formulation under normal storage conditions, typically at controlled room temperature and humidity, for an extended period. Samples are periodically analyzed to assess changes in chemical integrity and stability over time.

3. **Accelerated Stability Testing**: Accelerated stability testing involves storing the drug substance or formulation under accelerated conditions, such as higher temperatures and humidity, to accelerate degradation reactions. This helps predict long-term stability trends and estimate shelf-life more quickly.

4. **Specific Degradation Pathways**: Stability testing is designed to evaluate specific degradation pathways based on the known susceptibility of the drug substance or formulation to degradation under certain conditions.

Common degradation pathways include hydrolysis, oxidation, photolysis, and thermal degradation.

5. **Impurity Profiling**: Impurity profiling involves identifying and quantifying impurities that may arise during storage or manufacturing processes. Stability testing includes monitoring impurity levels and assessing their impact on product quality and safety.

6. **Stability-Indicating Assays**: Stability-indicating assays are analytical methods specifically developed to detect and quantify the drug substance and its degradation products accurately. These assays should be capable of separating the drug substance from its degradation products and impurities.

7. **Degradation Kinetics**: Stability testing involves assessing the kinetics of degradation reactions to determine degradation rates, half-life, and reaction mechanisms. This information helps predict stability under different storage conditions and establish appropriate storage recommendations.

8. **Container Closure Compatibility**: Stability testing includes evaluating the compatibility of the drug substance or formulation with its container closure system to ensure that it maintains chemical stability and integrity during storage. Compatibility studies assess factors such as leachables, extractables, and interaction between the formulation and packaging materials.

9. **Photostability Testing**: Photostability testing involves exposing the drug substance or formulation to controlled light conditions to assess its susceptibility to photodegradation. This helps ensure that the formulation remains chemically stable when exposed to light during storage or administration.

10. **Data Analysis and Interpretation**: Stability data obtained from chemical stability testing are analyzed to assess degradation trends,

establish degradation pathways, and determine shelf-life and storage conditions. Statistical methods may be used to analyze degradation kinetics and predict stability under different conditions.

Microbiological Stability Testing:

Microbiological stability testing in stability testing during product development, particularly in pre-formulation studies, focuses on assessing the susceptibility of drug substances or formulations to microbial contamination and growth over time. This type of testing helps ensure that pharmaceutical products remain free from microbial contamination during storage and use. Here's how microbiological stability testing is typically conducted:

1. **Microbial Contamination Control**: Ensure that all equipment, materials, and personnel involved in microbiological stability testing adhere to good microbiological practices to prevent contamination. Sterilize equipment, use aseptic techniques, and maintain a clean testing environment.

2. **Inoculation of Microorganisms**: Inoculate the drug substance or formulation with a standardized inoculum of microorganisms known to be relevant to the product's intended use or storage conditions. Common microorganisms include bacteria, yeast, and mold.

3. **Incubation Conditions**: Incubate the inoculated samples under controlled conditions, such as temperature, humidity, and time, to simulate storage conditions relevant to the product. Incubation parameters should be selected based on the product's intended storage conditions.

4. **Enumeration of Microbial Growth**: Periodically sample the inoculated samples and enumerate microbial growth using appropriate microbiological methods, such as viable plate counts, membrane filtration, or ATP bioluminescence assays. Assess changes in microbial

counts over time to determine the product's susceptibility to microbial contamination and growth.

5. **Identification of Microbial Isolates**: If microbial growth is observed, identify the microbial isolates to determine the types of microorganisms present and assess their potential impact on product quality and safety. Use phenotypic and/or molecular methods for microbial identification.

6. **Preservative Efficacy Testing**: For products containing preservatives, assess the efficacy of the preservative system in preventing microbial growth and contamination. Conduct preservative efficacy testing using challenge tests or antimicrobial effectiveness testing to ensure that the preservatives remain effective throughout the product's shelf-life.

7. **Antimicrobial Effectiveness Testing:** Conduct antimicrobial effectiveness testing to evaluate the product's ability to inhibit the growth of microorganisms. Use validated methods such as the USP <51> Antimicrobial Effectiveness Test or the European Pharmacopoeia (EP) antimicrobial efficacy tests.

8. **Endotoxin Testing**: If applicable, perform endotoxin testing to assess the presence of bacterial endotoxins in the product. Use validated methods such as the Limulus Amebocyte Lysate (LAL) assay to quantify endotoxin levels and ensure compliance with regulatory limits.

9. **Storage Stability Testing**: Evaluate the microbiological stability of the product under different storage conditions, including ambient temperature, refrigerated, and accelerated conditions. Assess changes in microbial counts and product integrity over time to determine shelf-life and storage recommendations.

10. **Regulatory Compliance**: Ensure that microbiological stability testing complies with regulatory requirements and guidelines, such as those outlined in pharmacopeial standards (e.g., USP, EP) and regulatory guidance documents. Include microbiological stability data in regulatory

submissions to demonstrate product safety and compliance with regulatory requirements.

Container Closure Integrity:

Container closure integrity (CCI) testing is a critical aspect of stability testing during product development, including pre-formulation studies. CCI testing ensures that the container closure system effectively maintains the integrity of the product throughout its shelf-life by preventing ingress of contaminants and egress of active ingredients or moisture. Here's how CCI testing is typically conducted during pre-formulation studies:

1. **Selection of Container Closure System**: Choose appropriate container closure systems based on the product's formulation and intended use. Consider factors such as compatibility with the product, protection against environmental factors (e.g., moisture, light), and regulatory requirements.

2. **Leak Detection Methods**: Select suitable leak detection methods to assess the integrity of the container closure system. Common methods include dye ingress tests, microbial ingress tests, vacuum decay tests, pressure decay tests, and helium leak tests. Each method has its advantages and limitations, and the choice depends on factors such as sensitivity, speed, and compatibility with the product.

3. **Test Method Validation**: Validate the selected leak detection method to ensure its accuracy, precision, specificity, and robustness. Validation parameters may include sensitivity, detection limits, linearity, repeatability, and reproducibility. Validation protocols should comply with regulatory requirements and guidelines.

4. **Sampling Plan**: Develop a sampling plan to ensure representative sampling of container closure systems from different batches and locations. Consider factors such as batch size, container type, and

production variability. Sample sizes and sampling frequencies should be sufficient to detect potential leaks reliably.

5. **Test Conditions:** Perform CCI testing under controlled conditions to ensure reproducibility and accuracy of results. Control parameters such as temperature, humidity, and test duration to simulate storage conditions and worst-case scenarios. Ensure that testing conditions are consistent with regulatory requirements and guidelines.

6. **Test Execution**: Conduct CCI testing according to validated test procedures and protocols. Perform tests on filled containers under simulated or actual storage conditions. Ensure that test equipment is calibrated and maintained properly to ensure accurate and reliable results.

7. **Data Analysis:** Analyze the test results to determine the presence or absence of leaks in the container closure system. Calculate leak rates or pressure differentials, as applicable, and compare the results against acceptance criteria or regulatory limits. Document all test data, observations, and calculations.

8. **Interpretation of Results**: Interpret the CCI test results to assess the integrity of the container closure system and its impact on product stability and quality. Identify any leaks or defects that may compromise product safety, efficacy, or shelf-life. Determine the root cause of leaks and implement corrective actions as necessary.

9. **Documentation and Reporting**: Document all aspects of CCI testing, including test procedures, protocols, results, and conclusions. Prepare a comprehensive CCI test report summarizing the testing process, results, interpretation, and any recommendations for corrective actions or improvements.

10. **Regulatory Compliance**: Ensure that CCI testing complies with regulatory requirements and guidelines, such as those outlined in pharmacopeial standards (e.g., USP <1207>) and regulatory guidance

documents. Include CCI test data in regulatory submissions to demonstrate product safety and compliance with regulatory requirements.

Data Analysis and Reporting:

Data analysis and reporting are crucial components of stability testing during product development, including pre-formulation studies. Proper analysis and reporting of stability data enable pharmaceutical developers to assess the stability profile of drug substances or formulations accurately, make informed decisions, and comply with regulatory requirements. Here's how data analysis and reporting are typically conducted:

1. **Data Compilation**: Gather all stability data obtained from testing throughout the study period, including physical, chemical, and microbiological stability data. Ensure that the data are complete, accurate, and well-documented.

2. **Data Verification**: Verify the accuracy and integrity of the stability data by reviewing raw data, laboratory notebooks, and electronic records. Confirm that data entry and transcription errors are corrected, and any discrepancies are resolved.

3. **Data Organization**: Organize the stability data into a structured format for analysis and reporting. Use spreadsheets, databases, or specialized software to manage and organize the data effectively.

4. **Statistical Analysis**: Conduct statistical analysis of stability data to identify trends, detect outliers, and assess variability. Common statistical methods include mean, standard deviation, regression analysis, and analysis of variance (ANOVA). Use appropriate statistical tests based on the nature of the data and study design.

5. **Trend Analysis**: Perform trend analysis to evaluate changes in stability parameters over time. Plot graphs or charts to visualize trends in physical appearance, chemical degradation, microbial growth, or other stability

indicators. Identify any significant deviations from expected stability trends.

6. **Comparison with Acceptance Criteria**: Compare stability data against established acceptance criteria, specifications, or regulatory guidelines. Determine whether the product meets predefined quality attributes, such as potency, purity, and microbial limits, throughout the study period.

7. **Shelf-Life Estimation**: Estimate the shelf-life of the product based on stability data and degradation kinetics. Use mathematical models, such as regression analysis or Arrhenius equation, to extrapolate stability data and predict shelf-life under different storage conditions.

8. **Out-of-Specification (OOS) Investigation**: Investigate any stability data that fall outside established acceptance criteria or specifications. Identify the root cause of OOS results, such as analytical errors, sample mishandling, or formulation issues. Implement corrective and preventive actions (CAPAs) to address identified deficiencies.

9. **Risk Assessment:** Perform risk assessment to evaluate the impact of stability deviations on product quality, safety, and efficacy. Consider factors such as patient risk, regulatory compliance, and business impact when assessing the severity of stability issues.

10. **Report Preparation**: Prepare a comprehensive stability report summarizing the study design, testing procedures, results, analysis, and conclusions. Clearly present the data and findings in a format suitable for regulatory submissions, internal reviews, or external stakeholders.

11. **Regulatory Compliance**: Ensure that data analysis and reporting comply with regulatory requirements and guidelines, such as those outlined in pharmacopeial standards (e.g., ICH guidelines) and regulatory guidance documents. Include relevant stability data and analyses in regulatory submissions to support product approval.

MCQs:

1. What is the primary goal of pre-formulation studies?

    A) To market pharmaceutical products

    B) To gather information about the drug substance for dosage form development

    C) To package the drug products

    D) To test the drug product on patients

2. Which technique is NOT used for solid-state characterization in pre-formulation studies?

    A) X-ray diffraction (XRD)

    B) Scanning electron microscopy (SEM)

    C) Blood testing

    D) Differential scanning calorimetry (DSC)

3. What does compatibility testing in pre-formulation studies aim to assess?

    A) The price of drug substances

    B) The strength of the drug

    C) The compatibility of the drug substance with excipients

    D) The color of the final product

4. Why is the study of organoleptic properties important in pre-formulation?

    A) They determine the chemical stability of the product.

    B) They affect patient acceptance and compliance.

    C) They help in pricing the product.

    D) They simplify the manufacturing process.

5. What is the role of surfactants in drug solubility enhancement?

    A) To increase the price of the drug

    B) To enhance the flavor of the drug

    C) To increase the melting point of the drug

    D) To reduce surface tension and improve dissolution rates

6. Which method is used to study crystal properties in pre-formulation studies?

A) High-Performance Liquid Chromatography (HPLC)

B) X-ray Powder Diffraction (XRPD)

C) Particle size analysis

D) Capillary electrophoresis

7. What is the significance of the BET method in pre-formulation studies?

A) It measures the bioavailability of the drug.

B) It is used to measure surface area.

C) It determines the odor of the drug.

D) It tests the viscosity of liquid formulations.

8. What does the shake flask method determine in pre-formulation studies?

A) The color of the drug substance

B) The dissolution rate of the drug

C) The solubility of the drug substance

D) The melting point of the drug

9. Which is NOT a focus of pre-formulation studies?

A) Determining the odor of drug substances

B) Assessing the economic impact of drug manufacturing

C) Characterizing physical and chemical properties of the drug

D) Testing the compatibility with excipients

10. Why is polymorphism studied in pre-formulation studies?

A) To assess the economic value of the drug

B) To identify the most stable crystalline form

C) To color the drug tablets

D) To test the flavor of the drug

11. What purpose does the study of impurity profiles serve in pre-formulation studies?

A) To color the drug substances

B) To understand the purity and safety of the drug substance

C) To determine the price of the drug substance

D) To understand the taste of the drug substance

12. What type of dosage forms does particle size most critically affect?

    A) Injectables

    B) Solids

    C) Gases

    D) Liquids

13. What aspect of drug substances does the pH solubility profile assess?

    A) Color change at different pH levels

    B) Taste variation at different pH levels

    C) Dissolution behavior at different pH levels

    D) Odor changes at different pH levels

14. What is the role of differential scanning calorimetry (DSC) in pre-formulation studies?

    A) It measures the weight of the drug substance.

    B) It assesses thermal properties.

    C) It determines the electrical charge of drug substances.

    D) It visualizes the drug substance.

15. What is evaluated during stability testing in pre-formulation studies?

    A) The marketing strategies for drug substances

    B) The degradation pathways and shelf-life

    C) The packaging color

    D) The price stability in the market

16. Which technique is not a part of solubility studies in pre-formulation?

    A) Turbidimetry

    B) Blood pressure monitoring

    C) Shake flask method

    D) Saturation solubility method

17. What does particle shape analysis in pre-formulation studies help to predict?

    A) The economic viability of the drug

B) The flavor of the drug

C) The behavior of drug substances in dosage forms

D) The packaging requirements

18. How does the dynamic vapor sorption technique contribute to pre-formulation studies?

    A) It measures the electrical resistance of drug substances.

    B) It studies moisture sorption behavior.

    C) It determines the viscosity of drug substances.

    D) It visualizes the molecular structure.

19. What is the primary focus of hot-stage microscopy in studying polymorphism?

    A) To observe melting behavior and phase transitions

    B) To measure the weight of the drug crystals

    C) To determine the electrical properties of crystals

    D) To assess the color changes under temperature

20. Which of the following is NOT assessed during the formulation screening phase of pre-formulation studies?

    A) Content uniformity

    B) Excipient compatibility

    C) Marketing strategies

    D) Stability under accelerated conditions

Short Answer Type Questions:

1. What is the purpose of compiling all stability data during stability testing?

2. How is data verification important in the context of stability testing?

3. Describe the role of data organization in stability testing.

4. What statistical methods are commonly used to analyze stability data?

5. Explain the process and purpose of trend analysis in stability testing.

6. Why is it necessary to compare stability data against established acceptance criteria?

7. How is the shelf-life of a product estimated based on stability data?

8. What is the significance of investigating Out-of-Specification (OOS) results in stability testing?

9. Describe what is involved in performing a risk assessment during stability testing.

10. What key elements should be included in a stability report?

11. Why is regulatory compliance important in stability testing?

12. How does data verification contribute to the integrity of stability testing results?

13. What tools or software are typically used for organizing stability data?

14. What is the importance of detecting outliers in stability data analysis?

15. What factors are considered when performing a risk assessment in stability testing?

16. How do changes in physical appearance impact the assessment of a drug's stability?

17. What role do mathematical models play in estimating the shelf-life of a pharmaceutical product?

18. What are the potential consequences of failing to resolve discrepancies in stability data?

19. How can stability data influence formulation optimization?

20. What are the challenges in ensuring regulatory compliance during stability testing?

Long Answer Type Questions:

1. Discuss the process and importance of compiling and verifying stability data in pre-formulation studies, and explain how this impacts the final product's development.

2. Describe the steps involved in organizing stability data and the significance of using specialized software in this process.

3. Explain the different statistical methods used for stability data analysis and how they contribute to understanding the stability profile of a drug.

4. Discuss the methodology and relevance of trend analysis in evaluating stability data, including examples of how trends can indicate potential issues.

5. Elaborate on the process of comparing stability data against acceptance criteria and how this ensures the quality and safety of pharmaceutical products.

6. Provide a detailed explanation of how shelf-life is estimated from stability data and the implications of incorrect estimations on the drug's market success.

7. Describe the investigation of Out-of-Specification (OOS) results, including steps to identify root causes and the importance of corrective actions.

8. Discuss the role of risk assessment in stability testing and how it aids in decision-making processes regarding drug development and formulation changes.

9. Explain the process of preparing a comprehensive stability report, including what information is crucial and how it should be presented.

10. Discuss the regulatory compliance requirements in stability testing and the consequences of non-compliance for pharmaceutical companies.

Answer Key:

1. (B) To gather information about the drug substance for dosage form development

2. (C) Blood testing

3. (C) The compatibility of the drug substance with excipients

4. (B) They affect patient acceptance and compliance.

5. (D) To reduce surface tension and improve dissolution rates

6. (B) X-ray Powder Diffraction (XRPD)

7. (B) It is used to measure surface area.

8. (C) The solubility of the drug substance

9. (B) Assessing the economic impact of drug manufacturing

10. (B) To identify the most stable crystalline form

11. (B) To understand the purity and safety of the drug substance

12. (B) Solids

13. (C) Dissolution behavior at different pH levels

14. (B) It assesses thermal properties.

15. (B) The degradation pathways and shelf-life

16. (B) Blood pressure monitoring

17. (C) The behavior of drug substances in dosage forms

18. (B) It studies moisture sorption behavior.

19. (A) To observe melting behavior and phase transitions

20. (C) Marketing strategies

CHAPTER – 3

PILOT PLANT SCALE UP

INTRODUCTION:

Pilot plant scale-up is a critical phase in the development of new processes, products, or technologies before full-scale production. It involves transitioning from laboratory-scale experimentation to larger-scale pilot plants to assess the feasibility, scalability, and performance of the process. Here's a detailed introduction to pilot plant scale-up:

1. **Definition:** Pilot plant scale-up refers to the process of increasing the scale of production from laboratory-scale to a larger, pilot-scale facility.

2. **Purpose:**

    a. **Evaluate scalability**: Determine if the process can be reliably scaled up to larger production levels.

    b. **Optimize process parameters**: Fine-tune operating conditions, equipment design, and materials to improve efficiency and product quality.

    c. **Assess feasibility**: Validate the economic viability and technical feasibility of the proposed process.

    d. **Gather data for commercialization:** Generate data necessary for designing full-scale production facilities and obtaining regulatory approvals.

3. **Key Considerations:**

    a. **Equipment selection**: Choose equipment that closely resembles full-scale production units to mimic real-world conditions accurately.

b. **Process optimization**: Adjust variables such as temperature, pressure, residence time, and feed rates to achieve optimal performance.

c. **Material compatibility**: Ensure that materials of construction are suitable for the intended process and compatible with the product.

d. **Safety and environmental impact**: Implement safety measures and assess environmental implications of the scaled-up process.

e. **Cost analysis**: Evaluate the cost implications of scaling up, including capital expenditure, operating costs, and potential savings.

4. **Steps in Pilot Plant Scale-Up:**

a. **Initial assessment**: Review laboratory-scale data and conduct feasibility studies to determine the need for pilot-scale testing.

b. **Design and construction**: Develop detailed engineering designs and construct the pilot plant according to specifications.

c. **Testing and optimization**: Conduct experiments using the pilot plant to optimize process parameters and assess performance.

d. **Data analysis**: Analyze data collected during pilot-scale trials to evaluate scalability, identify constraints, and make necessary adjustments.

e. **Scale-up strategy:** Develop a strategy for scaling up to full production based on the results obtained from pilot plant trials.

5. **Challenges:**

a. **Scale-up issues**: Differences in equipment performance, mixing characteristics, and heat transfer at larger scales can lead to unexpected challenges.

b. **Process variability**: Variations in raw materials, operating conditions, and environmental factors may affect process performance during scale-up.

c. **Cost constraints**: Limited budget for pilot-scale testing and equipment upgrades can pose challenges in achieving desired outcomes.

d. **Regulatory compliance**: Ensure compliance with regulations governing pilot-scale operations, including safety, environmental, and quality standards.

6. **Importance:**

a. **Risk mitigation**: Pilot plant scale-up helps identify and mitigate potential risks before investing in full-scale production facilities.

b. **Efficiency improvement**: By optimizing processes at a smaller scale, companies can improve efficiency and reduce costs in larger-scale operations.

c. **Quality assurance**: Testing in a pilot plant allows for better control over product quality and consistency, leading to improved market acceptance.

d. **Innovation facilitation**: Pilot plants provide a platform for innovation and experimentation, enabling the development of new products and processes.

CONCEPT OF PILOT PLANT SCALE UP

The concept of pilot plant scale-up is rooted in the need to bridge the gap between laboratory-scale research and full-scale industrial production. It involves transitioning from small-scale experimentation to larger-scale pilot plants to evaluate the feasibility, scalability, and performance of a process or product. Here's a detailed exploration of the concept:

1. **Transition from Laboratory to Pilot Scale:**

a. Laboratory-scale experiments are typically conducted on a small scale using bench-top equipment and small quantities of materials.

b. While laboratory experiments provide valuable insights into the fundamental aspects of a process or product, they may not accurately represent real-world conditions or challenges encountered at larger scales.

c. Pilot plant scale-up involves replicating the process on a larger scale using pilot-scale equipment to better simulate industrial conditions.

2. Feasibility and Scalability Assessment:

a. Pilot plant scale-up serves as a crucial stage in assessing the feasibility and scalability of a process or product before committing to full-scale production.

b. It helps identify potential challenges, such as equipment limitations, raw material variability, and process dynamics, that may arise during scale-up.

c. By testing the process at an intermediate scale, engineers and scientists can gather valuable data to inform decisions regarding process design, equipment selection, and operating parameters.

3. Optimization and Fine-Tuning:

a. Pilot plant scale-up provides an opportunity to optimize process parameters, refine operating conditions, and fine-tune equipment design to improve efficiency and product quality.

b. Through iterative experimentation and data analysis, researchers can identify optimal process conditions that maximize yield, minimize waste, and meet quality specifications.

c. Process optimization during pilot plant trials can lead to significant cost savings and performance improvements in full-scale production.

4. Risk Mitigation:

a. Pilot plant scale-up helps mitigate risks associated with scaling a process or product directly from the laboratory to industrial-scale production.

b. By conducting trials at an intermediate scale, companies can identify and address potential issues early in the development process, reducing the likelihood of costly setbacks or failures during full-scale production.

c. Risk mitigation strategies developed during pilot plant trials may include equipment modifications, process redesign, and contingency planning to address unforeseen challenges.

5. **Data Collection and Analysis:**

a. Pilot plant scale-up involves systematic data collection and analysis to evaluate process performance, assess scalability, and validate experimental results.

b. Data gathered during pilot-scale trials, such as production rates, material balances, energy consumption, and product quality metrics, are used to inform decision-making and process optimization.

c. Advanced data analytics techniques, such as statistical analysis, modeling, and simulation, may be employed to extract meaningful insights from experimental data and guide future scale-up efforts.

6. **Pathway to Commercialization:**

a. Successful pilot plant scale-up is often a critical milestone on the pathway to commercialization for new processes or products.

b. Data generated from pilot-scale trials provide valuable input for designing full-scale production facilities, estimating capital and operating costs, and securing regulatory approvals.

c. The knowledge and experience gained during pilot plant scale-up inform strategic decisions regarding market entry, production scale, and technology adoption, ultimately contributing to the successful commercialization of innovations.

SIGNIFICANCE OF PILOT PLANT SCALE UP

The significance of pilot plant scale-up lies in its pivotal role in the development, optimization, and commercialization of new processes, products, and technologies. Here's a detailed exploration of its significance:

1. **Risk Mitigation:**
   a. Pilot plant scale-up helps mitigate risks associated with scaling a process directly from laboratory experiments to full-scale production.
   b. By testing the process at an intermediate scale, companies can identify and address potential challenges early in the development process, reducing the likelihood of costly setbacks or failures during industrial-scale production.
   c. It allows for the exploration of various process parameters, equipment configurations, and operating conditions to optimize performance and minimize risks.

2. **Feasibility Assessment:**
   a. Pilot plant scale-up serves as a critical stage in assessing the feasibility of a new process or product on a larger scale.
   b. It provides insights into the scalability of the process, including its ability to maintain performance, efficiency, and product quality at increased production levels.
   c. By conducting trials in a pilot-scale environment, engineers and scientists can evaluate the technical, economic, and operational feasibility of the proposed process before committing to full-scale production.

3. **Process Optimization:**
   a. Pilot plant scale-up offers opportunities for process optimization and fine-tuning to improve efficiency, yield, and product quality.

b. Through iterative experimentation and data analysis, researchers can identify optimal process conditions, equipment designs, and material specifications that maximize performance and minimize resource consumption.

c. Optimization during pilot-scale trials can lead to significant cost savings, productivity gains, and competitive advantages in full-scale production.

4. Data Generation and Analysis:

a. Pilot plant scale-up generates valuable data that inform decision-making, process design, and scale-up strategies.

b. Data collected during pilot-scale trials, such as production rates, material balances, energy consumption, and product quality metrics, provide insights into process performance and scalability.

c. Advanced data analytics techniques, including statistical analysis, modeling, and simulation, can be used to extract meaningful insights from experimental data and guide further development efforts.

5. Technology Validation:

a. Pilot plant scale-up validates the technology readiness and performance of new processes or products in a real-world setting.

b. It allows companies to demonstrate the viability, reliability, and competitiveness of their innovations to stakeholders, investors, and regulatory authorities.

c. Successful pilot-scale trials build confidence in the technology and pave the way for commercialization by addressing concerns related to scalability, performance, and market acceptance.

6. Pathway to Commercialization:

a. Pilot plant scale-up is a crucial milestone on the pathway to commercialization for new processes, products, and technologies.

b. Data and insights generated from pilot-scale trials inform strategic decisions regarding market entry, production scale, investment priorities, and regulatory compliance.

c. Successful pilot plant scale-up accelerates the transition from research and development to full-scale production, enabling companies to capture market opportunities, generate revenue, and achieve sustainable growth.

DESIGN OF PILOT PLANT SCALE UP

Designing a pilot plant for scale-up involves careful consideration of various factors to ensure that the facility accurately simulates industrial-scale conditions while remaining flexible, cost-effective, and capable of generating reliable data. Here's a detailed exploration of the design aspects of a pilot plant for scale-up:

1. **Scale-Up Strategy:**

   a. Before designing the pilot plant, it's essential to define the scale-up strategy, including the target production capacity, process parameters, and performance objectives.

   b. Determine the level of scaling required (e.g., linear scale-up or non-linear scale-up) based on process characteristics and scalability considerations.

2. **Equipment Selection:**

   a. Choose equipment that closely resembles full-scale production units to replicate real-world conditions accurately.

   b. Consider factors such as capacity, material compatibility, operating conditions, and scalability when selecting equipment.

   c. Opt for modular and versatile equipment designs to accommodate process variations and future modifications.

3. **Process Layout and Flow:**

a. Design the layout of the pilot plant to facilitate smooth material flow, minimize cross-contamination, and optimize space utilization.

b. Arrange equipment and utilities in a logical sequence to reflect the process flow and minimize the need for material handling and transfer.

c. Incorporate provisions for cleaning, maintenance, and accessibility to ensure operational efficiency and safety.

4. Material Handling and Storage:

a. Include facilities for receiving, storing, and handling raw materials, intermediates, and finished products.

b. Design storage areas, silos, tanks, and handling equipment to accommodate varying quantities and types of materials while maintaining product integrity and quality.

c. Implement appropriate material handling procedures and safety measures to prevent spills, contamination, and workplace hazards.

5. Utilities and Infrastructure:

a. Provide utility connections, such as water, steam, electricity, and compressed air, to support process operations and equipment.

b. Size utility systems based on process requirements and anticipated loads, ensuring adequate capacity and redundancy to meet production demands.

c. Consider energy efficiency, environmental impact, and regulatory compliance when designing utility systems and infrastructure.

6. Control and Instrumentation:

a. Install instrumentation and control systems to monitor and control process parameters, equipment performance, and product quality.

b. Select sensors, analyzers, and control devices capable of accurately measuring critical variables and responding to dynamic process conditions.

c. Implement automation and data acquisition systems to collect real-time data, perform process optimization, and ensure reproducibility.

7. **Safety and Environmental Considerations:**

a. Incorporate safety features, such as emergency shutdown systems, ventilation, containment measures, and personal protective equipment, to mitigate risks and ensure a safe working environment.

b. Assess environmental impacts associated with pilot plant operations and implement measures to minimize emissions, waste generation, and resource consumption.

c. Comply with applicable regulations, codes, and standards related to occupational health, safety, and environmental protection.

8. **Flexibility and Scalability:**

a. Design the pilot plant with flexibility and scalability in mind to accommodate changes in process requirements, product formulations, and production volumes.

b. Use modular construction, interchangeable components, and adjustable settings to adapt to evolving needs and facilitate future expansions.

c. Plan for equipment upgrades, retrofitting, and reconfiguration to support process optimization and technology innovation over time.

9. **Documentation and Training:**

a. Develop comprehensive documentation, including standard operating procedures (SOPs), equipment manuals, and safety protocols, to guide pilot plant operations and maintenance.

b. Provide training and qualification programs for personnel involved in operating, maintaining, and troubleshooting pilot plant equipment and systems.

c. Foster a culture of safety, quality, and continuous improvement through regular training, audits, and knowledge sharing.

LAYOUT OF PILOT PLANT SCALE UP STUDY

Designing the layout of a pilot plant scale-up study involves organizing the pilot-scale facility in a manner that reflects the process flow, optimizes space utilization, and facilitates efficient operation and data collection. Here's a detailed breakdown of the layout considerations for a pilot plant scale-up study:

1. **Process Flow Analysis:**

   a. Begin by conducting a thorough analysis of the process flow to understand the sequence of operations, material handling requirements, and interactions between unit operations.

   b. Identify critical process steps, equipment interfaces, and material transfer points that influence the layout design.

2. **Zoning and Segmentation:**

   a. Divide the pilot plant facility into distinct zones or areas based on functional requirements, process stages, and safety considerations.

   b. Allocate separate zones for raw material handling, processing, intermediate storage, product finishing, utilities, and support services.

   c. Establish clear boundaries and workflow paths to minimize cross-contamination, safety hazards, and operational disruptions.

3. **Equipment Placement:**

   a. Arrange equipment and machinery in a logical sequence that mirrors the process flow and minimizes material handling.

   b. Position equipment with consideration for accessibility, maintenance requirements, and ergonomic considerations.

c. Group related equipment and unit operations together to streamline material flow, reduce downtime, and facilitate process monitoring and control.

4. Material Handling and Storage:

a. Designate designated areas for receiving, storing, and handling raw materials, intermediates, and finished products.

b. Select appropriate storage solutions, such as bins, silos, tanks, and pallet racks, based on material characteristics, quantity, and accessibility requirements.

c. Implement efficient material handling systems, such as conveyors, hoists, and forklifts, to transport materials between process units and storage areas.

5. Utility Distribution:

a. Plan the distribution of utilities, including water, steam, electricity, and compressed air, to support process operations and equipment.

b. Install utility connections strategically to minimize piping runs, pressure drops, and energy losses.

c. Ensure adequate capacity, redundancy, and flexibility in utility systems to accommodate process variations and future expansions.

6. Control and Instrumentation:

a. Integrate instrumentation and control systems throughout the pilot plant layout to monitor process parameters, equipment performance, and product quality.

b. Position sensors, analyzers, and control devices at critical points to capture real-time data and enable closed-loop control.

c. Centralize control panels, operator stations, and data acquisition systems for easy access and monitoring of pilot plant operations.

7. Safety and Emergency Preparedness:

a. Incorporate safety features and emergency response measures into the layout design to mitigate risks and ensure a safe working environment.

b. Install safety barriers, signage, and emergency stop controls to prevent accidents and unauthorized access to hazardous areas.

c. Establish emergency evacuation routes, assembly points, and communication systems to facilitate rapid response to incidents.

8. Flexibility and Scalability:

a. Design the pilot plant layout with flexibility and scalability in mind to accommodate changes in process requirements, equipment configurations, and production volumes.

b. Use modular construction, flexible piping connections, and adjustable equipment settings to facilitate process modifications and technology upgrades.

c. Plan for future expansions, equipment additions, and reconfigurations to support ongoing optimization and innovation initiatives.

9. Documentation and Training:

a. Develop detailed layout drawings, schematics, and equipment specifications to document the pilot plant configuration and operational procedures.

b. Provide comprehensive training and onboarding programs for personnel involved in pilot plant operations, maintenance, and safety protocols.

c. Establish protocols for documenting process deviations, equipment failures, and troubleshooting procedures to support continuous improvement efforts.

OPERATIONS OF PILOT PLANT SCALE UP

The operations of a pilot plant scale-up study involve executing a series of activities to simulate and evaluate the scaled-up process or product in a controlled environment. Here's a detailed breakdown of the operations involved in pilot plant scale-up:

1. **Preparation and Setup:**
    a. Ensure that the pilot plant facility is clean, organized, and equipped with all necessary materials, equipment, and utilities.
    b. Verify that safety protocols, operating procedures, and emergency response measures are in place and understood by personnel.
    c. Conduct pre-operational checks, inspections, and equipment calibrations to ensure readiness for pilot-scale trials.

2. **Material Handling and Preparation:**
    a. Receive, inspect, and prepare raw materials, intermediates, and additives required for the pilot-scale process.
    b. Weigh, measure, and document material quantities accurately to maintain process consistency and traceability.
    c. Transfer materials to designated storage areas, mixing vessels, or feed systems according to the process recipe and schedule.

3. **Process Operation and Monitoring:**
    a. Start up the pilot plant equipment and systems according to standard operating procedures (SOPs) and safety guidelines.
    b. Monitor process parameters, equipment performance, and product quality indicators continuously throughout the operation.
    c. Adjust control settings, operating conditions, and process parameters as needed to achieve desired outcomes and maintain process stability.

4. **Data Collection and Analysis:**

a. Collect real-time data on process variables, material flows, energy consumption, and product characteristics using sensors, meters, and instrumentation.

b. Record observations, measurements, and test results in logbooks, data sheets, or electronic databases for analysis and interpretation.

c. Analyze experimental data using statistical methods, modeling techniques, and software tools to assess process performance and identify trends or anomalies.

5. **Process Optimization and Troubleshooting:**

a. Evaluate process performance and identify opportunities for optimization, efficiency improvement, and quality enhancement.

b. Implement process modifications, parameter adjustments, and experimental interventions to address issues, overcome challenges, and achieve desired objectives.

c. Troubleshoot equipment malfunctions, process deviations, and quality issues promptly to minimize downtime and maximize productivity.

6. **Sampling and Product Analysis:**

a. Collect samples at regular intervals or key process stages for laboratory analysis, quality control testing, and product characterization.

b. Perform analytical tests, physical measurements, and sensory evaluations to assess product attributes, composition, and performance.

c. Compare experimental results against target specifications, quality standards, and regulatory requirements to ensure compliance and consistency.

7. **Documentation and Reporting:**

a. Document all aspects of pilot plant operations, including procedures, observations, deviations, and outcomes, in a comprehensive manner.

b. Maintain accurate records of material usage, production yields, equipment performance, and experimental conditions for future reference and analysis.

c. Prepare reports, summaries, and presentations summarizing the findings, conclusions, and recommendations of the pilot-scale trials for internal review, stakeholder communication, and decision-making.

8. **Shutdown and Cleanup:**

a. Safely shut down pilot plant equipment and systems in accordance with established procedures and safety protocols.

b. Conduct post-operational checks, inspections, and equipment maintenance tasks to ensure readiness for subsequent trials or shutdown periods.

c. Clean and sanitize process equipment, work areas, and utensils to prevent contamination, corrosion, and fouling between runs.

9. **Review and Feedback:**

a. Review the results, lessons learned, and insights gained from pilot-scale trials to inform future scale-up efforts, process refinements, and technology development.

b. Solicit feedback from stakeholders, team members, and subject matter experts to identify areas for improvement, innovation, and collaboration.

c. Incorporate feedback into pilot plant operations, procedures, and protocols to drive continuous improvement and optimize performance over time.

LARGE SCALE MANUFACTURING TECHNIQUES (FORMULA, EQUIPMENT, PROCESS, STABILITY AND QUALITY CONTROL) OF SOLIDS

Scaling up the manufacturing of solid products from laboratory-scale to large-scale production involves careful consideration of formulation, equipment selection, process design, stability assessment, and quality control measures. Here's a detailed exploration of each aspect in the context of pilot plant scale-up:

Formulation:

a. **Ingredients Selection**: Choose raw materials based on their availability, cost-effectiveness, and quality. Ensure consistency in the quality of ingredients from pilot scale to large-scale production.

b. **Formula Optimization**: Fine-tune the formulation to meet large-scale production requirements while maintaining product quality and stability.

c. **Compatibility Testing**: Verify compatibility of ingredients at larger scales to prevent issues such as phase separation, degradation, or unwanted reactions.

d. **Scaling Ratios**: Adjust ingredient proportions based on the scale-up factor to maintain product integrity and performance.

2. Equipment:

a. **Mixing Equipment**: Select industrial-scale mixers capable of handling larger volumes while ensuring uniform mixing and dispersion of ingredients.

b. **Granulation and Drying Equipment**: Utilize high-capacity granulators and dryers suitable for large-scale production to achieve desired particle size distribution and moisture content.

c. **Compression and Tableting Machines**: Invest in robust compression machines capable of producing tablets at the required throughput without compromising quality.

d. **Packaging Machinery**: Install packaging equipment suitable for bulk packaging of solids with features for accurate dosing, sealing, and labeling.

3. Process:

a. **Process Optimization**: Optimize process parameters such as mixing time, granulation duration, compression force, and drying temperature for large-scale production while maintaining product quality.

b. **Scale-Up Studies**: Conduct comprehensive scale-up studies to identify and address potential challenges arising from process scale-up.

c. **Validation**: Validate the scaled-up process through rigorous testing to ensure consistency in product quality, performance, and characteristics.

4. Stability and Quality Control:

a. **Stability Testing**: Perform accelerated and real-time stability studies on the scaled-up product to assess its shelf-life, degradation kinetics, and storage conditions.

b. **Quality Control Measures**: Implement robust quality control procedures at various stages of production to monitor critical quality attributes (CQAs) and ensure compliance with specifications.

c. **Analytical Techniques**: Employ advanced analytical techniques such as HPLC (High-Performance Liquid Chromatography), FTIR (Fourier Transform Infrared Spectroscopy), and microscopy for in-process monitoring and final product characterization.

d. **Process Monitoring**: Continuously monitor process parameters and product attributes during production to detect deviations and implement corrective actions promptly.

1. Equipment Selection:

a. **High-Capacity Ribbon Blenders or Paddle Mixers**: These are suitable for homogeneous blending of dry powders or granules at large scales.

They ensure uniform distribution of ingredients, critical for product consistency.

b. **Fluidized Bed Mixers**: For formulations requiring delicate handling or where heat-sensitive ingredients are involved, fluidized bed mixers can provide gentle yet thorough mixing.

2. Granulation and Drying Equipment:

a. **High-Capacity Fluid Bed Granulators and Dryers**: These are used for granulation and drying processes in a single unit, reducing processing time and ensuring uniform granule size and moisture content.

b. **Roller Compactors**: Ideal for granulating powders into larger, denser granules before final drying. They can handle high throughput rates and offer good control over granule size and density.

3. Compression and Tableting Machines:

a. **High-Speed Rotary Tablet Presses**: These machines are capable of producing large quantities of tablets per hour with precise control over tablet weight, hardness, and thickness.

b. **Multi-Station Tablet Presses**: For formulations requiring multiple layers or complex shapes, multi-station tablet presses offer flexibility and higher throughput.

4. Packaging Machinery:

a. **Automatic Filling and Sealing Machines:** These machines are essential for bulk packaging of solids into containers, sachets, or blister packs. They ensure accurate dosing and hermetic sealing to maintain product integrity.

b. **Labeling Machines**: To streamline the packaging process, labeling machines can be integrated to apply product labels accurately and efficiently.

5. Quality Control and Analytical Equipment:

a. **High-Performance Liquid Chromatography (HPLC) Systems**: These are used for quantitative analysis of active pharmaceutical ingredients (APIs) or other critical components in the final product.

b. **Moisture Analyzers**: Essential for determining moisture content in solids, ensuring compliance with specifications and stability requirements.

c. **Particle Size Analyzers**: Utilized for measuring particle size distribution, crucial for products where particle size affects dissolution rate or bioavailability.

6. Process Monitoring and Control Systems:

a. **Supervisory Control and Data Acquisition (SCADA) Systems**: These systems enable real-time monitoring and control of manufacturing processes, allowing operators to adjust parameters as needed to maintain product quality and consistency.

b. **Process Analytical Technology (PAT) Tools**: PAT tools such as NIR (Near-Infrared) spectroscopy or Raman spectroscopy can be integrated into production lines for in-line monitoring of critical parameters, reducing the need for offline sampling and analysis.

Process Design:

Designing the manufacturing process for large-scale production involves integrating formulation, equipment selection, process parameters, stability testing, and quality control measures. Here's a detailed breakdown:

1. Formulation:

a. **Ingredient Selection and Optimization**: Choose raw materials based on availability, cost, and quality. Optimize the formulation to ensure scalability while maintaining product performance and stability.

b. **Compatibility Testing**: Verify compatibility of ingredients at larger scales to prevent issues such as phase separation, degradation, or unwanted reactions.

c. **Scaling Ratios**: Adjust ingredient proportions based on the scale-up factor to maintain product integrity and performance.

2. Equipment Selection:

a. **Mixing Equipment**: Choose high-capacity mixers such as ribbon blenders or paddle mixers for homogeneous blending of powders or granules.

b. **Granulation and Drying Equipment**: Select equipment capable of handling larger volumes and ensuring uniform granule size and moisture content, such as fluid bed granulators and dryers.

c. **Compression and Tableting Machines**: Opt for high-speed rotary tablet presses or multi-station presses for efficient tablet production at large scales.

d. **Packaging Machinery**: Install automatic filling and sealing machines for bulk packaging, ensuring accurate dosing and hermetic sealing.

3. Process Parameters:

a. **Optimization**: Fine-tune process parameters such as mixing time, granulation duration, compression force, and drying temperature for large-scale production while maintaining product quality.

b. **Scale-Up Studies**: Conduct comprehensive scale-up studies to identify and address potential challenges arising from process scale-up.

c. **Validation**: Validate the scaled-up process through rigorous testing to ensure consistency in product quality, performance, and characteristics.

4. Stability and Quality Control:

a. **Stability Testing**: Perform accelerated and real-time stability studies to assess shelf-life, degradation kinetics, and storage conditions of the scaled-up product.

b. **Quality Control Measures**: Implement robust quality control procedures at various stages of production to monitor critical quality attributes (CQAs) and ensure compliance with specifications.

c. **Analytical Techniques**: Utilize advanced analytical techniques such as HPLC, FTIR, and microscopy for in-process monitoring and final product characterization.

d. **Process Monitoring**: Continuously monitor process parameters and product attributes during production to detect deviations and implement corrective actions promptly.

Stability Assessment:

Stability assessment is a critical aspect of large-scale manufacturing techniques for solids, ensuring that the final product maintains its quality, efficacy, and safety over its intended shelf-life. Here's a detailed breakdown of stability assessment considerations:

1. Formulation Stability:

a. **Ingredient Compatibility**: Verify the compatibility of ingredients at larger scales to prevent issues such as phase separation, degradation, or chemical interactions.

b. **Stability-Indicating Assays**: Develop and validate analytical methods capable of detecting degradation products or changes in critical quality attributes (CQAs) over time.

c. **Accelerated Stability Studies**: Conduct accelerated stability studies under elevated temperature and humidity conditions to predict long-term stability and degradation kinetics.

d. **Real-Time Stability Studies**: Perform real-time stability studies under recommended storage conditions to validate shelf-life claims and monitor changes in product attributes over time.

2. Equipment Stability:

a. **Equipment Calibration**: Regularly calibrate manufacturing equipment to ensure accurate and consistent processing conditions.

b. **Equipment Cleaning and Maintenance**: Implement robust cleaning and maintenance procedures to prevent contamination and ensure equipment integrity throughout the manufacturing process.

c. **Process Validation**: Validate equipment performance and process parameters to ensure reproducibility and consistency in product quality.

3. Process Stability:

a. **Process Optimization**: Optimize process parameters to minimize variability and maintain product consistency throughout large-scale production runs.

b. **Scale-Up Studies**: Conduct scale-up studies to identify and mitigate potential process-related issues, such as changes in mixing dynamics or drying kinetics, that may impact product stability.

c. **Process Monitoring**: Implement process monitoring systems to continuously monitor critical parameters such as temperature, humidity, and mixing speed to detect deviations and take corrective actions promptly.

4. Packaging Stability:

a. **Packaging Material Compatibility**: Select packaging materials compatible with the product formulation to prevent interactions that may affect product stability.

b. **Seal Integrity Testing**: Perform seal integrity testing to ensure hermetic sealing and prevent moisture ingress or contamination during storage.

c. **Package Testing**: Conduct package testing, including drop tests and stability testing under various storage conditions, to assess the integrity and stability of packaged products over time.

5. Quality Control Stability:

a. **Analytical Testing**: Utilize advanced analytical techniques such as HPLC, FTIR, and microscopy to monitor product stability and detect changes in critical quality attributes.

b. **Stability-Indicating Assays**: Develop and validate stability-indicating assays to assess product stability and shelf-life throughout the manufacturing process.

c. **Batch Testing**: Perform batch testing at regular intervals to ensure consistency in product quality and stability across different production batches.

Quality Control:

Quality control (QC) is crucial in large-scale manufacturing of solids to ensure that products meet specified standards for safety, efficacy, and consistency. Here's a detailed breakdown of QC considerations across formulation, equipment, process, stability, and quality control:

1. Formulation Quality Control:

a. **Raw Material Testing**: Perform incoming raw material testing to verify the quality, purity, and identity of ingredients.

b. **In-process Sampling**: Sample intermediate products during manufacturing to monitor critical quality attributes (CQAs) such as particle size, moisture content, and blend uniformity.

c. **Formulation Verification**: Confirm that the final formulation matches the approved recipe and specifications.

2. Equipment Quality Control:

a. **Equipment Calibration**: Regularly calibrate manufacturing equipment to ensure accurate and consistent processing conditions.

b. **Equipment Qualification**: Validate equipment performance to ensure it meets predefined acceptance criteria and regulatory requirements.

c. **Cleanliness Checks**: Conduct regular inspections and cleaning procedures to prevent cross-contamination and ensure equipment cleanliness.

3. Process Quality Control:

a. **Process Monitoring**: Continuously monitor process parameters such as temperature, pressure, and mixing speed to ensure adherence to specified operating conditions.

b. **In-process Testing**: Perform in-process testing to verify product quality and identify any deviations from established norms.

c. **Process Validation**: Validate manufacturing processes to ensure reproducibility and consistency in product quality.

4. Stability Quality Control:

a. **Stability Testing**: Conduct stability testing at regular intervals to assess product stability and shelf-life under various storage conditions.

b. **Accelerated Stability Studies:** Use accelerated stability studies to predict long-term stability and degradation kinetics.

c. **Real-Time Monitoring**: Monitor stability parameters in real-time to detect any changes in product attributes or degradation over time.

5. Final Product Quality Control:

a. **Finished Product Testing**: Perform comprehensive testing on finished products to ensure they meet specifications for identity, purity, potency, and safety.

b. **Analytical Testing**: Utilize advanced analytical techniques such as chromatography, spectroscopy, and microscopy to assess product quality and consistency.

c. **Batch Release**: Release products for distribution only after confirming compliance with established quality standards.

6. Documentation and Record-Keeping:

a. **Batch Records**: Maintain detailed batch records documenting all manufacturing steps, including formulation, equipment setup, process parameters, and quality control testing.

b. **Documentation Review**: Conduct thorough review and approval of batch records by qualified personnel to ensure accuracy and compliance with regulatory requirements.

c. **Retention of Samples**: Retain representative samples of each batch for future reference and testing as needed.

LARGE SCALE MANUFACTURING TECHNIQUES (FORMULA, EQUIPMENT, PROCESS, STABILITY AND QUALITY CONTROL) OF LIQUIDS

scaling up the manufacturing of liquid products from laboratory-scale to large-scale production involves several critical considerations including formulation, equipment selection, process design, stability assessment, and quality control. Let's delve into each aspect in detail:

1. **Formulation:**

a. **Ingredient Selection**: Choose raw materials based on their compatibility, solubility, stability, and intended functionality in the final product.

b. **Optimization**: Fine-tune the formulation to meet large-scale production requirements while maintaining product stability, efficacy, and desired attributes such as viscosity, pH, and color.

c. **Solvent Selection**: Select appropriate solvents or carriers to ensure uniform dissolution or dispersion of active ingredients and other components.

d. **Preservative Selection**: Incorporate preservatives to prevent microbial growth and ensure product stability throughout its shelf-life.

e. **Surfactants and Emulsifiers**: Include surfactants or emulsifiers as needed to stabilize emulsions or suspensions and improve product homogeneity.

2. **Equipment:**

a. **Mixing Equipment**: Choose high-capacity mixers such as emulsifiers, homogenizers, or agitators capable of handling larger volumes while ensuring uniform mixing and dispersion of ingredients.

b. **Emulsification Equipment**: Utilize high-shear mixers or emulsification systems to produce stable emulsions or dispersions.

c. **Filtration Equipment**: Install filtration systems for clarification or removal of particulate matter or impurities from the liquid product.

d. **Packaging Machinery**: Select filling and capping machines suitable for bulk packaging of liquids into bottles, containers, or other packaging formats.

3. Process Parameters:

a. **Temperature and Pressure Control**: Optimize temperature and pressure conditions to facilitate dissolution, mixing, or emulsification processes while maintaining product stability.

b. **Mixing Time and Speed**: Adjust mixing time and speed parameters to ensure thorough blending and dispersion of ingredients without causing degradation or phase separation.

c. **Homogenization Parameters**: Fine-tune homogenization parameters such as pressure and number of passes to achieve the desired droplet size distribution in emulsions or suspensions.

d. **Sterilization or Pasteurization**: Implement sterilization or pasteurization processes if required to ensure microbial safety and product stability.

4. Stability:

a. **Accelerated Stability Studies**: Conduct accelerated stability studies under elevated temperature and humidity conditions to assess product stability and degradation kinetics.

b. **Real-Time Stability Studies**: Perform real-time stability studies under recommended storage conditions to validate shelf-life claims and monitor changes in product attributes over time.

c. **Compatibility Testing**: Verify compatibility of ingredients and packaging materials to prevent interactions that may affect product stability or integrity.

5. Quality Control:

a. **Physical and Chemical Testing**: Implement comprehensive testing protocols to evaluate critical quality attributes (CQAs) such as viscosity, pH, density, clarity, and appearance.

b. **Microbiological Testing**: Conduct microbiological testing to ensure products meet microbial safety standards and to detect any microbial contamination.

c. **In-process Monitoring**: Continuously monitor process parameters and product attributes during production to detect deviations and ensure consistency in product quality.

d. **Batch Record Documentation**: Maintain detailed batch records documenting formulation, equipment setup, process parameters, and quality control testing for traceability and regulatory compliance.

Equipment Selection:

Equipment selection plays a crucial role in large-scale manufacturing techniques for liquids, ensuring efficient production while maintaining product quality, stability, and safety. Here's a detailed breakdown of equipment selection considerations across formulation, process parameters, stability, and quality control:

1. Mixing Equipment:

a. **High-Speed Mixers**: Choose high-speed mixers capable of handling larger volumes while ensuring thorough blending and dispersion of ingredients. Options include high-shear mixers, inline mixers, or planetary mixers.

b. **Emulsification Systems**: Utilize emulsification systems such as homogenizers or colloid mills to produce stable emulsions with uniform droplet size distribution.

c. **Agitators and Stirrers**: Install agitators or stirrers in mixing vessels to maintain product homogeneity and prevent sedimentation or phase separation during processing.

2. Filtration Equipment:

a. **Membrane Filtration Systems**: Select membrane filtration systems for clarification or removal of particulate matter or impurities from liquid products.

b. **Depth Filtration Systems**: Utilize depth filtration systems for coarse filtration or removal of larger particles before fine filtration or sterilization.

3. Filling and Packaging Equipment:

a. **Filling Machines**: Choose filling machines suitable for accurate dosing and filling of liquid products into bottles, containers, or other packaging formats. Options include piston fillers, gravity fillers, or vacuum fillers.

b. **Capping Machines**: Install capping machines capable of applying caps or closures securely to packaging containers to prevent leakage or contamination.

c. **Labeling Systems**: Integrate labeling systems for accurate application of product labels, batch numbers, and other required information onto packaging containers.

4. Heating and Cooling Equipment:

a. **Jacketed Tanks or Vessels**: Use jacketed tanks or vessels equipped with heating and cooling systems for precise temperature control during heating, cooling, or pasteurization processes.

b. **Heat Exchangers: Install** heat exchangers for rapid heating or cooling of liquid products using steam, hot water, or chilled water, minimizing processing time and energy consumption.

5. Process Monitoring and Control Systems:

a. **Temperature and Pressure Sensors**: Install temperature and pressure sensors at critical points in the process to monitor and control process parameters effectively.

b. **Automation Systems**: Implement automation systems such as programmable logic controllers (PLCs) or supervisory control and data acquisition (SCADA) systems for real-time monitoring and control of process variables.

c. **Safety Systems**: Ensure the integration of safety systems such as pressure relief valves, emergency shutdown systems, and leak detection sensors to prevent accidents and ensure operator safety.

Process Design:

Designing the manufacturing process for large-scale production of liquids involves integrating formulation, equipment selection, process parameters, stability considerations, and quality control measures. Here's a detailed breakdown:

1. Formulation:

a. **Ingredient Selection and Optimization**: Choose raw materials based on their compatibility, solubility, stability, and intended functionality in the final product. Optimize the formulation to ensure scalability while maintaining product stability, efficacy, and desired attributes.

b. **Solvent Selection**: Select appropriate solvents or carriers to ensure uniform dissolution or dispersion of active ingredients and other components.

c. **Preservative and Stabilizer Incorporation**: Include preservatives and stabilizers to prevent microbial growth and ensure product stability throughout its shelf-life.

d. **Emulsification Agents**: Incorporate emulsifiers or surfactants to stabilize emulsions or suspensions and improve product homogeneity.

2. Equipment Selection:

a. **Mixing Equipment**: Choose high-capacity mixers such as high-shear mixers, homogenizers, or agitators capable of handling larger volumes while ensuring thorough blending and dispersion of ingredients.

b. **Filtration Equipment**: Select membrane filtration systems for clarification or removal of particulate matter or impurities from liquid products.

c. **Filling and Packaging Machinery**: Install filling machines, capping machines, and labeling systems suitable for accurate dosing, sealing, and labeling of liquid products into bottles, containers, or other packaging formats.

3. Process Parameters:

a. **Temperature Control**: Optimize temperature control parameters to facilitate dissolution, mixing, or emulsification processes while maintaining product stability.

b. **Mixing Time and Speed**: Adjust mixing time and speed parameters to ensure thorough blending and dispersion of ingredients without causing degradation or phase separation.

c. **Homogenization Parameters**: Fine-tune homogenization parameters such as pressure and number of passes to achieve the desired droplet size distribution in emulsions or suspensions.

d. **Sterilization or Pasteurization**: Implement sterilization or pasteurization processes if required to ensure microbial safety and product stability.

4. Stability:

    a. **Accelerated Stability Studies**: Conduct accelerated stability studies under elevated temperature and humidity conditions to assess product stability and degradation kinetics.

    b. **Real-Time Stability Studies**: Perform real-time stability studies under recommended storage conditions to validate shelf-life claims and monitor changes in product attributes over time.

    c. **Compatibility Testing**: Verify compatibility of ingredients, packaging materials, and storage conditions to prevent interactions that may affect product stability or integrity.

5. Quality Control:

    a. **In-process Monitoring:** Continuously monitor process parameters and product attributes during production to detect deviations and ensure consistency in product quality.

    b. **Analytical Testing**: Implement comprehensive testing protocols to evaluate critical quality attributes (CQAs) such as viscosity, pH, density, clarity, and appearance.

    c. **Microbiological Testing**: Conduct microbiological testing to ensure products meet microbial safety standards and to detect any microbial contamination.

    d. **Batch Record Documentation**: Maintain detailed batch records documenting formulation, equipment setup, process parameters, and quality control testing for traceability and regulatory compliance.

Stability Assessment:

Stability assessment is crucial in large-scale manufacturing of liquids to ensure that the final products maintain their quality, efficacy, and safety over their intended shelf-life. Here's a detailed breakdown of stability assessment considerations across formulation, equipment, process parameters, and quality control:

1. **Formulation Stability:**

   a. **Ingredient Compatibility**: Verify compatibility of ingredients at larger scales to prevent issues such as phase separation, precipitation, or chemical interactions.

   b. **Stability-Indicating Assays**: Develop and validate analytical methods capable of detecting degradation products or changes in critical quality attributes (CQAs) over time.

   c. **Accelerated Stability Studies**: Conduct accelerated stability studies under elevated temperature and humidity conditions to predict long-term stability and degradation kinetics.

   d. **Real-Time Stability Studies**: Perform real-time stability studies under recommended storage conditions to validate shelf-life claims and monitor changes in product attributes over time.

2. **Equipment Stability:**

   a. **Equipment Calibration**: Regularly calibrate manufacturing equipment to ensure accurate and consistent processing conditions.

   b. **Equipment Qualification**: Validate equipment performance to ensure it meets predefined acceptance criteria and regulatory requirements.

   c. **Cleanliness Checks**: Conduct regular inspections and cleaning procedures to prevent contamination and ensure equipment integrity throughout the manufacturing process.

3. **Process Stability:**

   a. **Optimization:** Fine-tune process parameters such as temperature, agitation speed, and mixing time to minimize variability and maintain product consistency throughout large-scale production runs.

   b. **Scale-Up Studies**: Conduct scale-up studies to identify and mitigate potential process-related issues, such as changes in mixing dynamics or heat transfer characteristics, that may impact product stability.

c. **Process Monitoring:** Implement process monitoring systems to continuously monitor critical parameters and detect deviations from established norms.

4. Packaging Stability:

a. **Packaging Material Compatibility**: Select packaging materials compatible with the product formulation to prevent interactions that may affect product stability or integrity.

b. **Seal Integrity Testing**: Perform seal integrity testing to ensure hermetic sealing and prevent leakage or contamination during storage.

c. **Package Testing**: Conduct package testing, including drop tests and stability testing under various storage conditions, to assess the integrity and stability of packaged products over time.

5. Quality Control Stability:

a. **Analytical Testing:** Utilize advanced analytical techniques such as chromatography, spectroscopy, and microscopy to monitor product stability and detect changes in critical quality attributes.

b. **Stability-Indicating Assays**: Develop and validate stability-indicating assays to assess product stability and shelf-life throughout the manufacturing process.

c. **Batch Testing**: Perform batch testing at regular intervals to ensure consistency in product quality and stability across different production batches.

Quality Control:

Quality control (QC) is essential in large-scale manufacturing of liquids to ensure that products meet specified standards for safety, efficacy, and consistency. Here's a detailed breakdown of QC considerations across formulation, equipment, process parameters, stability, and quality control:

1. Formulation Quality Control:

a. **Raw Material Testing**: Conduct incoming raw material testing to verify the quality, purity, and identity of ingredients. Test for parameters such as pH, viscosity, density, and chemical composition.

b. **In-process Sampling**: Sample intermediate products during manufacturing to monitor critical quality attributes (CQAs) such as viscosity, pH, density, and color. Perform tests to ensure compliance with specifications.

c. **Formulation Verification**: Confirm that the final formulation matches the approved recipe and specifications through analytical testing and documentation.

2. Equipment Quality Control:

a. **Equipment Calibration**: Regularly calibrate manufacturing equipment, such as mixers, homogenizers, and filling machines, to ensure accurate and consistent processing conditions.

b. **Equipment Cleaning and Maintenance**: Implement robust cleaning and maintenance procedures to prevent contamination and ensure equipment integrity throughout the manufacturing process.

c. **Validation**: Validate equipment performance and process parameters to ensure reproducibility and consistency in product quality.

3. Process Quality Control:

a. **Process Monitoring**: Continuously monitor process parameters such as temperature, pressure, flow rate, and mixing speed to ensure adherence to specified operating conditions.

b. **In-process Testing**: Perform in-process testing to verify product quality and identify any deviations from established norms. Monitor CQAs to ensure consistency and uniformity of the product.

c. **Process Validation**: Validate manufacturing processes to ensure compliance with regulatory requirements and to demonstrate the ability to consistently produce quality products.

4. Stability Quality Control:

    a. **Accelerated Stability Studies**: Conduct accelerated stability studies under elevated temperature and humidity conditions to assess product stability and degradation kinetics.

    b. **Real-Time Stability Monitoring**: Monitor stability parameters in real-time during production to detect any changes in product attributes or degradation over time.

    c. **Compatibility Testing**: Verify compatibility of ingredients, packaging materials, and storage conditions to prevent interactions that may affect product stability.

5. Final Product Quality Control:

    a. **Physical and Chemical Testing**: Perform comprehensive testing on finished products to ensure they meet specifications for viscosity, pH, density, clarity, and appearance. Use analytical techniques such as chromatography, spectroscopy, and microscopy.

    b. **Microbiological Testing:** Conduct microbiological testing to ensure products meet microbial safety standards and to detect any microbial contamination.

    c. **Batch Release**: Release products for distribution only after confirming compliance with established quality standards.

6. Documentation and Record-Keeping:

    a. **Batch Records:** Maintain detailed batch records documenting all manufacturing steps, including formulation, equipment setup, process parameters, and quality control testing. Ensure records are accurate, complete, and readily accessible for review.

    b. **Quality Management System**: Implement a robust quality management system to ensure adherence to quality standards, regulatory requirements, and good manufacturing practices (GMP).

Large Scale Manufacturing Techniques (Formula, Equipment, Process, Stability And Quality Control) Of Semisolid

Scaling up the manufacturing of semi-solid products from laboratory-scale to large-scale production requires meticulous attention to formulation, equipment selection, process design, stability assessment, and quality control. Here's a detailed exploration of each aspect:

1. **Formulation:**

   a. **Ingredient Selection**: Choose raw materials such as active pharmaceutical ingredients (APIs), excipients, and bases based on their compatibility, solubility, stability, and intended functionality in the final semisolid product.

   b. **Optimization**: Fine-tune the formulation to meet large-scale production requirements while maintaining product stability, consistency, and desired attributes such as texture, viscosity, and drug release profile.

   c. **Base Selection**: Select appropriate bases (e.g., creams, gels, ointments) that provide desired rheological properties and enhance drug delivery.

   d. **Active Ingredient Incorporation**: Ensure uniform dispersion or dissolution of active ingredients within the base to achieve consistent dosing and therapeutic efficacy.

2. **Equipment:**

   a. **Mixing and Homogenization Equipment**: Choose high-capacity mixers, homogenizers, or emulsifiers capable of handling larger volumes while ensuring thorough blending and dispersion of ingredients. Consider factors such as shear forces and temperature control to maintain product stability.

   b. **Milling and Size Reduction Equipment**: Utilize colloid mills or high-shear mixers for size reduction of solid ingredients and to achieve uniform particle size distribution in the final product.

c. **Packaging Machinery**: Select filling and sealing equipment suitable for filling semisolid products into tubes, jars, or other packaging formats. Ensure accurate dosing, sealing integrity, and compatibility with the product's viscosity and texture.

3. Process Parameters:

a. **Temperature Control:** Optimize temperature control parameters to facilitate mixing, homogenization, and emulsification processes while maintaining product stability and consistency.

b. **Mixing Time and Speed**: Adjust mixing time and speed parameters to ensure thorough blending and dispersion of ingredients without causing degradation or phase separation.

c. **Homogenization Parameters**: Fine-tune homogenization parameters such as pressure and number of passes to achieve the desired particle size distribution and texture in the final semisolid product.

d. **Sterilization or Pasteurization**: Implement sterilization or pasteurization processes if required to ensure microbial safety and product stability.

4. Stability:

a. **Accelerated Stability Studies**: Conduct accelerated stability studies under elevated temperature and humidity conditions to assess product stability and degradation kinetics.

b. **Real-Time Stability Studies**: Perform real-time stability studies under recommended storage conditions to validate shelf-life claims and monitor changes in product attributes over time.

c. **Compatibility Testing**: Verify compatibility of ingredients, bases, and packaging materials to prevent interactions that may affect product stability or integrity.

5. Quality Control:

a. **In-process Monitoring**: Continuously monitor process parameters such as temperature, viscosity, and pH during production to detect deviations and ensure consistency in product quality.

b. **Analytical Testing**: Implement comprehensive testing protocols to evaluate critical quality attributes (CQAs) such as viscosity, pH, drug content, and microbiological purity.

c. **Microbiological Testing**: Conduct microbiological testing to ensure products meet microbial safety standards and to detect any microbial contamination.

d. **Batch Record Documentation**: Maintain detailed batch records documenting formulation, equipment setup, process parameters, and quality control testing for traceability and regulatory compliance.

Equipment Selection:

Equipment selection is crucial in large-scale manufacturing of semisolids to ensure efficient production while maintaining product quality, stability, and safety. Here's a detailed breakdown of equipment selection considerations across formulation, process parameters, stability, and quality control:

1. Mixing and Homogenization Equipment:

a. **High-Capacity Mixers**: Choose mixers capable of handling larger volumes while ensuring thorough blending and dispersion of ingredients. Options include high-shear mixers, planetary mixers, or sigma blade mixers.

b. **Homogenizers**: Utilize homogenizers to achieve uniform particle size distribution and texture in the final semisolid product. Choose options such as rotor-stator homogenizers or high-pressure homogenizers depending on the viscosity and consistency of the product.

2. Size Reduction Equipment:

a. **Colloid Mills**: Use colloid mills for size reduction of solid ingredients and to achieve uniform particle size distribution in the final product.

These mills are suitable for reducing particle size in suspensions or emulsions.

b. **High-Shear Mixers**: Consider high-shear mixers with appropriate milling attachments for size reduction of larger particles or agglomerates.

3. Filling and Packaging Machinery:

a. **Tube Filling Machines**: Select tube filling machines suitable for filling semisolid products into tubes with accurate dosing and sealing capabilities.

b. **Jar Filling Machines**: Choose jar filling machines for filling semisolids into jars or containers, ensuring consistent filling levels and sealing integrity.

c. **Sealing Equipment**: Install sealing equipment capable of hermetically sealing packaging containers to prevent leakage or contamination during storage.

4. Heating and Cooling Equipment:

a. **Jacketed Vessels**: Use jacketed vessels equipped with heating and cooling systems for precise temperature control during mixing, homogenization, or emulsification processes.

b. **Heat Exchangers**: Install heat exchangers for rapid heating or cooling of semisolid products, minimizing processing time and energy consumption.

5. Process Monitoring and Control Systems:

a. **Temperature and Pressure Sensors**: Install temperature and pressure sensors at critical points in the process to monitor and control process parameters effectively.

b. **Automation Systems**: Implement automation systems such as programmable logic controllers (PLCs) or supervisory control and data acquisition (SCADA) systems for real-time monitoring and control of process variables.

c. **Safety Systems**: Ensure integration of safety systems such as pressure relief valves, emergency shutdown systems, and leak detection sensors to prevent accidents and ensure operator safety.

Process Design:

Designing the manufacturing process for large-scale production of semisolids involves integrating formulation, equipment selection, process parameters, stability considerations, and quality control measures. Here's a detailed breakdown:

1. Formulation:

   a. **Ingredient Selection and Optimization**: Choose raw materials such as active pharmaceutical ingredients (APIs), excipients, and bases based on their compatibility, solubility, stability, and intended functionality in the final semisolid product.

   b. **Optimization**: Fine-tune the formulation to meet large-scale production requirements while maintaining product stability, consistency, and desired attributes such as texture, viscosity, and drug release profile.

   c. **Base Selection**: Select appropriate bases (e.g., creams, gels, ointments) that provide desired rheological properties and enhance drug delivery.

   d. **Active Ingredient Incorporation**: Ensure uniform dispersion or dissolution of active ingredients within the base to achieve consistent dosing and therapeutic efficacy.

2. Equipment Selection:

   a. **Mixing and Homogenization Equipment**: Choose high-capacity mixers, homogenizers, or emulsifiers capable of handling larger volumes while ensuring thorough blending and dispersion of ingredients. Consider factors such as shear forces and temperature control to maintain product stability.

b. **Size Reduction Equipment**: Utilize colloid mills or high-shear mixers for size reduction of solid ingredients and to achieve uniform particle size distribution in the final product.

c. **Filling and Packaging Machinery**: Select filling and sealing equipment suitable for accurate dosing, sealing integrity, and compatibility with the product's viscosity and texture.

3. Process Parameters:

a. **Temperature Control**: Optimize temperature control parameters to facilitate mixing, homogenization, and emulsification processes while maintaining product stability and consistency.

b. **Mixing Time and Speed**: Adjust mixing time and speed parameters to ensure thorough blending and dispersion of ingredients without causing degradation or phase separation.

c. **Homogenization Parameters**: Fine-tune homogenization parameters such as pressure and number of passes to achieve the desired particle size distribution and texture in the final semisolid product.

d. **Sterilization or Pasteurization**: Implement sterilization or pasteurization processes if required to ensure microbial safety and product stability.

4. Stability:

a. **Accelerated Stability Studies**: Conduct accelerated stability studies under elevated temperature and humidity conditions to assess product stability and degradation kinetics.

b. **Real-Time Stability Studies**: Perform real-time stability studies under recommended storage conditions to validate shelf-life claims and monitor changes in product attributes over time.

c. **Compatibility Testing**: Verify compatibility of ingredients, bases, and packaging materials to prevent interactions that may affect product stability or integrity.

5. Quality Control:

  a. **In-process Monitoring**: Continuously monitor process parameters such as temperature, viscosity, and pH during production to detect deviations and ensure consistency in product quality.

  b. **Analytical Testing**: Implement comprehensive testing protocols to evaluate critical quality attributes (CQAs) such as viscosity, pH, drug content, and microbiological purity.

  c. **Microbiological Testing**: Conduct microbiological testing to ensure products meet microbial safety standards and to detect any microbial contamination.

  d. **Batch Record Documentation**: Maintain detailed batch records documenting formulation, equipment setup, process parameters, and quality control testing for traceability and regulatory compliance.

Stability Assessment:

Stability assessment is critical in large-scale manufacturing of semisolids to ensure that the final products maintain their quality, efficacy, and safety over their intended shelf-life. Here's a detailed breakdown of stability assessment considerations across formulation, equipment, process parameters, and quality control:

1. Formulation Stability:

  a. **Ingredient Compatibility**: Verify compatibility of ingredients at larger scales to prevent issues such as phase separation, precipitation, or chemical interactions.

  b. **Stability-Indicating Assays:** Develop and validate analytical methods capable of detecting degradation products or changes in critical quality attributes (CQAs) over time.

  c. **Accelerated Stability Studies**: Conduct accelerated stability studies under elevated temperature and humidity conditions to predict long-term stability and degradation kinetics.

d. **Real-Time Stability Studies**: Perform real-time stability studies under recommended storage conditions to validate shelf-life claims and monitor changes in product attributes over time.

2. **Equipment Stability:**

   a. **Equipment Calibration**: Regularly calibrate manufacturing equipment to ensure accurate and consistent processing conditions.

   b. **Equipment Qualification**: Validate equipment performance to ensure it meets predefined acceptance criteria and regulatory requirements.

   c. **Cleanliness Checks**: Conduct regular inspections and cleaning procedures to prevent contamination and ensure equipment integrity throughout the manufacturing process.

3. **Process Stability:**

   a. **Optimization**: Fine-tune process parameters such as temperature, agitation speed, and mixing time to minimize variability and maintain product consistency throughout large-scale production runs.

   b. **Scale-Up Studies**: Conduct scale-up studies to identify and mitigate potential process-related issues, such as changes in mixing dynamics or heat transfer characteristics, that may impact product stability.

   c. **Process Monitoring:** Implement process monitoring systems to continuously monitor critical parameters and detect deviations from established norms.

4. **Packaging Stability:**

   a. **Packaging Material Compatibility**: Select packaging materials compatible with the product formulation to prevent interactions that may affect product stability or integrity.

   b. **Seal Integrity Testing**: Perform seal integrity testing to ensure hermetic sealing and prevent leakage or contamination during storage.

c. **Package Testing**: Conduct package testing, including stability testing under various storage conditions, to assess the integrity and stability of packaged products over time.

5. Quality Control Stability:

a. **Analytical Testing**: Utilize advanced analytical techniques such as chromatography, spectroscopy, and microscopy to monitor product stability and detect changes in critical quality attributes.

b. **Stability-Indicating Assays:** Develop and validate stability-indicating assays to assess product stability and shelf-life throughout the manufacturing process.

c. **Batch Testing**: Perform batch testing at regular intervals to ensure consistency in product quality and stability across different production batches.

Quality Control:

Scaling up manufacturing techniques for semi-solid formulations in a pilot plant requires meticulous attention to detail in various aspects including formula development, equipment selection, process optimization, stability testing, and quality control measures. Here's a detailed breakdown of each aspect:

Formula Development:

1. **Ingredient Selection**: Choose ingredients based on their compatibility, stability, and desired rheological properties for the semi-solid formulation. Common ingredients include gelling agents (e.g., carbomers, cellulose derivatives), emollients, humectants, preservatives, and active ingredients.

2. **Formula Optimization**: Experiment with different ingredient ratios and processing conditions to achieve the desired viscosity, spreadability, texture, and stability of the semi-solid product.

3. **Stability Testing**: Conduct stability studies to assess the physical, chemical, and microbiological stability of the formulation under various storage conditions (e.g., temperature, humidity, light exposure) over time.

Equipment Selection:

1. **Mixing Equipment**: Choose suitable mixing equipment such as planetary mixers, homogenizers, or propeller mixers capable of effectively dispersing and blending ingredients to achieve uniformity in the semi-solid formulation.

2. **Heating and Cooling Equipment**: Select equipment like jacketed vessels or steam jacketed kettles for precise temperature control during heating, melting, and cooling stages of the manufacturing process.

3. **Packaging Equipment**: Choose filling and packaging machinery suitable for semi-solid products, ensuring accurate filling, sealing, and labeling of containers.

Process Optimization:

1. **Batch Size Optimization**: Determine the optimal batch size based on equipment capacity, processing time, and resource availability to maximize efficiency while maintaining product consistency.

2. **Process Parameters:** Establish critical process parameters such as mixing speed, temperature profiles, and mixing duration to ensure reproducibility and uniformity in product quality.

3. **Cleaning and Sanitization Procedures**: Develop robust cleaning and sanitization protocols for equipment and facilities to prevent cross-contamination and ensure product safety and compliance with regulatory standards.

Stability Testing:

1. **Accelerated Stability Studies**: Conduct accelerated stability testing to predict the long-term stability of the semi-solid formulation by subjecting

samples to elevated temperatures and humidity conditions for a defined period.

2. **Real-time Stability Studies**: Perform real-time stability testing under ambient storage conditions to monitor changes in physical appearance, viscosity, pH, and microbial growth over an extended period.

3. **Formulation Optimization**: Adjust the formulation or packaging based on stability testing results to enhance product stability and shelf-life.

Quality Control Measures:

1. **Raw Material Testing**: Implement stringent quality control measures for incoming raw materials through testing for identity, purity, potency, and microbial contamination to ensure consistency and safety.

2. **In-process Testing**: Conduct in-process testing at critical control points during manufacturing to monitor parameters such as viscosity, pH, temperature, and homogeneity to detect deviations and ensure product quality.

3. **Finished Product Testing:** Perform comprehensive testing of finished products, including physical attributes (e.g., appearance, texture), chemical composition (e.g., active ingredient content), microbial quality, and stability to verify compliance with specifications and regulatory requirements.

Documentation and Record-keeping:

1. **Batch Records**: Maintain detailed batch records documenting all manufacturing steps, including formulation, equipment calibration, processing parameters, in-process testing results, and deviations encountered, to facilitate traceability and troubleshooting.

2. **Quality Documentation**: Generate certificates of analysis (CoA) for each batch of semi-solid product, summarizing test results and confirming compliance with specifications and regulatory standards.

3. **Regulatory Compliance**: Ensure adherence to Good Manufacturing Practices (GMP) and other relevant regulatory guidelines throughout the manufacturing process, including documentation practices, facility cleanliness, and personnel hygiene.

LARGE SCALE MANUFACTURING TECHNIQUES (FORMULA, EQUIPMENT, PROCESS, STABILITY AND QUALITY CONTROL) OF PARENTERAL DOSAGE FORMS

Large-scale manufacturing of parenteral dosage forms, such as injections, requires meticulous attention to formulation, equipment selection, process design, stability assessment, and quality control to ensure product safety, efficacy, and compliance with regulatory standards. Here's a detailed exploration of each aspect:

1. **Formulation:**
   a. Formulating parenteral dosage forms involves selecting suitable ingredients, such as active pharmaceutical ingredients (APIs), solvents, stabilizers, buffers, and preservatives, to achieve the desired drug concentration, pH, osmolarity, and stability.
   b. Consider factors such as solubility, compatibility, particle size, and sterility when formulating parenteral products.
   c. Conduct compatibility studies, solubility assessments, and stability testing at laboratory scale to optimize the formulation and ensure product safety and efficacy.

2. **Equipment Selection:**
   a. Choose equipment suitable for manufacturing parenteral dosage forms, such as stainless steel tanks, mixing vessels, filtration systems, filling machines, and lyophilizers, based on process requirements and product specifications.

b. Select equipment designed for aseptic processing, with features such as closed systems, laminar airflow, sterilization capabilities, and automated controls.

c. Consider factors such as equipment capacity, precision, accuracy, and cleanliness when selecting equipment for pilot plant scale-up.

3. **Process Design:**

a. Design the manufacturing process for parenteral dosage forms to ensure sterility, uniformity, and reproducibility of the final product while minimizing contamination risks and product losses.

b. Define process parameters, such as temperature, pressure, filtration rates, and filling volumes, to achieve desired product characteristics and meet regulatory requirements.

c. Incorporate process validation protocols, environmental monitoring, and aseptic techniques to verify process performance and compliance with current Good Manufacturing Practices (cGMP) regulations.

4. **Stability Assessment:**

a. Evaluate the physical, chemical, and microbiological stability of parenteral dosage forms under various storage conditions to ensure product integrity, potency, and safety.

b. Conduct stability testing, accelerated aging studies, and container closure integrity testing to determine product shelf-life, degradation kinetics, and packaging compatibility.

c. Monitor critical stability indicators such as pH, osmolality, particle size, and microbial contamination to assess product quality over time.

5. **Quality Control:**

a. Implement quality control measures to monitor and maintain product quality throughout the manufacturing process, from raw material receipt to finished product release.

b. Establish specifications, test methods, and acceptance criteria for key quality attributes such as sterility, endotoxin levels, particulate matter, and container closure integrity.

c. Perform in-process checks, sampling, and testing at critical control points to detect deviations, non-conformities, and out-of-specification results.

d. Document all quality control activities, deviations, corrective actions, and product disposition decisions in accordance with cGMP regulations and regulatory requirements.

NEW ERA OF DRUG PRODUCTS: OPPORTUNITIES AND CHALLENGES

The emergence of new drug products brings both opportunities and challenges to the field of pilot plant scale-up. Let's explore these in detail:

1. **Opportunities:**

   a. **Innovative Formulations**: New drug products offer opportunities to develop innovative formulations that improve patient outcomes, enhance drug delivery, and address unmet medical needs. These formulations may include nanoparticles, liposomes, micelles, and other advanced delivery systems.

   b. **Personalized Medicine**: Advances in genomics, proteomics, and biomarker research enable the development of personalized medicine tailored to individual patient characteristics. Pilot plant scale-up allows for the production of small batches of personalized therapies for clinical trials and patient-specific treatments.

   c. **Biologics and Biosimilars**: The growing demand for biologics and biosimilars presents opportunities for pilot plant scale-up to support the manufacturing of complex biological products, such as monoclonal antibodies, recombinant proteins, and cell therapies. These products offer new treatment modalities for various diseases.

d. **Advanced Manufacturing Technologies**: Technological advancements, such as continuous manufacturing, 3D printing, and artificial intelligence, enhance the efficiency, flexibility, and cost-effectiveness of drug manufacturing. Pilot plant scale-up allows for the evaluation and implementation of these technologies in real-world production settings.

e. **Regulatory Flexibility**: Regulatory agencies increasingly recognize the importance of innovation and flexibility in drug development and manufacturing. Pilot plant scale-up offers an opportunity to work closely with regulatory authorities to address challenges and streamline the approval process for new drug products.

2. **Challenges**:

   a. **Complexity of Formulations**: New drug products often involve complex formulations, including biologics, nanoparticles, and combination therapies. Scaling up these formulations requires specialized equipment, expertise, and process optimization to ensure product quality and consistency.

   b. **Manufacturing Complexity**: Biologics, cell therapies, and other advanced drug products have unique manufacturing requirements, such as stringent temperature control, aseptic processing, and sterile filtration. Pilot plant scale-up must address these challenges to maintain product safety and efficacy.

   c. **Regulatory Compliance**: Regulatory requirements for new drug products are evolving, particularly for biologics, biosimilars, and advanced therapies. Pilot plant scale-up must navigate complex regulatory pathways, including compliance with Good Manufacturing Practices (GMP), validation requirements, and product characterization standards.

d. **Cost and Resource Constraints**: Scaling up new drug products can be costly and resource-intensive, particularly for small and medium-sized companies with limited budgets and infrastructure. Pilot plant scale-up must balance cost considerations with the need for quality, safety, and regulatory compliance.

e. **Technology Transfer**: Transferring technology from research laboratories to pilot plant and commercial-scale facilities poses challenges related to equipment compatibility, process scalability, and data reproducibility. Pilot plant scale-up requires effective technology transfer strategies and collaboration between research, development, and manufacturing teams.

MCQs

1. What is the primary purpose of pilot plant scale-up?

    A) To decrease production costs

    B) To evaluate scalability of a process

    C) To reduce the time for product development

    D) To diminish the importance of laboratory experiments

2. Which of the following is NOT a key consideration in pilot plant scale-up?

    A) Equipment selection

    B) Process optimization

    C) Brand marketing

    D) Material compatibility

3. What is involved in the initial assessment step of pilot plant scale-up?

    A) Designing the full-scale production facility

B) Reviewing laboratory-scale data and conducting feasibility studies

C) Immediate commencement of full-scale production

D) Disregarding laboratory findings

4. What does the testing and optimization step in pilot plant scale-up focus on?

    A) Analyzing market trends

    B) Optimizing financial investments

    C) Conducting experiments to optimize process parameters

    D) Expanding the production line immediately

5. Which of the following best describes a challenge in pilot plant scale-up related to equipment?

    A) Marketing strategies for product launch

    B) Differences in equipment performance at larger scales

    C) Immediate reduction in production costs

    D) Simplification of process dynamics

6. What is the importance of risk mitigation in pilot plant scale-up?

    A) To prevent all potential financial losses

    B) To ensure that no new products are developed

    C) To identify and address potential risks before full-scale production

    D) To avoid any changes to the process

7. What is a major goal of feasibility assessment in pilot plant scale-up?

    A) To finalize product pricing and distribution channels

    B) To assess the scalability and maintain efficiency at increased production levels

    C) To diminish research and development activities

    D) To reduce interaction with regulatory authorities

8. How does data analysis help in pilot plant scale-up?

    A) By promoting the product on social media

    B) By evaluating scalability and identifying constraints

    C) By ignoring all previous research data

D) By focusing solely on financial aspects

9. What role does process optimization play during pilot plant trials?

    A) It is overlooked as it is not critical

    B) It aims to maximize yield and minimize waste

    C) It focuses on reducing employee efficiency

    D) It deals exclusively with external business conditions

10. How do pilot plants contribute to innovation?

    A) By restricting new ideas

    B) By providing a platform for experimentation

    C) By solely focusing on profit maximization

    D) By avoiding any risks

11. What does the design and construction step in pilot plant scale-up involve?

    A) Developing marketing campaigns

    B) Immediate mass production

    C) Developing detailed engineering designs and constructing the pilot plant

    D) Consulting only external stakeholders

12. What does the optimization and fine-tuning phase focus on in pilot plant scale-up?

    A) Decreasing employee numbers

    B) Optimizing process parameters and refining operating conditions

    C) Reducing the size of the plant

    D) Outsourcing production to other companies

13. Why are advanced data analytics techniques used during pilot plant scale-up?

    A) To reduce the workforce

    B) To gather and analyze large amounts of data

    C) To create advertisements

    D) To immediately sell the pilot plant

14. What is a challenge associated with process variability during pilot plant scale-up?

   A) The exact replication of laboratory conditions

   B) Variations in raw materials affecting process performance

   C) Increased marketing activities

   D) The complete automation of processes

15. What is a direct benefit of testing in a pilot plant?

   A) Increased complexity in production

   B) Better control over product quality and consistency

   C) Reduction in data collection

   D) Ignoring environmental impacts

16. Which statement best describes the scale-up issue in pilot plants?

   A) There is no change in performance across different scales.

   B) There is increased simplification of process parameters.

   C) Larger scales can lead to unexpected challenges due to changes in equipment performance.

   D) Scale-up always guarantees decreased production costs.

17. What is meant by "data generation and analysis" in the context of pilot plant scale-up?

   A) It refers to creating promotional content for advertising.

   B) It involves collecting and analyzing data to evaluate process performance.

   C) It pertains to disregarding any data from pilot trials.

   D) It is about minimizing the use of data in decision-making.

18. What is the primary focus when designing a pilot plant for scale-up regarding utilities and infrastructure?

   A) Prioritizing aesthetic design over functionality

   B) Providing necessary utility connections like water and electricity

   C) Avoiding any form of environmental assessment

D) Focusing solely on the administrative areas of the plant

19. What role does material handling play in pilot plant design?

   A) It is generally ignored as it does not impact the scale-up.

   B) It involves creating a system for efficient transfer and storage of materials.

   C) It focuses only on reducing costs of materials.

   D) It ensures that only the minimum required materials are used.

20. How does the design of the pilot plant affect safety and environmental considerations?

   A) Safety and environmental impacts are usually not considered.

   B) It includes implementing measures to minimize emissions and waste.

   C) It promotes maximum utilization of hazardous materials.

   D) It focuses on maximizing environmental harm to reduce costs.

Short Answer Type Questions

1. What is the primary objective of pilot plant scale-up in process development?

2. How does equipment selection impact the scalability of a process in a pilot plant?

3. Describe the role of material compatibility in pilot plant scale-up.

4. What are the key considerations for safety and environmental impact during pilot plant scale-up?

5. How does the initial assessment step in pilot plant scale-up contribute to the overall process?

6. What is the significance of process optimization in pilot plant trials?

7. Explain how pilot plant scale-up assists in risk mitigation before full-scale production.

8. What kind of data is primarily focused on during the data analysis step of pilot plant scale-up?

9. How does pilot plant scale-up facilitate innovation in product development?

10. What challenges might arise due to scale-up issues related to equipment performance?

11. How does variability in raw materials impact the process during pilot plant scale-up?

12. Discuss the importance of regulatory compliance in the context of pilot plant scale-up.

13. What role does cost analysis play during the scale-up process?

14. Describe the significance of feasibility assessment in pilot plant scale-up.

15. How does the design and construction step affect the scale-up process?

16. Explain the importance of testing and optimization in pilot plant scale-up.

17. What are the potential impacts of process variability on pilot plant scale-up?

18. How can pilot plant trials contribute to the pathway to commercialization?

19. What factors should be considered when designing a pilot plant for scale-up?

20. Describe the challenges associated with transferring technology from laboratory to pilot plant scale.

Long Answer Type Questions

1. Discuss the systematic approach involved in the transition from laboratory-scale research to pilot plant scale-up, emphasizing the assessment of scalability and feasibility.

2. Explain the critical steps in designing and constructing a pilot plant, focusing on the importance of mimicking real-world conditions.

3. Analyze the role of advanced data analytics in optimizing processes during pilot plant scale-up and how this impacts the final product quality.

4. Describe the various risks associated with direct scale-up from lab to full production and how pilot plant trials help mitigate these risks.

5. Detail the optimization and fine-tuning phases in a pilot plant trial and their significance in improving process efficiency and product yield.

6. Explain the importance of material handling and utility considerations in the design of a pilot plant and their impact on operational efficiency.

7. Discuss the implications of environmental and safety considerations in pilot plant scale-up and how they influence plant design and operation.

8. Provide a detailed analysis of how pilot plant scale-up contributes to innovation in the pharmaceutical industry, particularly in the development of new drugs.

9. Explore the challenges and strategies involved in ensuring regulatory compliance during the pilot plant scale-up of new pharmaceutical products.

10. Discuss the critical aspects of quality control in pilot plant scale-up and how they ensure the product meets required standards before full-scale production.

Answer Key:

1. (B) To evaluate scalability of a process

2. (C) Brand marketing

3. (B) Reviewing laboratory-scale data and conducting feasibility studies

4. (C) Conducting experiments to optimize process parameters

5. (B) Differences in equipment performance at larger scales

6. (C) To identify and address potential risks before full-scale production

7. (B) To assess the scalability and maintain efficiency at increased production levels

8. (B) By evaluating scalability and identifying constraints

9. (B) It aims to maximize yield and minimize waste

10.(B) By providing a platform for experimentation

11.(C) Developing detailed engineering designs and constructing the pilot plant

12.(B) Optimizing process parameters and refining operating conditions

13.(B) To gather and analyze large amounts of data

14.(B) Variations in raw materials affecting process performance

15.(B) Better control over product quality and consistency

16.(C) Larger scales can lead to unexpected challenges due to changes in equipment performance

17.(B) It involves collecting and analyzing data to evaluate process performance

18.(B) Providing necessary utility connections like water and electricity

19.(B) It involves creating a system for efficient transfer and storage of materials

20.(B) It includes implementing measures to minimize emissions and waste

CHAPTER – 4

PHARMACEUTICAL PACKAGING

INTRODUCTION:

Pharmaceutical packaging plays a crucial role in ensuring the safety, efficacy, and quality of pharmaceutical products. It encompasses a wide range of materials, designs, and technologies aimed at protecting medications from external factors that could compromise their integrity, such as moisture, light, air, and contamination. Here's a detailed introduction to pharmaceutical packaging:

1. **Purpose and Importance:**
   a. **Protection**: Pharmaceutical packaging serves to protect medications from physical, chemical, and biological damage during storage, transportation, and use.
   b. **Preservation**: It helps maintain the stability and potency of drugs by preventing exposure to moisture, oxygen, light, and other degrading factors.
   c. **Information**: Packaging provides essential information to healthcare professionals and patients, including dosage instructions, expiry dates, batch numbers, and safety warnings.
   d. **Compliance**: Packaging must adhere to regulatory requirements and standards to ensure product safety, efficacy, and legality.

2. **Types of Pharmaceutical Packaging:**
   a. **Primary Packaging**: Directly in contact with the pharmaceutical product, such as bottles, vials, ampoules, blisters, and syringes.
   b. **Secondary Packaging**: Outer packaging used for additional protection, identification, and branding, including boxes, cartons, labels, and leaflets.

c. **Tertiary Packaging**: Bulk packaging for transportation and storage, like pallets, shrink wrap, and containers.

3. **Materials:**

   a. **Plastics**: Commonly used for bottles, containers, and blister packs due to their versatility, lightweight, and barrier properties.

   b. **Glass**: Preferred for its inertness and ability to preserve drug stability, often used for vials and ampoules.

   c. **Aluminum**: Offers excellent barrier properties against light, moisture, and gases, commonly used in blister packs and closures.

   d. **Paper and Cardboard**: Used for secondary packaging and labels, providing printing surfaces for essential information and branding.

   e. **Films and Foils**: Provide barrier properties against moisture, oxygen, and light, used in blister packs and sachets.

4. **Packaging Considerations:**

   a. **Safety**: Packaging should ensure the safety of both the product and the user, including child-resistant closures and tamper-evident features.

   b. **Stability**: Packaging materials and designs must maintain the stability and potency of the pharmaceutical product throughout its shelf life.

   c. **Compatibility**: Packaging should be compatible with the drug formulation to prevent interactions that could affect efficacy or safety.

   d. **Ease of Use**: Packaging should be user-friendly, facilitating accurate dosing and administration by healthcare professionals and patients.

   e. **Regulatory Compliance**: Packaging must comply with various regulatory requirements, including Good Manufacturing Practices (GMP), labeling regulations, and international standards.

5. **Innovations and Trends:**

   a. **Smart Packaging**: Integration of sensors and indicators for monitoring product integrity, temperature, and tampering.

   b. **Sustainable Packaging**: Adoption of eco-friendly materials and designs to reduce environmental impact, such as recyclable plastics and biodegradable alternatives.

   c. **Patient-Centric Packaging**: Designs focused on improving medication adherence and patient convenience, including easy-open packaging and dose reminder systems.

PHARMACEUTICAL DOSAGE FORM AND THEIR PACKAGING REQUIREMENTS

Pharmaceutical dosage forms refer to the various forms in which pharmaceutical products are manufactured and administered to patients. Each dosage form has unique characteristics and requirements for packaging to ensure stability, safety, efficacy, and patient convenience. Here's an overview of common pharmaceutical dosage forms and their corresponding packaging requirements:

1. **Solid Dosage Forms:**

   - **Tablets:** Solid, compressed formulations containing active pharmaceutical ingredients (APIs) and excipients. Packaging requirements include:

      1. Protection from moisture, light, and air to prevent degradation.
      2. Child-resistant and tamper-evident packaging for safety.
      3. Unit-dose packaging for convenience and accurate dosing.

   b. **Capsules**: Gelatin or polymer shells containing powdered or liquid medication. Packaging considerations are similar to tablets, focusing on protection and convenience.

c. **Powders**: Dry formulations for reconstitution or direct administration. Packaging must prevent moisture ingress and provide accurate dosing mechanisms.

d. **Granules**: Small, solid particles for oral administration. Packaging requirements include moisture protection and accurate dosing devices.

2. **Liquid Dosage Forms:**

a. **Solutions**: Homogeneous mixtures of API(s) dissolved in a solvent. Packaging must be leak-proof, light-resistant, and provide accurate measuring devices for dosing.

b. **Suspensions**: Dispersions of finely divided solid particles in a liquid medium. Packaging should prevent settling, maintain stability, and provide accurate dosing.

c. **Emulsions**: Dispersions of immiscible liquids, such as oil and water, stabilized with emulsifiers. Packaging requirements include stability against phase separation and protection from light and air.

d. **Syrups and Elixirs**: Concentrated solutions containing sweeteners or flavoring agents. Packaging should prevent microbial contamination, maintain stability, and provide accurate dosing devices.

3. **Semi-Solid Dosage Forms:**

a. **Ointments**: Viscous, semisolid preparations for topical application. Packaging should ensure microbial integrity, prevent oxidation, and facilitate controlled dispensing.

b. **Creams**: Emulsions of oil and water with a semi-solid consistency. Packaging must maintain stability, prevent microbial growth, and provide hygienic dispensing.

c. **Gels:** Semi-solid systems containing gelling agents for topical or mucosal application. Packaging requirements include stability against leakage, microbial contamination, and degradation.

4. **Specialized Dosage Forms:**
   a. **Aerosols**: Pressurized dosage forms for inhalation or topical application. Packaging must withstand pressure, prevent leakage, and provide accurate dosing mechanisms.
   b. **Transdermal Patches**: Drug-in-adhesive or reservoir systems for controlled delivery through the skin. Packaging should ensure drug stability, adhesion, and protection from moisture and light.
   c. **Implants and Injections**: Parenteral dosage forms requiring sterile packaging, such as vials, ampoules, and prefilled syringes. Packaging must maintain sterility, prevent breakage, and facilitate aseptic administration.

PHARMACEUTICAL PACKAGING MATERIALS

Pharmaceutical packaging materials are carefully selected to ensure the integrity, stability, and safety of pharmaceutical products. These materials must provide protection against external factors such as moisture, light, oxygen, and contamination while maintaining the efficacy of the medication. Here's an in-depth look at common pharmaceutical packaging materials:

1. **Plastics:**
   a. **Polyethylene (PE**): Used for bottles, containers, and closures due to its flexibility, durability, and chemical resistance.
   b. **Polypropylene (PP**): Provides good barrier properties against moisture and gases, commonly used for containers, closures, and blister packs.
   c. **Polyethylene Terephthalate (PET):** Lightweight and transparent, suitable for bottles, blister packs, and film coatings.

d. **Polyvinyl Chloride (PVC):** Offers excellent barrier properties and is commonly used for blister packs, tubes, and intravenous bags.

e. **Polystyrene (PS):** Used for containers, vials, and trays due to its clarity, rigidity, and ease of molding.

2. **Glass:**

   a. **Type I Borosilicate Glass**: Preferred for its inertness and ability to preserve drug stability, commonly used for vials and ampoules.

   b. **Type II and Type III Glass**: Also used for packaging pharmaceuticals, with varying degrees of chemical resistance and durability.

3. **Metals:**

   a. **Aluminum**: Provides excellent barrier properties against light, moisture, and gases, commonly used for blister packs, closures, and tubes.

   b. **Tinplate and Aluminum Foils**: Used for sealing and protecting pharmaceutical products in containers and blister packs.

4. **Paper and Cardboard:**

   a. **Carton Board**: Used for secondary packaging such as boxes and cartons, providing strength, printability, and barrier properties.

   b. **Paper**: Used for labels, inserts, and package inserts, providing printing surfaces for essential information and branding.

5. **Films and Foils:**

   a. **Polyethylene (PE) Film**: Provides moisture barrier properties and is commonly used as inner seals in bottle caps and closures.

   b. **Polyvinyl Chloride (PVC) Film**: Used for blister packs and sachets, offering barrier properties against moisture and gases.

   c. **Aluminum Foil**: Provides excellent barrier properties against light, moisture, and gases, commonly used in blister packs and strip packs.

d. **Polyethylene Terephthalate (PET) Film**: Provides strength, clarity, and moisture barrier properties, used for blister packs and labels.

6. **Rubber and Elastomers:**

   a. **Natural Rubber**: Used for closures and stoppers in vials and bottles, providing a secure seal and compatibility with pharmaceutical formulations.

   b. **Synthetic Elastomers (e.g., Butyl Rubber):** Offers chemical resistance and compatibility with various drug formulations, commonly used for closures and seals.

7. **Specialized Materials:**

   a. **Desiccants:** Absorb moisture to maintain the stability of pharmaceutical products, commonly included in packaging for moisture-sensitive drugs.

   b. **Tyvek®:** Provides microbial barrier properties and tear resistance, commonly used as packaging material for sterile medical devices and parenteral products.

MEDICAL DEVICE PACKAGING

Medical device packaging is an integral aspect of pharmaceutical packaging, particularly for products such as syringes, catheters, implants, and diagnostic tools. The packaging of medical devices serves several critical functions beyond simply containing the product; it ensures sterility, protects against damage during transportation and storage, and provides information to healthcare professionals and patients. Here's a detailed look at medical device packaging in pharmaceutical packaging:

1. **Sterility Assurance:**

   a. Medical devices that come into contact with the body or bodily fluids must be sterile to prevent infections. Packaging for these devices must maintain sterility throughout manufacturing, transportation, and storage.

b. Sterile packaging typically involves using materials and processes that prevent microbial contamination, such as sterile barrier systems, including pouches, trays, and blister packs.

c. Packaging materials must be compatible with sterilization methods such as steam, ethylene oxide (EtO), gamma radiation, or electron beam sterilization.

2. Protection and Safety:

a. Medical devices are often fragile and sensitive to environmental factors such as moisture, light, temperature, and mechanical stress. Packaging must protect devices from damage during handling, transportation, and storage.

b. Protective packaging materials may include rigid containers, cushioning materials, wraps, and films designed to absorb shock and vibration.

c. Child-resistant and tamper-evident features may be incorporated into packaging to enhance safety, particularly for devices containing hazardous materials or medications.

3. Information and Instructions:

a. Medical device packaging must provide essential information to healthcare professionals and patients, including product identification, instructions for use, warnings, and precautions.

b. Packaging may include labels, inserts, package inserts, and instructions for assembly, operation, and disposal.

c. Clear and concise labeling is essential to ensure proper handling, administration, and disposal of medical devices, especially for self-administered devices used by patients at home.

4. **Regulatory Compliance:**

   a. Medical device packaging must comply with regulatory requirements and standards, such as those set forth by regulatory agencies like the U.S. Food and Drug Administration (FDA) and the European Medicines Agency (EMA).

   b. Regulations may include guidelines for sterile packaging, labeling, quality control, traceability, and documentation.

   c. Packaging validation and testing are essential to demonstrate compliance with regulatory requirements and ensure the safety and efficacy of medical devices.

5. **Specialized Packaging Technologies:**

   a. Active Packaging: Incorporates technologies such as desiccants, oxygen scavengers, and antimicrobial agents to extend shelf life and maintain product integrity.

   b. Smart Packaging: Integration of sensors and indicators to monitor product conditions such as temperature, humidity, and tampering.

   c. Sustainable Packaging: Adoption of eco-friendly materials and designs to reduce environmental impact and improve sustainability.

ENTERAL PACKAGING

Enteral packaging refers to the packaging of pharmaceutical products that are intended for administration via the gastrointestinal tract, primarily through the mouth or feeding tubes. Enteral medications are commonly used for patients who cannot take medications orally or require nutritional support. Enteral packaging serves several critical functions, including ensuring product stability, accuracy of dosing, safety, and ease of administration. Here's a detailed overview of enteral packaging in pharmaceutical packaging:

1. **Types of Enteral Products:**

   a. **Liquid Formulations**: Including solutions, suspensions, and emulsions, packaged in bottles, sachets, or unit-dose containers.

b. **Powder Formulations**: Often used for reconstitution with water or other liquids before administration, packaged in single-dose packets or bulk containers.

c. **Pre-filled Syringes**: Ready-to-use syringes containing liquid medications, commonly used for accurate dosing and convenience.

d. **Nutritional Supplements**: Including enteral feeds, meal replacements, and oral nutritional supplements, packaged in cans, bottles, or tetra packs.

2. **Packaging Requirements:**

a. **Product Stability**: Enteral packaging must protect medications and nutritional products from degradation due to exposure to light, moisture, oxygen, and temperature fluctuations.

b. **Safety and Sterility**: Packaging should ensure the sterility of products intended for administration to vulnerable patient populations, such as those with compromised immune systems.

c. **Accurate Dosing**: Packaging must facilitate accurate measurement and administration of enteral medications and nutritional products, especially for patients with specific dosage requirements.

d. **Compatibility:** Packaging materials must be compatible with the formulation of the product to prevent interactions that could affect stability or efficacy.

e. **Ease of Use**: Packaging should be user-friendly, allowing for easy administration by healthcare professionals and caregivers, including clear labeling and instructions.

f. **Tamper Resistance**: Enteral packaging may include tamper-evident features to ensure the integrity of the product and protect against tampering or contamination.

3. **Packaging Materials:**

a. **Plastics**: Commonly used for bottles, containers, and unit-dose packets due to their flexibility, durability, and barrier properties.

b. **Glass**: Preferred for certain liquid formulations due to its inertness and ability to maintain product stability.

c. **Aluminum Foil:** Provides excellent barrier properties against light, moisture, and gases, commonly used in sachets and blister packs.

d. **Paper and Cardboard**: Used for secondary packaging, labels, and instructions, providing printing surfaces for essential information and branding.

e. **Polyethylene Terephthalate (PET) Film**: Provides strength, clarity, and moisture barrier properties, used for bottle labels and packaging seals.

4. **Regulatory Compliance:**

a. Enteral packaging must comply with regulatory requirements and standards specific to pharmaceutical products, including Good Manufacturing Practices (GMP) and labeling regulations.

b. Regulations may include guidelines for sterility assurance, quality control, traceability, and documentation to ensure the safety and efficacy of enteral products.

ASEPTIC PACKAGING SYSTEMS

Aseptic packaging systems are crucial in pharmaceutical packaging, especially for products that require sterile conditions to maintain their integrity and efficacy. These systems are designed to prevent microbial contamination during the packaging process and maintain sterility throughout storage and distribution. Aseptic packaging is commonly used for liquid formulations, injectable drugs, and biological products that cannot withstand terminal sterilization processes. Here's a detailed overview of aseptic packaging systems in pharmaceutical packaging:

1. **Principles of Aseptic Packaging:**

a. **Sterile Environment**: Aseptic packaging systems operate in controlled environments with low levels of airborne particles and microorganisms to prevent contamination.

b. **Sterile Components**: Packaging materials, containers, closures, and equipment must be sterilized before use to ensure product sterility.

c. **Sterile Handling**: Operators must follow strict aseptic techniques to minimize the risk of contamination during the packaging process, including wearing sterile gowns, gloves, and masks.

d. **Barrier Systems:** Aseptic packaging systems may incorporate barrier technologies such as laminar airflow, isolators, and sterile connectors to maintain sterility and prevent microbial ingress.

e. **Sterilization Methods:** Equipment and packaging components may be sterilized using methods such as steam sterilization, gamma irradiation, or hydrogen peroxide vapor.

2. **Components of Aseptic Packaging Systems:**

   a. **Filling Equipment**: Aseptic filling machines are designed to fill sterile liquid products into containers without compromising sterility. These machines may use technologies such as peristaltic pumps, piston fillers, or rotary fillers.

   b. **Sterile Containers**: Containers such as vials, ampoules, syringes, and bags are made from materials such as glass or plastic and are sterilized before filling.

   c. **Sterile Closures**: Closures such as caps, stoppers, and seals must maintain sterility and provide a secure barrier to prevent microbial ingress after filling.

   d. **Packaging Materials**: Films, laminates, and labels used for aseptic packaging must be sterilized and compatible with the product to maintain sterility and stability.

3. **Aseptic Filling Techniques:**

   a. **Isobaric Filling**: Maintains constant pressure in the container during filling to minimize foaming and splashing, reducing the risk of contamination.

   b. **Pre-sterilized Components**: Some aseptic filling systems use pre-sterilized components such as pre-filled syringes or sterile connectors to simplify the packaging process and minimize contamination risks.

   c. **Closed Systems**: Aseptic filling lines may incorporate closed systems that isolate the product from the environment, reducing the risk of microbial contamination during filling and sealing.

4. **Validation and Monitoring:**

   a. **Process Validation**: Aseptic packaging processes must be validated to demonstrate their effectiveness in maintaining sterility and preventing contamination.

   b. **Environmental Monitoring**: Regular monitoring of the packaging environment, including air quality, surface cleanliness, and personnel gowning, is essential to ensure compliance with sterility requirements.

   c. **Microbial Testing:** Finished products undergo microbial testing to confirm their sterility and compliance with regulatory standards.

5. **Regulatory Compliance:**

   a. Aseptic packaging systems must comply with regulatory requirements and standards, such as Good Manufacturing Practices (GMP), Annex 1 of the EU GMP, and the FDA's Aseptic Processing Guidance.

   b. Regulatory agencies conduct inspections and audits to ensure compliance with aseptic processing requirements and to verify the sterility and safety of pharmaceutical products.

CONTAINER CLOSURE SYSTEMS

Container closure systems play a critical role in pharmaceutical packaging, serving as the primary barrier between the pharmaceutical product and the external environment. These systems must maintain product integrity, prevent contamination, and ensure patient safety throughout the product's shelf life. Here's a detailed overview of container closure systems in pharmaceutical packaging:

1. **Components of Container Closure Systems:**
   a. **Primary Packaging**: Directly in contact with the pharmaceutical product, including vials, ampoules, bottles, syringes, cartridges, and blister packs.
   b. **Closures:** Caps, stoppers, seals, and lids used to seal the primary packaging and prevent product leakage and contamination.
   c. **Sealing Materials**: Gaskets, liners, and coatings used to provide a secure seal between the container and closure, ensuring product integrity and sterility.

2. **Functions of Container Closure Systems:**
   a. **Containment**: Prevents leakage and spillage of the pharmaceutical product, protecting it from contamination and environmental factors.
   b. **Protection:** Shields the product from moisture, light, oxygen, and other degrading factors that could compromise its stability and efficacy.
   c. **Sterility Assurance**: Maintains the sterility of sterile products and prevents microbial ingress during storage, transportation, and use.
   d. **Safety**: Ensures the safety of both the product and the user by preventing tampering, accidental ingestion, and exposure to hazardous materials.

3. **Types of Container Closure Systems:**

a. **Closures for Liquid Formulations**: Screw caps, rubber stoppers, and crimp seals used for bottles, vials, and ampoules containing liquid medications.

b. **Closures for Solid Dosage Forms**: Child-resistant caps, foil blister packs, and heat-sealed pouches used for tablets, capsules, and powders.

c. **Prefilled Syringe Systems**: Ready-to-use syringes with preattached needles and needle shields, sealed with caps or tip caps to maintain sterility.

d. **Parenteral Containers**: Glass vials, plastic bottles, and prefilled syringes used for injectable drugs, sealed with rubber stoppers, aluminum caps, or plastic plungers.

4. **Materials Used in Container Closure Systems:**

a. **Glass**: Preferred for its inertness, transparency, and ability to maintain product stability, commonly used for vials, ampoules, and parenteral containers.

b. **Plastics**: Polyethylene, polypropylene, and cyclic olefin polymers (COP) are commonly used for bottles, syringes, and blister packs due to their flexibility, durability, and barrier properties.

c. **Rubber:** Natural rubber and synthetic elastomers such as bromobutyl and chlorobutyl rubber are used for closures and stoppers, providing a secure seal and compatibility with pharmaceutical formulations.

d. **Metals:** Aluminum, tinplate, and stainless steel are used for caps, seals, and foil blister packs, offering excellent barrier properties against moisture, light, and gases.

5. **Regulatory Considerations:**

a. Container closure systems must comply with regulatory requirements and standards set forth by regulatory agencies such as the U.S. Food and Drug Administration (FDA), European Medicines Agency (EMA), and International Organization for Standardization (ISO).

b. Regulations include guidelines for container integrity, sterility assurance, compatibility testing, extractables and leachables, and closure system performance.

6. Quality Control and Testing:

a. Container closure systems undergo rigorous quality control and testing to ensure their integrity, compatibility, and performance.

b. Testing may include container closure integrity testing (CCIT), extractables and leachables studies, accelerated aging studies, and microbiological testing for sterility assurance.

ISSUES FACING MODERN DRUG PACKAGING

Modern drug packaging faces several challenges and issues that impact product safety, efficacy, regulatory compliance, and patient convenience. These challenges arise from various factors, including technological advancements, regulatory requirements, environmental concerns, and the evolving needs of healthcare stakeholders. Here's a detailed overview of some of the key issues facing modern drug packaging in pharmaceutical packaging:

1. Counterfeiting and Tampering:

a. Counterfeiting and tampering pose significant risks to patient safety and public health, as counterfeit drugs may contain harmful ingredients or incorrect dosages.

b. Pharmaceutical packaging must incorporate anti-counterfeiting and tamper-evident features such as holographic labels, RFID tags, and unique serial numbers to prevent unauthorized access and ensure product authenticity.

2. Child-Resistant Packaging:

a. Medications and household products must be packaged in child-resistant containers to prevent accidental ingestion by children, reducing the risk of poisoning and overdose.

b. Designing effective child-resistant packaging while maintaining accessibility for adult users presents a challenge for pharmaceutical packaging designers.

3. **Sustainability and Environmental Impact:**

a. Pharmaceutical packaging contributes to environmental pollution through the generation of plastic waste, greenhouse gas emissions, and depletion of natural resources.

b. There is growing pressure to develop sustainable packaging solutions, including recyclable materials, biodegradable polymers, and reduced packaging volumes, to minimize environmental impact and meet regulatory requirements.

4. **Drug Stability and Shelf Life:**

a. Pharmaceutical products are susceptible to degradation due to exposure to light, moisture, oxygen, and temperature fluctuations during storage and transportation.

b. Packaging materials and designs must be selected to provide adequate protection and stability for drugs throughout their shelf life, ensuring product efficacy and safety.

5. **Patient Adherence and Convenience:**

a. Complex packaging designs, difficult-to-open containers, and unclear labeling can hinder patient adherence to medication regimens and lead to medication errors.

b. Patient-centric packaging solutions, such as easy-open blister packs, color-coded labels, and medication reminder systems, are needed to improve patient convenience and adherence.

6. **Regulatory Compliance:**

   a. Pharmaceutical packaging must comply with stringent regulatory requirements and standards set forth by regulatory agencies such as the FDA, EMA, and ISO.

   b. Compliance with Good Manufacturing Practices (GMP), labeling regulations, child-resistant packaging requirements, and serialization mandates presents challenges for pharmaceutical manufacturers and packaging suppliers.

7. **Supply Chain Complexity:**

   a. Globalization and complex supply chains increase the risk of product diversion, theft, and counterfeiting during transportation and distribution.

   b. Implementing track-and-trace technologies, such as barcoding, RFID, and blockchain, can enhance supply chain visibility and security, but integration challenges and cost implications remain.

8. **Cost Pressures and Market Competition:**

   a. Pharmaceutical companies face cost pressures and competitive pressures to reduce packaging costs while maintaining product quality and safety.

   b. Balancing cost-effectiveness with packaging innovation, sustainability, and regulatory compliance is a challenge for pharmaceutical manufacturers.

SELECTION OF PHARMACEUTICAL PACKAGING MATERIALS

The selection of pharmaceutical packaging materials is a critical aspect of pharmaceutical packaging design, as it directly impacts the stability, safety, efficacy, and regulatory compliance of pharmaceutical products. Several factors must be considered when choosing packaging materials, including compatibility with the drug formulation, protection against environmental factors, ease of manufacturing, cost-effectiveness, and sustainability. Here's a detailed overview of the selection process for pharmaceutical packaging materials:

1. **Compatibility with Drug Formulation:**
   a. The packaging material must be compatible with the specific characteristics of the drug formulation, including its chemical composition, pH, solubility, and stability.
   b. Compatibility testing, such as extractables and leachables studies, is conducted to evaluate potential interactions between the drug and packaging material, ensuring product safety and efficacy.

2. **Barrier Properties:**
   a. Packaging materials must provide barrier properties against moisture, light, oxygen, and other environmental factors that could degrade the drug formulation.
   b. Barrier properties are critical for maintaining product stability and shelf life, especially for sensitive pharmaceuticals prone to degradation.

3. **Safety and Regulatory Compliance:**
   a. Packaging materials must comply with regulatory requirements and standards set forth by regulatory agencies such as the FDA, EMA, and ISO.
   b. Compliance with Good Manufacturing Practices (GMP), pharmacopeial standards, and labeling regulations is essential to ensure product safety, quality, and legality.

4. **Protection and Stability:**
   a. Packaging materials should protect pharmaceutical products from physical, chemical, and biological damage during storage, transportation, and use.

b. Stability testing is conducted to assess the compatibility of packaging materials with the drug formulation and their ability to maintain product stability under various conditions.

5. **Ease of Manufacturing and Processing:**
   a. Packaging materials should be compatible with manufacturing processes such as molding, extrusion, printing, and sterilization.
   b. Ease of processing and compatibility with high-speed packaging equipment can improve manufacturing efficiency and reduce production costs.

6. **Cost-Effectiveness:**
   a. Packaging materials should be cost-effective and provide value for money while meeting quality and performance requirements.
   b. Considerations such as material cost, production efficiency, packaging waste, and total cost of ownership are evaluated to determine cost-effectiveness.

7. **Sustainability and Environmental Impact:**
   a. There is growing pressure to adopt sustainable packaging materials and practices to reduce environmental impact and meet corporate sustainability goals.
   b. Sustainable packaging options include recyclable plastics, biodegradable polymers, renewable materials, and lightweight designs that minimize packaging waste and carbon footprint.

8. **Aesthetics and Branding:**
   a. Packaging materials play a crucial role in product presentation, branding, and consumer perception.
   b. Aesthetic considerations such as color, texture, transparency, and printability contribute to the overall visual appeal and marketability of pharmaceutical products.

EVALUATION OF PHARMACEUTICAL PACKAGING MATERIALS

The evaluation of pharmaceutical packaging materials is a crucial step in ensuring the safety, efficacy, and quality of pharmaceutical products. This process involves comprehensive testing and analysis to assess the suitability of packaging materials for specific drug formulations and intended applications. Here's a detailed overview of the evaluation process for pharmaceutical packaging materials:

1. **Compatibility Testing:**
    a. Compatibility testing evaluates the interaction between the drug formulation and packaging materials to ensure product stability and safety.
    b. Studies may include extractables and leachables testing to identify and quantify substances that migrate from the packaging material into the drug product.
    c. Compatibility testing also assesses the physical and chemical compatibility of packaging materials with the drug formulation, including pH, solubility, and degradation pathways.

2. **Barrier Properties:**
    a. Barrier properties testing measures the ability of packaging materials to protect pharmaceutical products from environmental factors such as moisture, light, oxygen, and microbial contamination.
    b. Techniques such as permeability testing, moisture vapor transmission rate (MVTR) testing, and light transmission testing evaluate the barrier performance of packaging materials under simulated conditions.

3. **Physical Properties:**

a. Physical properties testing assesses the mechanical strength, durability, and integrity of packaging materials to ensure they can withstand handling, transportation, and storage.

b. Tests may include tensile strength, puncture resistance, tear resistance, and impact resistance to evaluate the physical properties of packaging films, foils, and containers.

4. Chemical Properties:

a. Chemical properties testing evaluates the chemical composition, purity, and stability of packaging materials to ensure they do not introduce contaminants or impurities into the drug product.

b. Techniques such as Fourier-transform infrared spectroscopy (FTIR), gas chromatography-mass spectrometry (GC-MS), and high-performance liquid chromatography (HPLC) are used to analyze packaging materials for chemical compatibility and impurity profiling.

5. Biological Safety:

a. Biological safety testing assesses the potential for packaging materials to cause adverse reactions or microbial contamination in pharmaceutical products.

b. Tests may include biocompatibility testing, cytotoxicity testing, and microbial challenge testing to evaluate the biological safety of packaging materials and components.

6. Regulatory Compliance:

a. Packaging materials must comply with regulatory requirements and standards set forth by regulatory agencies such as the FDA, EMA, and ISO.

b. Compliance with Good Manufacturing Practices (GMP), pharmacopeial standards, and labeling regulations is essential to ensure product safety, quality, and legality.

7. **Environmental Impact:**

   a. Environmental impact assessments evaluate the sustainability and eco-friendliness of packaging materials, considering factors such as recyclability, biodegradability, and carbon footprint.

   b. Life cycle assessments (LCAs) quantify the environmental impact of packaging materials from raw material extraction to end-of-life disposal, helping identify opportunities for improvement and optimization.

8. **Performance Testing:**

   a. Performance testing assesses the functionality and usability of packaging materials, including ease of opening, closure integrity, and compatibility with packaging equipment.

   b. Tests may include drop testing, vibration testing, and simulated transportation testing to evaluate the performance of packaging materials under real-world conditions.

QUALITY CONTROL TEST OF CONTAINERS

Quality control tests of containers in pharmaceutical packaging are essential to ensure the integrity, safety, and compliance of pharmaceutical products. These tests evaluate the physical, chemical, and mechanical properties of containers to ensure they meet regulatory requirements and maintain product stability throughout storage, transportation, and use. Here's a detailed overview of the quality control tests conducted on containers in pharmaceutical packaging:

Visual Inspection:

Visual inspection plays a crucial role in quality control tests for containers used in pharmaceutical packaging. Here's a detailed overview of the process:

1. **Preparation**: Before beginning the inspection, ensure that the inspection area is clean, well-lit, and free from any distractions. Gather all necessary

equipment such as magnifying glasses, light sources, and inspection checklists.

2. **Sample Selection**: Random samples of containers are typically selected from each batch for inspection. The number of samples selected may vary depending on regulatory requirements and internal quality standards.

3. **External Inspection**:

    a. **General Appearance**: Examine the external surface of the container for any defects such as scratches, dents, or discoloration.

    b. **Labels and Printing**: Check for accurate labeling, legibility of printed information (e.g., drug name, strength, expiration date), alignment, and adherence to regulatory requirements.

    c. **Seals and Closures**: Inspect the integrity of seals and closures to ensure they are properly applied and secure.

4. **Internal Inspection:**

    a. **Cleanliness**: Ensure that the interior of the container is clean and free from any foreign particles or residues.

    b. **Clarity:** For transparent containers, check for clarity and absence of haze or cloudiness that could affect visibility of the contents.

    c. **Defects**: Look for any defects such as cracks, chips, or irregularities that could compromise the integrity of the container.

5. **Functional Tests**: Some containers may undergo functional tests to ensure proper functionality of features such as closures, dispensing mechanisms, or child-resistant features.

6. **Documentation**: Record all findings meticulously, including any deviations or defects observed during the inspection process. This documentation is essential for traceability and quality assurance purposes.

7. **Decision Making**: Based on the inspection results, containers may be categorized as either acceptable or rejected. Acceptable containers meet all specified criteria and can proceed to the next stage of the packaging

process. Rejected containers are segregated and investigated further to determine the root cause of the defects.

8. **Follow-up Actions**: In case of rejected containers, appropriate corrective actions are taken to address the issues identified during the inspection. This may involve rework, repair, or disposal of the defective containers.

9. **Quality Assurance**: Continuous monitoring and improvement of the visual inspection process are essential to ensure consistency and reliability in detecting defects and maintaining product quality.

10. **Regulatory Compliance**: It's crucial to ensure that the visual inspection process complies with relevant regulatory requirements, such as those outlined in pharmacopeial standards or Good Manufacturing Practices (GMP).

Dimensional Measurements:

Dimensional measurements are critical in ensuring the quality and integrity of containers used in pharmaceutical packaging. Here's a detailed overview of how dimensional measurements are conducted as part of quality control tests:

1. **Equipment Preparation:**
   a. **Calibrated measuring instruments**: Use precision measuring tools such as calipers, micrometers, rulers, or gauges that are calibrated according to international standards.
   b. **Reference standards**: Have reference samples or standards available to compare measurements and ensure accuracy.

2. **Sample Selection:**
   a. **Random sampling**: Select representative samples from each batch of containers for measurement. The number of samples may vary based on regulatory requirements and internal quality standards.

3. **Measurement Parameters:**

a. **Outer Dimensions:** Measure the external dimensions of the container, including length, width, height, and diameter, depending on the container's shape.

b. **Inner Dimensions**: For containers with internal components (e.g., vials, bottles with necks), measure inner dimensions such as inner diameter or depth.

c. **Wall Thickness:** Measure the thickness of the container walls at various points to ensure uniformity and compliance with specifications.

4. **Measurement Techniques:**

a. **Direct Measurement:** Use measuring tools to directly measure dimensions such as length, width, and diameter.

b. **Indirect Measurement**: Employ techniques like displacement or volume measurements for irregularly shaped containers or those with complex geometries.

5. **Tolerance Limits:**

a. Refer to specifications and regulatory guidelines to determine acceptable tolerance limits for each dimension.

b. Tolerance limits may vary based on the type of container, its intended use, and regulatory requirements.

6. **Data Collection:**

a. Record measurements accurately, ensuring proper units (e.g., millimeters, inches) and precision (e.g., decimal places) are documented.

b. Use data recording systems or software to maintain consistency and traceability of measurements.

7. **Comparison and Analysis:**

a. Compare measured dimensions against specified tolerances and reference standards.

b. Analyze measurement data to identify any deviations from specifications and assess the impact on product quality and performance.

8. Decision Making:

a. Based on measurement results, containers are classified as either conforming or non-conforming.

b. Conforming containers meet all dimensional specifications and can proceed to the next stage of the packaging process.

c. Non-conforming containers may require further evaluation, corrective actions, or rejection, depending on the severity of deviations.

9. Documentation and Reporting:

a. Document all measurement data, including deviations, in quality control records or reports.

b. Provide detailed documentation of measurement procedures, equipment used, and results for traceability and audit purposes.

10. Continuous Improvement:

- Regularly review and improve measurement techniques, equipment calibration processes, and quality control procedures to enhance accuracy and efficiency.

Container Closure Integrity Testing (CCIT):

Container Closure Integrity Testing (CCIT) is a critical quality control test used in pharmaceutical packaging to ensure the integrity of sealed containers and prevent contamination or leakage. Here's a detailed overview of CCIT:

1. **Purpose**: The primary objective of CCIT is to verify that the closure system of pharmaceutical containers effectively prevents the ingress of contaminants and maintains the integrity of the product throughout its shelf life.

2. **Regulatory Requirements**: CCIT is often mandated by regulatory authorities such as the FDA (Food and Drug Administration) and EMA (European Medicines Agency) as part of Good Manufacturing Practices (GMP) for pharmaceutical packaging.

3. **Methods of CCIT**:

    a. **Dye Immersion Test**: This method involves immersing the sealed container in a dye solution under vacuum or pressure. If there are leaks in the container closure system, the dye will penetrate into the container, indicating a failure.

    b. **Pressure Decay Test:** In this method, the container is pressurized with a gas, and any decrease in pressure over time indicates a leak in the closure system.

    c. **High Voltage Leak Detection (HVLD):** HVLD involves applying a high voltage across the container closure system and detecting any electrical discharge caused by breaches in the closure integrity.

    d. **Headspace Gas Analysis**: This method measures the concentration of gases (e.g., helium) in the headspace of the container. An increase in gas concentration indicates a leak in the closure system.

    e. **Mass Extraction Test (Vacuum Decay)**: Vacuum is applied to the sealed container, and any increase in mass due to the ingress of air indicates a leak.

    f. **Microbial Ingress Test**: This method involves inoculating the exterior of the container with microbial agents and incubating the container to detect any microbial ingress through leaks in the closure system.

4. **Selection of Test Method**: The choice of CCIT method depends on various factors such as the type of container, closure system, product characteristics, regulatory requirements, and sensitivity of the test method.

5. **Validation of CCIT**: CCIT methods must be validated to demonstrate their reliability, sensitivity, and reproducibility. Validation studies involve establishing acceptance criteria, conducting method validation experiments, and documenting the results in a validation report.

6. **Routine Testing**: After validation, CCIT is performed routinely on samples from each batch of pharmaceutical products to verify the integrity of the container closure system.

7. **Data Analysis and Interpretation**: The results of CCIT are analyzed to determine whether the container closure system meets the specified acceptance criteria. Any deviations or failures are investigated, and appropriate corrective actions are taken.

8. **Documentation and Reporting: All** CCIT activities, including test methods, results, deviations, and corrective actions, are documented thoroughly in quality control records or reports.

9. **Continuous Improvement**: Pharmaceutical manufacturers continuously evaluate and improve CCIT methods and procedures to enhance the reliability and effectiveness of container closure integrity testing.

Mechanical Strength Testing:

Mechanical strength testing is a crucial quality control test used in the pharmaceutical industry to assess the physical robustness and integrity of containers used for packaging drugs. Here's a detailed overview of mechanical strength testing in quality control:

1. **Purpose**: The primary objective of mechanical strength testing is to ensure that containers used in pharmaceutical packaging can withstand the stresses and handling encountered during manufacturing, storage, transportation, and use without compromising the integrity of the product.

2. **Types of Containers Tested**: Mechanical strength testing applies to various types of containers commonly used in pharmaceutical packaging, including vials, bottles, ampoules, blister packs, and syringes.

3. **Common Mechanical Strength Tests:**

   a. **Compression Test**: This test evaluates the resistance of the container to axial or radial compression forces. The container is subjected to increasing compressive loads until failure or deformation occurs.

   b. **Burst Test**: In a burst test, the container is pressurized internally until it ruptures. This test assesses the ability of the container closure system to withstand internal pressure without leaking or bursting.

   c. **Drop Test**: Drop testing simulates the impact of accidental drops during handling or transportation. Containers filled with appropriate placeholders or simulated products are dropped from specified heights onto various surfaces to assess their ability to withstand impact forces.

   d. **Top Load Test**: This test evaluates the resistance of containers to vertical loads applied to the top surface. It is particularly relevant for containers stacked during storage or transportation.

   e. **Vacuum Test**: Vacuum testing assesses the ability of the container closure system to maintain its seal under negative pressure conditions. The container is evacuated, and any loss of vacuum indicates a breach in the closure system.

4. **Test Equipment**: Mechanical strength testing requires specialized equipment designed to apply controlled forces and measure various parameters such as load, displacement, pressure, and deformation. Common equipment includes universal testing machines, burst testers, drop testers, and vacuum chambers.

5. **Test Conditions and Standards**: Mechanical strength tests are conducted under controlled environmental conditions (e.g., temperature,

humidity) as per relevant regulatory standards, such as those outlined in pharmacopeias (e.g., USP, EP) or industry guidelines.

6. **Sampling and Acceptance Criteria**: Samples for mechanical strength testing are selected from each batch of containers based on statistically valid sampling plans. Acceptance criteria are defined in terms of maximum allowable deformation, pressure, or failure load.

7. **Validation and Calibration**: Test equipment used for mechanical strength testing must be validated to ensure accuracy, precision, and reliability. Regular calibration and maintenance of equipment are essential to maintain measurement integrity.

8. **Data Analysis and Reporting**: Test results are analyzed to determine whether the containers meet specified acceptance criteria. Any deviations or failures are investigated, documented, and reported in quality control records or reports.

9. **Continuous Improvement**: Pharmaceutical manufacturers continuously evaluate and improve mechanical strength testing procedures, methods, and equipment to enhance reliability, efficiency, and product quality.

Chemical Compatibility Testing:

Chemical compatibility testing is a critical quality control test used in the pharmaceutical industry to assess the interaction between pharmaceutical products and the materials used in packaging containers. Here's a detailed overview of chemical compatibility testing in quality control:

1. **Purpose**: The primary objective of chemical compatibility testing is to ensure that the materials used in pharmaceutical packaging do not adversely affect the quality, safety, or efficacy of the drug product. It involves assessing potential interactions between the drug formulation and the container materials, such as leaching of substances, adsorption, or degradation.

2. **Types of Container Materials:** Chemical compatibility testing applies to various container materials commonly used in pharmaceutical packaging, including glass, plastics (e.g., polyethylene, polypropylene, polyethylene terephthalate), metals (e.g., aluminum, stainless steel), and elastomers (e.g., rubber, silicone).

3. **Test Methods:**

   a. **Extractables and Leachables Studies**: This involves extracting substances from the container material using appropriate solvents and analyzing the extract for potential leachables that could migrate into the drug product.

   b. **Immersion Studies**: Containers are immersed in the drug product or relevant simulants under controlled conditions (e.g., temperature, duration) to simulate long-term storage or exposure. The drug product is then analyzed for any changes in composition or quality.

   c. **Accelerated Aging Studies**: Containers are subjected to accelerated aging conditions (e.g., elevated temperature, humidity) to simulate long-term storage conditions. The drug product is then evaluated for any changes in stability, potency, or quality.

   d. **Compatibility Testing with Specific Formulations**: Some drug formulations may be particularly sensitive to certain container materials or additives. Compatibility testing is conducted using the actual drug formulation to assess any adverse effects.

4. **Selection of Test Conditions**: Test conditions, including temperature, duration, and choice of extraction solvents or simulants, are selected based on regulatory requirements, industry guidelines, and the intended use of the packaging material.

5. **Analytical Techniques:**

a. Various analytical techniques are employed to detect and quantify potential interactions between the drug product and container materials, including chromatography (e.g., HPLC, GC), spectroscopy (e.g., UV-Vis, FTIR), mass spectrometry, and microscopy.

b. These techniques allow for the identification and quantification of leachables, changes in drug potency or degradation products, and any physical changes in the container material.

6. **Acceptance Criteria**: Acceptance criteria for chemical compatibility testing are established based on regulatory requirements, pharmacopeial standards (e.g., USP, EP), and industry best practices. These criteria ensure that any observed interactions do not exceed acceptable limits and do not compromise the quality, safety, or efficacy of the drug product.

7. **Validation and Documentation**: Chemical compatibility testing methods must be validated to ensure their reliability, sensitivity, and reproducibility. Detailed documentation of test protocols, results, and interpretations is essential for regulatory compliance and product quality assurance.

8. **Continuous Monitoring and Improvement**: Pharmaceutical manufacturers continuously monitor and evaluate the chemical compatibility of packaging materials, particularly for new formulations or changes in packaging materials. Any observed issues are addressed promptly through corrective actions or adjustments to packaging materials or processes.

Extractables and Leachables Studies:

Extractables and leachables studies are comprehensive tests conducted as part of quality control in pharmaceutical packaging to assess the potential migration of substances from the packaging material into the drug product. Here's a detailed overview of extractables and leachables studies:

1. **Purpose:**
   a. **Extractables**: The purpose of extractables testing is to identify and quantify substances that can be extracted from the packaging material under extreme conditions (e.g., elevated temperature, prolonged exposure to solvents). These substances may include additives, processing aids, residual monomers, or other impurities present in the packaging material.
   b. **Leachables**: Leachables testing aims to evaluate the migration of substances from the packaging material into the drug product under normal storage and use conditions. Leachables are substances that are released from the packaging material and can potentially contaminate the drug product, leading to safety or efficacy concerns.

2. **Study Design:**
   a. **Selection of Packaging Material:** Identify the specific packaging material(s) used for the container closure system, such as glass, plastics, metals, or elastomers.
   b. **Extraction Conditions**: Establish extraction conditions that mimic the worst-case scenario for potential migration, including temperature, duration, and choice of extraction solvents.
   c. **Analytical Techniques**: Employ appropriate analytical techniques such as chromatography (e.g., HPLC, GC), spectroscopy (e.g., FTIR, UV-Vis), mass spectrometry, and microscopy to analyze extracted substances.
   d. **Control Samples**: Include control samples to account for background levels of extractables and potential interferences from analytical procedures.

3. **Test Execution:**

a. **Extraction**: The packaging material is subjected to extraction conditions (e.g., heating, immersion in solvents) to release extractable substances.

b. **Analysis:** The extract is analyzed using validated analytical methods to identify and quantify extractable substances. Peaks corresponding to extractables are compared against reference standards or databases for identification.

c. **Quantification**: Extractable levels are quantified based on calibration curves or external standards. The results are reported in terms of concentration or mass of extractables per unit area or volume of packaging material.

d. **Risk Assessment**: Evaluate the potential health risks associated with identified extractables, considering factors such as toxicological profiles, exposure levels, and regulatory limits.

4. **Leachables Study:**

a. **Selection of Conditions**: Determine storage and use conditions that represent the intended use of the drug product (e.g., temperature, duration).

b. **Exposure**: The packaging material is in contact with the drug product under controlled conditions (e.g., storage time, temperature) to allow leaching of substances.

c. **Analysis**: Analyze the drug product for the presence of leachables using the same analytical methods employed in extractables testing.

d. **Evaluation:** Compare the profile and levels of leachables detected in the drug product against safety thresholds or regulatory limits to assess potential risks to patient safety and product quality.

5. **Reporting and Documentation:**

a. Document all aspects of the extractables and leachables study, including study design, analytical methods, results, and interpretations.

b. Prepare a comprehensive report summarizing the findings and conclusions of the study, including any identified risks and recommendations for mitigation.

6. **Regulatory Compliance:**

a. Ensure that extractables and leachables studies comply with relevant regulatory requirements, such as those outlined in pharmacopeias (e.g., USP, EP) and regulatory guidelines (e.g., FDA, EMA).

b. Provide documentation of extractables and leachables testing as part of regulatory submissions for new drug products or changes to packaging materials.

Container Closure System Functionality:

Container closure system functionality testing is a critical quality control measure in pharmaceutical packaging to ensure that the packaging effectively maintains the integrity and stability of the drug product throughout its shelf life. Here's a detailed overview of this process:

1. **Purpose:**

a. The primary purpose of container closure system functionality testing is to assess the ability of the packaging to prevent contamination, maintain product sterility, and protect the drug product from external factors such as moisture, light, and oxygen.

b. It also evaluates the functionality of closures (e.g., caps, seals) to ensure they are secure, tamper-evident, and child-resistant if required.

2. **Test Parameters:**

a. **Seal Integrity**: Assess the integrity of seals between the container and closure to prevent leakage or ingress of contaminants. This may involve visual inspection, dye penetration tests, or pressure/vacuum tests.

b. **Tamper Evidence**: Verify that tamper-evident features, such as seals or closures, function as intended to provide visible evidence of tampering.

c. **Child-Resistance**: Test the child-resistant features of closures to ensure they require a deliberate action to open, reducing the risk of accidental ingestion by children.

d. **Compatibility**: Evaluate compatibility between the container closure system and the drug product to ensure that no adverse interactions occur, such as chemical degradation or physical instability.

3. **Test Methods:**

a. **Visual Inspection**: Examine the container closure system for any visible defects, irregularities, or signs of damage that could compromise functionality.

b. **Dye Penetration Test**: Submerge the sealed container closure system in a colored dye solution and apply pressure or vacuum to detect any leaks through the closure.

c. **Pressure/Vacuum Decay Test**: Apply pressure or vacuum to the sealed container closure system and monitor any changes in pressure over time, indicating a leak or loss of seal integrity.

d. **Torque Test**: Measure the torque required to open or close the closure to ensure it meets specified requirements for ease of use and seal integrity.

e. **Functionality Testing**: Evaluate the functionality of special features such as child-resistant closures, flip caps, or dispensing mechanisms to ensure they operate as intended.

4. **Acceptance Criteria:**

   a. Define acceptance criteria based on regulatory requirements, industry standards, and product-specific considerations. Criteria may include maximum allowable leakage rates, torque values, or visual inspection criteria.

   b. Criteria should also consider factors such as intended storage conditions, shelf life, and the risk of microbial contamination or product degradation.

5. **Sampling:**

   a. Select representative samples from each batch of packaging materials or finished products for functionality testing. The number of samples and sampling plan should be based on statistical principles and risk assessment.

6. **Documentation and Reporting:**

   a. Document all aspects of container closure system functionality testing, including test methods, results, deviations, and corrective actions taken.

   b. Prepare detailed reports summarizing the testing procedures, findings, and conclusions, which may be included in batch records, quality control documentation, or regulatory submissions.

7. **Regulatory Compliance:**

   a. Ensure that container closure system functionality testing complies with relevant regulatory requirements, such as those outlined in pharmacopeias, Good Manufacturing Practices (GMP), and specific regulatory guidelines for pharmaceutical packaging.

Regulatory Compliance:

Regulatory compliance is a critical aspect of quality control testing for containers in pharmaceutical packaging. Here's a detailed overview of regulatory compliance considerations:

1. **Applicable Regulations:**
   a. Pharmaceutical packaging must comply with various regulations and standards established by regulatory authorities such as the Food and Drug Administration (FDA) in the United States, the European Medicines Agency (EMA) in Europe, and other regulatory agencies worldwide.
   b. Relevant regulations include Good Manufacturing Practices (GMP), which outline requirements for the design, manufacturing, and control of pharmaceutical packaging materials to ensure product quality and safety.

2. **Pharmacopeial Standards:**
   a. Pharmaceutical packaging materials are often subject to standards outlined in pharmacopeias such as the United States Pharmacopeia (USP), European Pharmacopoeia (EP), and other national pharmacopeias.
   b. These standards provide specifications for materials, testing methods, and acceptance criteria for pharmaceutical packaging, including containers, closures, and packaging systems.

3. **Quality Control Testing Requirements:**
   a. Regulatory authorities and pharmacopeial standards prescribe specific quality control tests for pharmaceutical packaging materials to ensure their suitability for use.
   b. Quality control tests may include dimensional measurements, visual inspection, mechanical strength testing, chemical compatibility testing, container closure integrity testing (CCIT), and functionality testing, among others.

4. **Validation and Documentation:**

   a. Quality control tests must be validated to demonstrate their accuracy, reliability, and consistency. Validation protocols should be developed and executed according to regulatory guidelines and industry best practices.

   b. Comprehensive documentation of quality control activities, including test protocols, results, deviations, and corrective actions, is essential for regulatory compliance and product traceability.

5. **Change Control:**

   a. Any changes to packaging materials, manufacturing processes, or quality control procedures must be evaluated for their impact on product quality, safety, and regulatory compliance.

   b. Change control procedures should be implemented to manage and document changes effectively, including risk assessments, validation studies, and regulatory submissions as necessary.

6. **Supplier Qualification:**

   a. Pharmaceutical manufacturers are responsible for ensuring the quality and regulatory compliance of packaging materials supplied by external vendors.

   b. Supplier qualification processes should include assessment of vendors' quality management systems, compliance with regulatory requirements, and performance in meeting quality specifications.

7. **Audits and Inspections:**

   a. Regulatory authorities conduct audits and inspections of pharmaceutical manufacturing facilities to assess compliance with regulatory requirements, including those related to packaging materials.

   b. Preparation for regulatory inspections should include documentation of quality control testing procedures, training records, validation studies, and any corrective actions taken in response to previous inspections.

8. **Post-Market Surveillance:**
    a. Pharmaceutical manufacturers are obligated to monitor the performance of packaging materials in the market and report any adverse events or quality issues to regulatory authorities.
    b. Post-market surveillance activities may include complaints handling, product recalls, and ongoing assessment of packaging material performance through stability studies and product testing.

QUALITY CONTROL TEST OF CLOSURES

Quality control tests of closures in pharmaceutical packaging are crucial to ensure the integrity, functionality, and safety of container closure systems. Closures play a vital role in maintaining the sterility, stability, and security of pharmaceutical products, and thorough testing is necessary to identify any defects or potential issues that could compromise product quality. Here's a detailed overview of the quality control tests conducted on closures in pharmaceutical packaging:

Visual Inspection:

Visual inspection is a critical quality control test for closures used in pharmaceutical packaging to ensure their integrity, functionality, and compliance with regulatory requirements. Here's a detailed overview of visual inspection in quality control testing of closures:

1. **Preparation:**
    a. Establish a dedicated inspection area equipped with appropriate lighting and magnification tools (e.g., magnifying glasses, microscopes) to facilitate detailed examination.
    b. Ensure that inspectors are trained in visual inspection techniques and familiar with closure specifications and acceptance criteria.

2. **Sampling:**

a. Select representative samples of closures from each batch for inspection, following statistically valid sampling plans based on batch size and regulatory requirements.

3. **External Inspection:**

    a. **General Appearance**: Examine the external surface of closures for any defects, including scratches, dents, discoloration, or foreign particles.

    b. **Dimensional Accuracy**: Verify that closures meet dimensional specifications, including diameter, height, and overall dimensions.

    c. **Color and Transparency**: Assess color consistency and transparency (if applicable) to ensure uniformity and compliance with specified requirements.

    d. **Surface Finish**: Check for smoothness, uniform texture, and absence of rough or uneven surfaces that could affect functionality or aesthetics.

4. **Functional Inspection:**

    a. **Thread Integrity**: Inspect the threading mechanism of closures (e.g., screw caps, snap caps) to ensure proper engagement and functionality.

    b. **Seal Integrity:** Verify the integrity of seals, gaskets, or liners to ensure a tight seal with the container and prevent leakage or contamination.

    c. **Tamper-Evident Features**: Assess the functionality of tamper-evident features, such as tear bands, breakable caps, or shrink bands, to provide visible evidence of tampering.

5. **Labeling and Printing:**

    a. Check for accurate labeling and printing on closures, including legibility, alignment, and adherence to regulatory requirements.

b. Verify that any printed information (e.g., product name, strength, expiration date) is clear, complete, and correctly positioned.

6. Special Features Inspection:

a. Some closures may have special features or functionalities, such as child-resistant mechanisms, dispensing systems, or resealable closures. Inspect these features to ensure they operate as intended.

7. Documentation:

a. Record all inspection findings meticulously, including any defects or deviations observed during the visual inspection process.

b. Maintain comprehensive documentation of inspection results, including photographs, diagrams, or detailed descriptions of defects.

8. Decision Making:

a. Based on the inspection results, closures are categorized as either acceptable or rejected. Acceptable closures meet all specified criteria and can proceed to the next stage of the packaging process.

b. Rejected closures are segregated, investigated further to determine the root cause of defects, and appropriate corrective actions are taken.

9. Quality Assurance:

a. Continuous monitoring and improvement of the visual inspection process are essential to ensure consistency and reliability in detecting defects and maintaining closure quality.

10. Regulatory Compliance:

- Ensure that the visual inspection process complies with relevant regulatory requirements, such as those outlined in pharmacopeial standards or Good Manufacturing Practices (GMP).

Dimensional Measurements:

Dimensional measurements are essential in quality control tests for closures used in pharmaceutical packaging to ensure their proper fit, functionality, and compliance with specifications. Here's a detailed overview of dimensional measurements in quality control testing of closures:

1. **Selection of Measurement Parameters:**
   a. Identify key dimensional parameters specific to the closure design, such as diameter, height, thread pitch, thread depth, or any other critical dimensions specified by regulatory standards or internal requirements.

2. **Equipment Preparation:**
   a. Utilize calibrated measuring instruments suitable for the specific dimensions of closures being tested. This may include micrometers, calipers, gauges, or other precision measuring tools.
   b. Ensure that the measuring instruments are calibrated according to recognized standards and have the necessary accuracy and precision for the intended measurements.

3. **Sampling:**
   a. Select representative samples of closures from each batch for dimensional measurements, following statistically valid sampling plans based on batch size and regulatory requirements.

4. **Measurement Techniques:**
   a. **Direct Measurement:** Use measuring instruments to directly measure dimensions such as diameter, height, or thread parameters of the closure.
   b. **Non-Destructive Testing**: Perform measurements without altering or damaging the closure, ensuring that it remains suitable for use in packaging pharmaceutical products.

5. **Measurement Process:**

a. Conduct measurements in a controlled environment to minimize environmental influences on the accuracy of measurements, such as temperature and humidity.

b. Take multiple measurements at different locations on each closure to account for variations in dimensions and ensure representative sampling.

c. Record measurement values accurately, including units (e.g., millimeters, inches) and precision (e.g., decimal places), to maintain consistency and traceability.

6. **Comparison with Specifications:**

a. Compare measured dimensions against specified tolerance limits defined by regulatory standards, pharmacopeial requirements, or internal quality control specifications.

b. Evaluate whether the measured dimensions fall within acceptable ranges and comply with established criteria for closure functionality and performance.

7. **Documentation:**

a. Maintain detailed records of dimensional measurements, including measurement data, sample identification, measurement techniques used, and any deviations from specifications.

b. Document any corrective actions taken in response to deviations or out-of-specification results, including retesting, adjustment of manufacturing processes, or rejection of non-conforming closures.

8. **Validation and Calibration:**

a. Validate measurement techniques and procedures to ensure accuracy, precision, and reproducibility of dimensional measurements.

b. Regularly calibrate measuring instruments to maintain measurement integrity and traceability, following established calibration schedules and procedures.

9. Continuous Improvement:

a. Continuously evaluate and improve dimensional measurement techniques, equipment calibration processes, and quality control procedures to enhance accuracy, efficiency, and reliability in closure testing.

Torque Testing:

Torque testing is an important quality control test for closures used in pharmaceutical packaging to ensure that they meet specified torque requirements for proper sealing, opening, and closure. Here's a detailed overview of torque testing in quality control:

1. Purpose:

a. The primary purpose of torque testing is to measure the torque (rotational force) required to open or close closures, such as screw caps or snap caps, to ensure they meet specified requirements for functionality and seal integrity.

b. Torque testing helps ensure that closures can be properly sealed to prevent leakage or contamination of pharmaceutical products while also ensuring ease of opening for end-users.

2. Selection of Testing Equipment:

a. Use a torque testing instrument or torque analyzer capable of accurately measuring the rotational force applied to closures.

b. Ensure that the torque testing equipment is calibrated according to recognized standards to maintain measurement accuracy and reliability.

3. Sampling:

a. Select representative samples of closures from each batch for torque testing, following statistically valid sampling plans based on batch size and regulatory requirements.

4. Testing Procedure:

a. Secure the closure in the torque testing equipment according to the manufacturer's instructions, ensuring proper alignment and positioning.

b. Apply a controlled rotational force to the closure in either the opening or closing direction, depending on the intended use of the closure.

c. Measure and record the torque required to achieve full opening or closure of the closure, typically in units such as inch-pounds or Newton-meters.

d. Repeat the test on multiple closures to ensure consistency and repeatability of results.

5. Comparison with Specifications:

a. Compare the measured torque values against specified torque requirements defined by regulatory standards, pharmacopeial requirements, or internal quality control specifications.

b. Evaluate whether the measured torque values fall within acceptable ranges and comply with established criteria for closure functionality and performance.

6. Acceptance Criteria:

a. Define acceptance criteria for torque testing based on factors such as closure type, intended use, and regulatory requirements.

b. Acceptance criteria may include minimum and maximum torque values for sealing, opening, or resealing closures, as well as consistency of torque across multiple samples.

7. **Documentation:**

   a. Maintain detailed records of torque testing, including measurement data, sample identification, testing procedures, and any deviations from specifications.

   b. Document any corrective actions taken in response to deviations or out-of-specification results, including adjustments to manufacturing processes or rejection of non-conforming closures.

8. **Validation and Calibration:**

   a. Validate torque testing procedures and equipment to ensure accuracy, precision, and reproducibility of measurements.

   b. Regularly calibrate torque testing equipment according to established calibration schedules and procedures to maintain measurement integrity.

9. **Continuous Improvement:**

   a. Continuously evaluate and improve torque testing techniques, equipment calibration processes, and quality control procedures to enhance accuracy, efficiency, and reliability in closure testing.

Seal Integrity Testing:

Seal integrity testing is a critical quality control test for closures used in pharmaceutical packaging to ensure that they effectively seal the container and maintain the integrity of the packaged product. Here's a detailed overview of seal integrity testing in quality control:

1. **Purpose:**

   a. The primary purpose of seal integrity testing is to verify that closures form a tight and secure seal with the container, preventing leakage, contamination, or tampering of the pharmaceutical product.

b. Seal integrity testing helps ensure the stability, efficacy, and safety of the packaged product throughout its shelf life.

2. **Selection of Testing Methods:**

   a. Various methods can be used to assess seal integrity, including non-destructive and destructive techniques. Common methods include dye penetration testing, pressure decay testing, vacuum decay testing, and microbial ingress testing.

   b. The selection of the testing method depends on factors such as closure type, container material, regulatory requirements, and the sensitivity of the product being packaged.

3. **Non-Destructive Testing Methods:**

   a. **Dye Penetration Testing**: This method involves applying a colored dye solution to the closure-sealing interface. Any leakage or breach in the seal allows the dye to penetrate, resulting in visible staining that indicates a seal defect.

   b. **Pressure Decay Testing**: Closures are pressurized, and any decrease in pressure over time indicates a leak in the seal. This method is suitable for closures with a flexible seal, such as stoppers or septa.

4. **Destructive Testing Methods:**

   a. **Vacuum Decay Testing**: In this method, a vacuum is applied to the sealed container, and any increase in pressure over time indicates a leak in the seal. This method is suitable for closures with a rigid seal, such as screw caps or crimp seals.

   b. **Microbial Ingress Testing**: This method involves inoculating the external surface of the closure with microbial agents and incubating the sealed container. Any microbial growth inside the container indicates a breach in the seal.

5. **Testing Procedure:**

a. Prepare samples of closures sealed onto containers containing a suitable test medium or placeholder.

b. Apply the selected testing method according to the specified procedure, ensuring that testing conditions (e.g., pressure, temperature) are controlled and consistent.

c. Record the testing parameters and observations, including any indications of leakage or breach in the seal.

6. Comparison with Specifications:

a. Compare the results of seal integrity testing against specified acceptance criteria defined by regulatory standards, pharmacopeial requirements, or internal quality control specifications.

b. Evaluate whether the tested closures meet the specified requirements for seal integrity and compliance with regulatory standards.

7. Acceptance Criteria:

a. Define acceptance criteria for seal integrity testing based on factors such as closure type, container material, product characteristics, and regulatory requirements.

b. Acceptance criteria may include maximum allowable leakage rates, absence of visible dye penetration, or absence of microbial growth inside the container.

8. Documentation:

a. Maintain detailed records of seal integrity testing, including testing parameters, results, sample identification, and any deviations from specifications.

b. Document any corrective actions taken in response to deviations or out-of-specification results, including adjustments to manufacturing processes or rejection of non-conforming closures.

9. **Validation and Calibration:**

   a. Validate seal integrity testing procedures and equipment to ensure accuracy, precision, and reproducibility of results.

   b. Regularly calibrate testing equipment according to established calibration schedules and procedures to maintain measurement integrity.

Closure Removal Force Testing:

Closure removal force testing is a critical quality control test for closures used in pharmaceutical packaging to ensure they meet specified requirements for ease of opening while maintaining proper seal integrity. Here's a detailed overview of closure removal force testing in quality control:

1. **Purpose:**

   a. The primary purpose of closure removal force testing is to measure the force required to open closures, such as screw caps, snap caps, or flip caps, from their sealed position on the container.

   b. Closure removal force testing helps ensure that closures can be opened easily by end-users while providing sufficient resistance to prevent unintentional opening and maintain seal integrity during storage and transportation.

2. **Selection of Testing Equipment:**

   a. Use a closure removal force testing instrument capable of accurately measuring the force required to open closures.

   b. Ensure that the testing equipment is calibrated according to recognized standards to maintain measurement accuracy and reliability.

3. **Sampling:**

   a. Select representative samples of closures from each batch for closure removal force testing, following statistically valid sampling plans based on batch size and regulatory requirements.

4. **Testing Procedure:**

   a. Secure the closure and container assembly in the closure removal force testing equipment according to the manufacturer's instructions, ensuring proper alignment and positioning.

   b. Apply a controlled force to the closure in the opening direction to simulate the action of an end-user opening the closure.

   c. Measure and record the force required to fully open the closure, typically in units such as Newtons or pounds-force.

   d. Repeat the test on multiple closures to ensure consistency and repeatability of results.

5. **Comparison with Specifications:**

   a. Compare the measured closure removal force values against specified requirements defined by regulatory standards, pharmacopeial requirements, or internal quality control specifications.

   b. Evaluate whether the measured closure removal force values fall within acceptable ranges and comply with established criteria for closure functionality and performance.

6. **Acceptance Criteria:**

   a. Define acceptance criteria for closure removal force testing based on factors such as closure type, intended use, and regulatory requirements.

   b. Acceptance criteria may include maximum and minimum closure removal force values to ensure ease of opening while maintaining seal integrity.

7. **Documentation:**

   a. Maintain detailed records of closure removal force testing, including measurement data, sample identification, testing procedures, and any deviations from specifications.

b. Document any corrective actions taken in response to deviations or out-of-specification results, including adjustments to manufacturing processes or rejection of non-conforming closures.

8. **Validation and Calibration:**

   a. Validate closure removal force testing procedures and equipment to ensure accuracy, precision, and reproducibility of measurements.

   b. Regularly calibrate testing equipment according to established calibration schedules and procedures to maintain measurement integrity.

9. **Continuous Improvement:**

   a. Continuously evaluate and improve closure removal force testing techniques, equipment calibration processes, and quality control procedures to enhance accuracy, efficiency, and reliability in closure testing.

Chemical Compatibility Testing:

Chemical compatibility testing is a crucial quality control test for closures used in pharmaceutical packaging to ensure that they do not interact adversely with the drug product or its formulation. Here's a detailed overview of chemical compatibility testing in quality control:

1. **Purpose:**

   a. The primary purpose of chemical compatibility testing is to assess potential interactions between the closure material and the pharmaceutical product it will contain.

   b. This testing helps ensure that the closure material does not release harmful substances (leachables) into the drug product, which could compromise its safety, efficacy, or stability.

2. **Selection of Test Conditions:**

a. Identify the specific closure material(s) used in the packaging, such as plastics (e.g., polyethylene, polypropylene), elastomers (e.g., rubber, silicone), or metals (e.g., aluminum, stainless steel).

b. Determine the appropriate test conditions, including temperature, duration, and choice of extraction solvents, based on regulatory requirements, industry guidelines, and the intended use of the closure material.

3. **Test Methods:**

   a. **Extractables Studies**: Conduct extractables studies to identify and quantify substances that can be extracted from the closure material under extreme conditions (e.g., elevated temperature, prolonged exposure to solvents).

   b. **Immersion Studies**: Perform immersion studies where closures are exposed to the drug product or relevant simulants under controlled conditions to simulate long-term storage or exposure.

   c. **Accelerated Aging Studies**: Subject closures to accelerated aging conditions (e.g., elevated temperature, humidity) to simulate long-term storage conditions and assess potential changes in material properties.

   d. **Compatibility Testing with Specific Formulations**: Conduct compatibility testing using the actual drug formulation to assess any adverse effects or interactions with the closure material.

4. **Analytical Techniques:**

   a. Employ various analytical techniques to detect and quantify potential leachables, changes in material properties, or degradation products. These may include chromatography (e.g., HPLC, GC), spectroscopy (e.g., FTIR, UV-Vis), mass spectrometry, and microscopy.

b. These techniques allow for the identification and quantification of leachables, changes in closure material properties, and any physical changes in the closure material.

5. **Acceptance Criteria:**

   a. Establish acceptance criteria for chemical compatibility testing based on regulatory requirements, pharmacopeial standards (e.g., USP, EP), and industry best practices.

   b. These criteria ensure that any observed interactions or leachables do not exceed acceptable limits and do not compromise the quality, safety, or efficacy of the drug product.

6. **Documentation and Reporting:**

   a. Maintain comprehensive documentation of chemical compatibility testing protocols, results, and interpretations.

   b. Prepare detailed reports summarizing the findings and conclusions of the testing, including any identified risks and recommendations for mitigation.

7. **Regulatory Compliance:**

   a. Ensure that chemical compatibility testing complies with relevant regulatory requirements, such as those outlined in pharmacopeias, Good Manufacturing Practices (GMP), and specific regulatory guidelines for pharmaceutical packaging.

Biological Safety:

Biological safety testing is a critical aspect of quality control for closures used in pharmaceutical packaging to ensure that they do not pose any risks of biological contamination to the drug product or end-users. Here's a detailed overview of biological safety testing in quality control:

1. **Purpose:**

   a. The primary purpose of biological safety testing is to evaluate closures for potential contamination by microorganisms, endotoxins, or other biological hazards that could compromise the safety, efficacy, or stability of the pharmaceutical product.

   b. This testing ensures that closures meet stringent biological safety standards and do not introduce biological contaminants during storage, handling, or use.

2. Selection of Test Methods:

   a. Identify appropriate test methods for biological safety testing based on regulatory requirements, pharmacopeial standards, and industry best practices.

   b. Common biological safety tests for closures may include sterility testing, endotoxin testing, and bioburden testing.

3. Sterility Testing:

   a. Sterility testing assesses whether closures are free from viable microorganisms, including bacteria, fungi, and spores.

   b. Closure samples are subjected to culture-based methods, such as membrane filtration or direct inoculation, followed by incubation under appropriate conditions to detect microbial growth.

4. Endotoxin Testing:

   a. Endotoxin testing evaluates the presence of bacterial endotoxins, such as lipopolysaccharides (LPS), which can cause adverse reactions in patients.

   b. Closure samples are tested using methods such as the Limulus Amebocyte Lysate (LAL) assay, which detects the presence of endotoxins by coagulating with lysate from horseshoe crab blood.

5. Bioburden Testing:

   a. Bioburden testing quantifies the total microbial load present on closure surfaces or within packaging materials.

b. Closure samples are swabbed or rinsed with suitable neutralizing agents, and the recovered microorganisms are enumerated using microbiological culture methods.

6. **Acceptance Criteria:**

   a. Define acceptance criteria for biological safety testing based on regulatory requirements, pharmacopeial standards, and industry guidelines.

   b. Acceptance criteria typically specify maximum allowable microbial counts, absence of microbial growth in sterility testing, and compliance with specified endotoxin limits.

7. **Validation and Control of Test Methods:**

   a. Validate biological safety testing methods to ensure accuracy, precision, and reliability of results.

   b. Implement appropriate controls, including positive and negative controls, to validate the effectiveness of the testing method and ensure the integrity of test results.

8. **Documentation and Reporting:**

   a. Maintain comprehensive documentation of biological safety testing protocols, procedures, results, and interpretations.

   b. Prepare detailed reports summarizing the findings and conclusions of the testing, including any deviations from acceptance criteria and corrective actions taken.

9. **Regulatory Compliance:**

   a. Ensure that biological safety testing complies with relevant regulatory requirements, such as those outlined in pharmacopeias, Good Manufacturing Practices (GMP), and specific regulatory guidelines for pharmaceutical packaging.

Regulatory Compliance:

Regulatory compliance is paramount in the quality control testing of closures used in pharmaceutical packaging to ensure the safety, efficacy, and integrity of the packaged drug products. Here's a detailed overview of regulatory compliance considerations:

1. **Applicable Regulations:**
   a. Pharmaceutical packaging must comply with various regulations and standards established by regulatory authorities such as the Food and Drug Administration (FDA) in the United States, the European Medicines Agency (EMA) in Europe, and other regulatory agencies worldwide.
   b. Relevant regulations include Good Manufacturing Practices (GMP), which outline requirements for the design, manufacturing, and control of pharmaceutical packaging materials.

2. **Pharmacopeial Standards:**
   a. Pharmaceutical packaging materials are often subject to standards outlined in pharmacopeias such as the United States Pharmacopeia (USP), European Pharmacopoeia (EP), and other national pharmacopeias.
   b. These standards provide specifications for materials, testing methods, and acceptance criteria for pharmaceutical packaging, including closures.

3. **Quality Control Testing Requirements:**
   a. Regulatory authorities and pharmacopeial standards prescribe specific quality control tests for closures to ensure their suitability for use.
   b. Quality control tests may include dimensional measurements, visual inspection, mechanical strength testing, chemical compatibility testing, biological safety testing, and closure integrity testing.

4. **Validation and Documentation:**

   a. Quality control tests must be validated to demonstrate their accuracy, reliability, and consistency. Validation protocols should be developed and executed according to regulatory guidelines and industry best practices.

   b. Comprehensive documentation of quality control activities, including test protocols, results, deviations, and corrective actions, is essential for regulatory compliance and product traceability.

5. **Change Control:**

   a. Any changes to closure materials, manufacturing processes, or quality control procedures must be evaluated for their impact on product quality, safety, and regulatory compliance.

   b. Change control procedures should be implemented to manage and document changes effectively, including risk assessments, validation studies, and regulatory submissions as necessary.

6. **Supplier Qualification:**

   a. Pharmaceutical manufacturers are responsible for ensuring the quality and regulatory compliance of closure materials supplied by external vendors.

   b. Supplier qualification processes should include assessment of vendors' quality management systems, compliance with regulatory requirements, and performance in meeting quality specifications.

7. **Audits and Inspections:**

   a. Regulatory authorities conduct audits and inspections of pharmaceutical manufacturing facilities to assess compliance with regulatory requirements, including those related to closure quality control.

   b. Preparation for regulatory inspections should include documentation of quality control testing procedures, training records, validation studies, and any corrective actions taken in response to previous inspections.

8. **Post-Market Surveillance:**

    a. Pharmaceutical manufacturers are obligated to monitor the performance of closures in the market and report any adverse events or quality issues to regulatory authorities.

    b. Post-market surveillance activities may include complaints handling, product recalls, and ongoing assessment of closure performance through stability studies and product testing.

QUALITY CONTROL TEST OF SECONDARY PACKING MATERIALS

Quality control tests of secondary packaging materials in pharmaceutical packaging are essential to ensure the integrity, safety, and compliance of pharmaceutical products throughout the distribution chain. Secondary packaging materials provide additional protection, identification, and information for the primary pharmaceutical containers and must undergo rigorous testing to meet regulatory requirements and maintain product quality. Here's a detailed overview of the quality control tests conducted on secondary packing materials in pharmaceutical packaging:

1. **Visual Inspection:**

    a. Visual inspection assesses the overall appearance and condition of secondary packaging materials, including boxes, cartons, labels, and inserts.

    b. Inspectors look for defects such as tears, creases, printing errors, misalignments, and discolorations that could affect package integrity or product presentation.

    c. Automated vision systems may be used for high-speed inspection of secondary packaging materials to ensure consistency and accuracy.

2. **Dimensional Measurements:**

   a. Dimensional measurements evaluate the physical dimensions of secondary packaging materials to ensure they meet specifications and provide proper fit and functionality.

   b. Measurements may include box dimensions, label size, fold and crease accuracy, and alignment with primary packaging containers.

   c. Proper dimensional measurements ensure compatibility with packaging equipment and facilitate efficient handling, storage, and distribution.

3. **Print Quality and Legibility:**

   a. Print quality testing assesses the clarity, accuracy, and legibility of text, graphics, and barcodes printed on secondary packaging materials.

   b. Tests evaluate factors such as font size, color contrast, line thickness, barcode readability, and adherence to regulatory requirements for labeling and product identification.

   c. Proper print quality and legibility are essential for ensuring accurate product information, traceability, and regulatory compliance.

4. **Barcode Verification:**

   a. Barcode verification ensures the accuracy and readability of barcodes printed on secondary packaging materials, including labels, cartons, and inserts.

   b. Verification tests assess factors such as barcode symbology, data accuracy, quiet zones, and print contrast to ensure compliance with industry standards and regulatory requirements.

   c. Proper barcode verification ensures accurate product identification, tracking, and traceability throughout the supply chain.

5. **Packaging Material Strength and Durability:**

a. Strength and durability testing evaluate the mechanical properties of secondary packaging materials to ensure they provide adequate protection and support for pharmaceutical products.

b. Tests may include burst strength testing, compression testing, and tear resistance testing to assess the strength, resilience, and resistance to damage of packaging materials.

c. Proper material strength and durability are essential for protecting pharmaceutical products from physical damage during handling, transportation, and storage.

6. **Chemical Compatibility:**

a. Chemical compatibility testing assesses the interaction between secondary packaging materials and pharmaceutical products to prevent contamination or degradation of the drug formulation.

b. Materials are exposed to simulated drug formulations under accelerated conditions, followed by analysis to identify potential extractables or leachables that could affect product quality.

c. Chemical compatibility testing ensures that secondary packaging materials do not adversely affect product stability, safety, or efficacy.

7. **Regulatory Compliance:**

a. Quality control tests of secondary packaging materials must comply with regulatory requirements and standards set forth by regulatory agencies such as the FDA, EMA, and ISO.

b. Compliance with Good Manufacturing Practices (GMP), pharmacopeial standards, and labeling regulations is essential to ensure product safety, quality, and legality.

Multiple-choice questions (MCQs)

1. What is the primary purpose of pharmaceutical packaging?

A) Branding

B) Transportation only

C) Ensuring safety, efficacy, and quality of pharmaceutical products

D) Increasing product price

2. Which type of packaging is in direct contact with the pharmaceutical product?

A) Primary Packaging

B) Secondary Packaging

C) Tertiary Packaging

D) None of the above

3. Which material is commonly used for making bottles, vials, and ampoules due to its inert properties?

A) Plastics

B) Glass

C) Aluminum

D) Paper

4. Which regulatory body sets guidelines for pharmaceutical packaging in the USA?

A) ISO

B) EMA

C) FDA

D) WHO

5. What is the purpose of child-resistant closures in pharmaceutical packaging?

A) To enhance visual appeal

B) To reduce cost

C) To increase safety by preventing children from opening them

D) To make packaging easier to open

6. Which of the following is NOT a typical method of sterilization used in sterile medical device packaging?

A) Steam

B) Ethylene oxide

C) Heavy metal catalysis

D) Gamma radiation

7. What kind of packaging system is commonly used for products that require sterile conditions to maintain their efficacy and integrity?

   A) Aseptic packaging systems

   B) Active packaging systems

   C) Simple packaging systems

   D) Basic packaging systems

8. What is tested through compatibility testing in pharmaceutical packaging?

   A) Brand compatibility

   B) Material interaction with the drug formulation

   C) Package attractiveness

   D) Cost efficiency

9. What is the primary purpose of desiccants in pharmaceutical packaging?

   A) To add weight

   B) To absorb moisture

   C) To improve taste

   D) To color the packaging

10. What is the function of the barrier properties of pharmaceutical packaging materials?

   A) To prevent external elements like moisture and light from degrading the product

   B) To make the packaging look attractive

   C) To reduce the cost of packaging

   D) To increase the ease of transport

11. Which of the following packaging materials is known for its excellent barrier properties against light, moisture, and gases?

A) Cardboard

B) Aluminum

C) Glass

D) Paper

12. In which form are aerosols packaged?

A) Solid

B) Liquid

C) Gas

D) Pressurized dosage forms

13. What does smart packaging in pharmaceuticals typically feature?

A) Colors and patterns

B) Sensors and indicators

C) Simple designs

D) Biodegradable materials

14. What does the term "compatibility" refer to in the context of pharmaceutical packaging?

A) Compatibility between different brands

B) Interaction between the packaging material and the drug

C) The fit between the box and the shelf

D) Price alignment with competitors

15. What is a primary requirement for pharmaceutical packaging that involves oral administration of the drug?

A) Opacity

B) High durability

C) Child resistance

D) Light emission

16. What is the primary role of tertiary packaging in pharmaceuticals?

A) Direct contact with drugs

B) Information display

C) Bulk handling and transportation

D) Individual doses distribution

17. Which of the following is NOT a function of secondary packaging in pharmaceuticals?

   A) Containment of the drug

   B) Providing additional protection

   C) Offering branding space

   D) Dispensing the drug

18. What type of testing might include testing for the effects of light exposure on a drug product?

   A) Sterility testing

   B) Stability testing

   C) Pressure testing

   D) Compatibility testing

19. Which material is preferred for its flexibility and chemical resistance in pharmaceutical packaging?

   A) Polyethylene (PE)

   B) Tinplate

   C) Stainless steel

   D) Cardboard

20. What is the purpose of patient-centric packaging designs?

   A) To reduce packaging costs

   B) To minimize environmental impact

   C) To improve patient adherence and convenience

   D) To simplify manufacturing processes

Short answer type questions (subjective):

1. Why is pharmaceutical packaging critical for maintaining the efficacy and safety of products?

2. What are the main functions of primary packaging in the pharmaceutical industry?

3. Describe the role of secondary packaging in pharmaceuticals.

4. Explain the importance of tertiary packaging in the distribution of pharmaceutical products.

5. What are the key properties of plastics that make them suitable for pharmaceutical packaging?

6. Why is glass considered an ideal material for certain pharmaceutical packaging applications?

7. How does aluminum contribute to pharmaceutical packaging, especially in terms of barrier properties?

8. What are the challenges associated with using paper and cardboard in pharmaceutical packaging?

9. Explain the function of films and foils in enhancing the barrier properties of pharmaceutical packaging.

10. Describe the regulatory requirements for child-resistant closures in pharmaceutical packaging.

11. How do smart packaging technologies contribute to pharmaceutical packaging?

12. What are the benefits of using sustainable materials in pharmaceutical packaging?

13. Describe how patient-centric packaging designs improve patient adherence.

14. How does the pharmaceutical industry ensure that packaging materials are safe and compatible with drug formulations?

15. What are the challenges in designing pharmaceutical packaging for global markets?

16. How do aseptic packaging systems maintain the sterility of pharmaceutical products?

17. Explain the role of container closure systems in maintaining product integrity.

18. Discuss the impact of modern challenges such as counterfeiting on pharmaceutical packaging design.

19. What considerations are taken into account when selecting materials for pharmaceutical packaging?

20. How is the stability of pharmaceutical products tested in relation to their packaging?

Long answer type questions (subjective):

1. Discuss the various types of materials used in pharmaceutical packaging and the criteria for their selection.

2. Explain the technological advancements in pharmaceutical packaging and how they address the needs of modern healthcare.

3. Analyze the role of regulatory bodies in shaping the standards and practices of pharmaceutical packaging.

4. Evaluate the impact of environmental concerns on the development of pharmaceutical packaging materials.

5. Describe the process of compatibility testing for pharmaceutical packaging and its significance in ensuring drug safety.

6. Discuss the challenges and solutions in designing packaging for sensitive pharmaceuticals that are prone to degradation.

7. Explain the principles and components of aseptic packaging systems and their importance in pharmaceutical manufacturing.

8. Analyze the relationship between packaging design and patient adherence to treatment regimens.

9. Discuss the advancements in barrier technology within pharmaceutical packaging and their impact on drug stability.

10.Evaluate the role of innovation in pharmaceutical packaging in response to global health challenges.

Answer Key for the MCQs:

1. C) Ensuring safety, efficacy, and quality of pharmaceutical products
2. A) Primary Packaging
3. B) Glass
4. C) FDA
5. C) To increase safety by preventing children from opening them
6. C) Heavy metal catalysis
7. A) Aseptic packaging systems
8. B) Material interaction with the drug formulation
9. B) To absorb moisture
10.A) To prevent external elements like moisture and light from degrading the product
11.B) Aluminum
12.D) Pressurized dosage forms
13.B) Sensors and indicators
14.B) Interaction between the packaging material and the drug
15.C) Child resistance
16.C) Bulk handling and transportation
17.A) Containment of the drug
18.B) Stability testing
19.A) Polyethylene (PE)
20.C) To improve patient adherence and convenience

CHAPTER – 5

TECHNOLOGY TRANSFER

INTRODUCTION:

Technology transfer refers to the process of transferring knowledge, technologies, skills, or innovations developed in one organization, institution, or country to another for further development, commercialization, or utilization. It plays a crucial role in fostering innovation, economic growth, and societal progress by enabling the dissemination and application of valuable knowledge and expertise.

Here's a detailed introduction to technology transfer:

1. **Definition and Scope**: Technology transfer encompasses a wide range of activities, including the licensing of intellectual property rights (patents, copyrights, and trademarks), collaborative research and development agreements, joint ventures, spin-offs, and the exchange of personnel between organizations or countries. It involves the transmission of technological know-how, innovations, and best practices from research institutions, universities, or businesses to other entities, such as startups, industries, or governments.

2. **Types of Technology Transfer**:

   a. **Intra-organizational Transfer**: Transfer of technology within the same organization or institution, such as from R&D departments to production units.

   b. **Inter-organizational Transfer**: Transfer between different organizations, including academia-industry collaborations, public-private partnerships, or international collaborations.

   c. **International Transfer**: Transfer of technology across national borders, often involving licensing agreements, foreign direct investment, or technology diffusion through trade and globalization.

3. **Key Stakeholders:**

   a. **Technology Owners:** Entities possessing intellectual property rights or proprietary technologies, such as research institutions, universities, or corporations.

   b. **Recipients or Licensees**: Organizations or individuals seeking access to technology for commercialization, innovation, or research purposes.

   c. **Intermediaries:** Entities facilitating technology transfer activities, including technology transfer offices, venture capitalists, technology brokers, or government agencies.

4. **Motivations for Technology Transfer:**

   a. **Commercialization and Market Access:** Expanding market reach and revenue generation through the licensing or sale of technology.

   b. **Innovation and Collaboration**: Leveraging external expertise and resources to enhance innovation capacity and accelerate product development.

   c. **Knowledge Dissemination**: Sharing scientific breakthroughs, research findings, and technological advancements for the benefit of society.

   d. **Economic Development**: Stimulating economic growth, job creation, and industry competitiveness by fostering entrepreneurship and technology-based industries.

5. **Challenges and Barriers:**

   a. **Intellectual Property Rights:** Negotiating licensing terms, protecting intellectual property, and resolving conflicts over ownership rights.

b. **Cultural and Organizational Differences**: Addressing divergent priorities, values, and operating procedures between technology providers and recipients.

c. **Legal and Regulatory Frameworks**: Navigating complex legal and regulatory environments, including export controls, antitrust laws, and technology transfer policies.

d. **Resource Constraints**: Limited funding, infrastructure, or human capital to support technology transfer activities, especially in developing countries or small enterprises.

6. **Best Practices and Strategies:**

a. **Developing Clear Policies and Procedures**: Establishing transparent guidelines for technology transfer, including intellectual property management, licensing terms, and dispute resolution mechanisms.

b. **Building Strategic Partnerships**: Cultivating mutually beneficial collaborations with industry partners, investors, government agencies, and international organizations to leverage complementary strengths and resources.

c. **Capacity Building and Training**: Investing in workforce development, technical assistance, and entrepreneurship education to enhance the capabilities of technology transfer professionals and stakeholders.

d. **Promoting Open Innovation**: Embracing open-source initiatives, collaborative research platforms, and technology-sharing networks to facilitate the exchange of ideas and accelerate innovation diffusion.

DEVELOPMENT OF TECHNOLOGY BY R & D

The development of technology through Research and Development (R&D) is a fundamental aspect of technology transfer. R&D activities are often the initial stages in creating innovative solutions, products, or processes that have the potential for commercialization or societal impact. Here's a detailed exploration of how R&D contributes to technology transfer:

R&D Process:

The Research and Development (R&D) process is a fundamental stage in the development of technology before it can be transferred for commercialization or practical application. The R&D process involves systematic investigation, experimentation, and innovation to advance scientific knowledge, develop new technologies, and solve complex problems. Here's a detailed exploration of the R&D process in the development of technology for technology transfer:

1. **Identifying Needs and Opportunities:**
   a. **Market Research:** Conduct market research and analysis to identify emerging trends, unmet needs, and opportunities for innovation in target industries or markets. Understand customer requirements, market dynamics, competitive landscapes, and regulatory environments to inform R&D priorities and technology development efforts.
   b. **Stakeholder Engagement**: Engage stakeholders, including customers, end-users, industry partners, and domain experts, to gather insights, feedback, and input on potential technology solutions. Collaborate with stakeholders to define problem statements, user requirements, and performance criteria that guide R&D efforts.

2. **Conceptualization and Idea Generation:**
   a. **Brainstorming and Ideation**: Foster a culture of creativity and innovation within the R&D team through brainstorming sessions, ideation workshops, and collaborative problem-solving activities. Generate a diverse range of ideas, concepts, and hypotheses that have the potential to address identified needs and opportunities.

b. **Feasibility Analysis**: Conduct feasibility studies and preliminary assessments to evaluate the technical, economic, and market feasibility of potential technology concepts. Assess factors such as technical complexity, resource requirements, intellectual property landscape, and commercialization potential to prioritize ideas for further development.

3. **Research and Experimentation:**

   a. **Literature Review**: Conduct a comprehensive literature review to review existing knowledge, research findings, and technological advancements relevant to the R&D project. Identify gaps, opportunities, and insights that inform research hypotheses, experimental designs, and technology development strategies.

   b. **Experimental Design**: Develop experimental plans, methodologies, and protocols to test hypotheses, validate concepts, and gather empirical data. Design experiments that systematically investigate key variables, parameters, and factors influencing the technology's performance, functionality, and feasibility.

   c. **Prototyping and Proof-of-Concept**: Build prototypes or proof-of-concept models to demonstrate the feasibility, functionality, and potential of the technology. Prototyping allows researchers to validate design concepts, assess performance metrics, and iterate on design iterations based on feedback and experimentation results.

4. **Data Analysis and Interpretation:**

   a. **Data Collection**: Collect, record, and analyze experimental data generated from research and experimentation activities. Utilize quantitative and qualitative analysis techniques, statistical methods, and data visualization tools to extract meaningful insights, trends, and patterns from the data.

b. **Interpretation and Insights**: Interpret research findings, experimental results, and data analysis outputs to draw conclusions, make inferences, and generate actionable insights. Assess the implications of the findings on technology development decisions, hypothesis validation, and future research directions.

5. **Iterative Development and Optimization:**

   a. **Iterative Design**: Iterate on technology designs, prototypes, and experimental setups based on feedback, evaluation results, and iterative testing. Incorporate design modifications, optimizations, and refinements to improve performance, functionality, and usability iteratively.

   b. **Validation and Verification**: Validate technology designs, features, and performance through systematic testing, validation studies, and verification protocols. Ensure that the technology meets specified requirements, standards, and user needs before proceeding to the next stage of development.

6. **Documentation and Intellectual Property Protection:**

   a. **Documenting Research Findings**: Document research methodologies, experimental procedures, results, and conclusions in detailed technical reports, lab notebooks, and research publications. Maintain accurate records of data, observations, and analyses to support future technology transfer activities, patent filings, and regulatory submissions.

   b. **Intellectual Property Management**: Protect intellectual property assets generated during the R&D process through patents, copyrights, trademarks, or trade secrets. Work closely with legal counsel and intellectual property experts to identify, assess, and protect valuable intellectual property rights associated with the technology.

7. **Collaboration and Knowledge Sharing:**

   a. **Interdisciplinary Collaboration**: Foster interdisciplinary collaboration and knowledge sharing among researchers, scientists, engineers, and domain experts involved in the R&D project. Collaborate across organizational boundaries, departments, and disciplines to leverage diverse expertise, perspectives, and resources.

   b. **Dissemination of Findings**: Disseminate research findings, insights, and innovations through internal reports, presentations, scientific publications, and conference presentations. Share knowledge and best practices with external stakeholders, academic partners, industry collaborators, and the broader scientific community to promote collaboration and facilitate technology transfer.

8. **Regulatory Compliance and Ethical Considerations:**

   a. **Regulatory Compliance**: Ensure compliance with applicable laws, regulations, and ethical standards governing research, experimentation, and technology development. Adhere to ethical principles, research integrity guidelines, and regulatory requirements related to human subjects, animal welfare, environmental protection, and data privacy.

   b. **Risk Assessment and Mitigation**: Identify, assess, and mitigate potential risks associated with the R&D project, including technical, safety, ethical, and regulatory risks. Implement risk management strategies, safety protocols, and compliance measures to protect stakeholders and ensure responsible conduct of research.

Innovation and Technology Creation:

Innovation and technology creation are at the heart of the development of technology through research and development (R&D) for eventual technology transfer. This process involves generating new ideas, concepts, and solutions to address existing challenges or opportunities, and transforming them into tangible technologies with practical applications. Here's a detailed exploration of innovation and technology creation in the context of R&D for technology transfer:

1. **Identifying Opportunities for Innovation:**
   a. **Market Analysis**: Conduct market research to identify emerging trends, unmet needs, and opportunities for innovation in specific industries or sectors. Analyze market dynamics, customer preferences, competitor offerings, and regulatory landscapes to uncover areas ripe for technological advancement.
   b. **Technology Scanning**: Scan technology landscapes, scientific literature, and patent databases to identify existing solutions, breakthroughs, and intellectual property relevant to the target area of innovation. Evaluate gaps, limitations, or opportunities for improvement that can be addressed through new technological developments.
   c. **Stakeholder Engagement**: Engage stakeholders, including customers, end-users, industry partners, and domain experts, to gather insights, feedback, and input on potential innovation opportunities. Collaborate with stakeholders to co-create solutions that address real-world problems and meet user needs effectively.

2. **Idea Generation and Conceptualization:**
   a. **Brainstorming and Ideation**: Foster a culture of creativity and innovation within the R&D team through brainstorming sessions, design thinking workshops, and collaborative problem-solving activities. Generate a wide range of ideas, concepts, and hypotheses that have the potential to address identified opportunities or challenges.

b. **Technology Roadmapping**: Develop technology roadmaps that outline the strategic direction, goals, and milestones for innovation initiatives. Define a clear vision for technology development, prioritize innovation projects, and allocate resources based on strategic objectives, market potential, and technical feasibility.

3. **Research and Exploration:**

    a. **Exploratory Research**: Conduct exploratory research to explore novel concepts, technologies, and approaches that have the potential to drive innovation. Explore fundamental scientific principles, experimental techniques, and cutting-edge technologies that may inspire new ideas or solutions.

    b. **Proof-of-Concept Studies**: Conduct proof-of-concept studies to validate the feasibility and viability of innovative ideas or technologies. Build prototypes, conduct feasibility studies, and perform preliminary experiments to demonstrate the technical feasibility, functionality, and potential value of the innovation.

4. **Collaborative Innovation and Open Innovation:**

    a. **Collaborative Partnerships**: Form collaborative partnerships and alliances with external stakeholders, including academia, industry, government agencies, and research institutions, to leverage complementary expertise, resources, and perspectives. Collaborate on joint research projects, consortia, or open innovation platforms to accelerate technology development and enhance innovation outcomes.

    b. **Open Innovation Practices**: Embrace open innovation practices that involve sharing ideas, knowledge, and resources with external collaborators, partners, and the broader innovation ecosystem. Engage in crowdsourcing, hackathons, challenge competitions, and open-source initiatives to tap into diverse talent pools, foster creativity, and drive breakthrough innovations.

5. **Iterative Design and Optimization:**
   a. **Iterative Prototyping**: Adopt an iterative approach to technology development, where prototypes are designed, tested, and refined through multiple iterations. Solicit feedback from end-users, stakeholders, and experts to identify areas for improvement, iterate on design features, and enhance user experience iteratively.
   b. **Design Thinking**: Apply design thinking methodologies to empathize with end-users, define problem statements, ideate innovative solutions, prototype concepts, and test prototypes in real-world contexts. Design thinking fosters a user-centered approach to innovation, ensuring that technology solutions address genuine user needs and preferences effectively.

6. **Cross-Disciplinary Collaboration:**
   a. **Interdisciplinary Teams**: Form interdisciplinary teams composed of experts from diverse disciplines, including engineering, science, design, business, and social sciences. Foster collaboration and knowledge sharing across disciplines to combine different perspectives, approaches, and methodologies in technology development.
   b. **Translational Research: Promote** translational research that bridges the gap between basic research and applied innovation. Translate scientific discoveries, academic research findings, and theoretical concepts into practical technologies with real-world applications through interdisciplinary collaboration and cross-sector partnerships.

7. **Risk-Taking and Experimentation:**

a. **Tolerance for Failure**: Cultivate a culture of risk-taking, experimentation, and learning within the R&D organization. Encourage experimentation, exploration, and iteration by providing a supportive environment where failure is seen as an opportunity for learning and improvement.

b. **Agile Methodologies: Adopt** agile methodologies and rapid prototyping techniques that enable quick iteration, adaptation, and validation of ideas. Embrace an iterative, incremental approach to innovation that allows for rapid experimentation, feedback incorporation, and course correction based on real-time insights.

8. **Intellectual Property Management and Commercialization:**

a. **Intellectual Property Strategy**: Develop a comprehensive intellectual property strategy to protect and monetize innovative technologies generated through R&D efforts. File patents, copyrights, trademarks, or trade secrets to secure intellectual property rights and create barriers to entry for competitors.

b. **Technology Transfer and Commercialization**: Facilitate technology transfer and commercialization of innovative technologies by licensing intellectual property rights to industry partners, startups, or spin-off companies. Collaborate with technology transfer offices, venture capitalists, and industry accelerators to identify commercialization opportunities, secure funding, and bring innovations to market.

Intellectual Property Generation:

Intellectual property (IP) generation is a critical aspect of the development of technology through research and development (R&D) for eventual technology transfer. Intellectual property encompasses patents, copyrights, trademarks, and trade secrets that protect innovations, inventions, and creative works. Here's a detailed exploration of intellectual property generation in the context of R&D for technology transfer:

1. **Invention Disclosure:**
   a. **Identification of Innovations**: R&D teams identify novel innovations, discoveries, or inventions that have the potential for commercialization or practical application. These innovations may arise from experimental findings, design improvements, process optimizations, or new product concepts developed during the R&D process.
   b. **Documentation and Disclosure**: R&D personnel document their inventions, discoveries, or innovations in invention disclosure forms or reports. These documents provide detailed descriptions, drawings, experimental data, and other relevant information that support the claims and novelty of the invention.

2. **Patentability Assessment:**
   a. **Prior Art Search**: Conduct a prior art search to assess the novelty and non-obviousness of the invention compared to existing technologies, patents, publications, and prior art in the relevant field. This search helps determine the patentability and potential scope of protection for the invention.
   b. **Patentability Analysis**: Analyze the results of the prior art search to evaluate the patentability of the invention based on criteria such as novelty, inventive step, industrial applicability, and patent eligibility. Assess the strengths, weaknesses, opportunities, and threats associated with pursuing patent protection for the invention.

3. **Patent Drafting and Filing:**
   a. **Drafting Patent Applications**: Prepare patent applications that describe the invention in detail, including its technical features, functionality, advantages, and potential applications. Draft claims

that define the scope of protection sought for the invention and support them with sufficient disclosure and enablement.

    b. **Filing Patent Applications**: File patent applications with the relevant intellectual property offices, such as the United States Patent and Trademark Office (USPTO) or the European Patent Office (EPO). Follow procedural requirements, deadlines, and formalities for patent filing to secure priority rights and initiate the examination process.

4. **Intellectual Property Protection Strategies:**

    a. **Portfolio Management**: Develop a strategic portfolio of intellectual property assets that align with organizational goals, R&D priorities, and commercialization strategies. Manage the IP portfolio proactively, including maintaining, updating, and optimizing patent filings, maintenance fees, and licensing agreements.

    b. **Global Protection**: Consider international patent protection strategies to secure intellectual property rights in key markets, regions, or jurisdictions relevant to technology transfer and commercialization efforts. File international patent applications under the Patent Cooperation Treaty (PCT) or regional patent systems to streamline the process of obtaining foreign patents.

5. **Commercialization and Technology Transfer:**

    a. **Licensing and Technology Transfer**: Leverage intellectual property assets to facilitate technology transfer and commercialization initiatives. Enter into licensing agreements, technology transfer agreements, or collaborative partnerships with industry partners, startups, or investors interested in commercializing the technology.

b. **Spin-Off Ventures**: Explore spin-off ventures, startup incubators, or entrepreneurship programs as avenues for commercializing intellectual property assets developed through R&D. Create spin-off companies or startups that leverage patented technologies to develop innovative products, services, or solutions for the market.

6. **Enforcement and Defense:**

   a. **Monitoring and Enforcement**: Monitor the marketplace for potential infringement of intellectual property rights associated with patented technologies. Identify unauthorized use, reproduction, or distribution of patented inventions and take appropriate enforcement actions, such as cease-and-desist letters, litigation, or licensing negotiations.

   b. **Defensive Strategies**: Develop defensive strategies to protect intellectual property rights and mitigate risks of infringement or challenges to patent validity. Build a strong patent portfolio, establish defensive patent pools, or engage in cross-licensing agreements with competitors to deter litigation and enhance market competitiveness.

7. **Collaboration and Technology Transfer Offices:**

   a. **Technology Transfer Offices (TTOs)**: Collaborate with technology transfer offices within research institutions, universities, or government agencies to facilitate intellectual property management and technology transfer activities. TTOs provide expertise, resources, and support for patenting, licensing, and commercialization efforts.

   b. **Collaborative Partnerships**: Form collaborative partnerships with industry, academia, and government agencies to leverage intellectual property assets for technology transfer and commercialization. Collaborate on joint research projects, consortia, or technology transfer programs that promote innovation, knowledge exchange, and economic development.

Collaboration and Technology Transfer:

Collaboration and technology transfer are integral components of the development of technology through research and development (R&D) for eventual commercialization or practical application. Collaboration involves partnering with external stakeholders, such as industry partners, academic institutions, government agencies, and research organizations, to leverage complementary expertise, resources, and capabilities. Technology transfer refers to the process of transferring knowledge, innovations, and intellectual property from R&D activities to end-users, industry partners, or other entities for commercialization or societal benefit. Here's a detailed exploration of collaboration and technology transfer in the context of R&D for technology development:

1. **Identifying Collaborative Opportunities:**

    a. **Strategic Alignment**: Identify potential collaborators whose expertise, resources, and objectives align with the goals and priorities of the technology development initiative. Seek partners with complementary strengths, capabilities, and networks that can enhance the innovation ecosystem and accelerate technology transfer.

    b. **Industry Partnerships**: Form strategic partnerships with industry stakeholders, including technology companies, manufacturers, suppliers, and service providers, to leverage industry expertise, market insights, and commercialization pathways. Collaborate on joint R&D projects, technology licensing agreements, or product development initiatives to bring innovations to market.

    c. **Academic Collaborations**: Collaborate with academic institutions, research centers, and universities to access cutting-edge research, specialized facilities, and academic expertise in relevant scientific disciplines. Partner on joint research projects, collaborative grants, or technology transfer programs that bridge the gap between academic research and industry application.

d. **Government Initiatives**: Participate in government-sponsored initiatives, funding programs, and consortia that promote collaboration, technology transfer, and innovation-driven economic development. Engage with government agencies, innovation hubs, and technology clusters to access funding, infrastructure, and regulatory support for technology development and commercialization.

2. **Establishing Collaborative Partnerships:**

a. **Memoranda of Understanding (MoUs)**: Formalize collaborative partnerships through memoranda of understanding (MoUs), partnership agreements, or joint venture agreements that outline the terms, objectives, and responsibilities of each party. Clarify the roles, expectations, and contributions of collaborators in the technology development and transfer process.

b. **Consortia and Alliances**: Join industry consortia, technology alliances, or research networks that facilitate collaboration, knowledge sharing, and resource pooling among multiple stakeholders. Participate in pre-competitive research initiatives, standardization efforts, or market development programs that foster collaboration and innovation in specific industries or sectors.

c. **Technology Transfer Offices (TTOs):** Collaborate with technology transfer offices within research institutions, universities, or government agencies to facilitate technology transfer and commercialization activities. TTOs provide expertise, resources, and support for intellectual property management, patent licensing, startup incubation, and industry engagement.

d. **Open Innovation Platforms**: Embrace open innovation platforms, crowdsourcing initiatives, or innovation challenges that invite external stakeholders to contribute ideas, expertise, and resources to technology development projects. Engage with startups, entrepreneurs, and innovators through open innovation programs that foster collaboration, creativity, and co-creation.

3. **Knowledge Exchange and Transfer:**

   a. **Technology Licensing**: Transfer technology through licensing agreements that grant rights to use, develop, or commercialize intellectual property assets generated through R&D activities. Negotiate licensing terms, royalties, and revenue-sharing arrangements with licensees to facilitate technology transfer and monetize intellectual property.

   b. **Technology Demonstrations**: Showcase technology prototypes, proof-of-concept models, or pilot projects to potential collaborators, investors, or end-users to demonstrate the feasibility, functionality, and value proposition of the technology. Organize technology demonstrations, roadshows, or industry showcases to attract interest and investment in technology transfer initiatives.

   c. **Capacity Building**: Build capacity and capabilities within collaborating organizations through training, knowledge transfer, and skill development programs. Share best practices, technical expertise, and industry insights to empower collaborators to contribute effectively to technology development, commercialization, and adoption.

   d. **Technology Access and Transfer Mechanisms**: Establish mechanisms for accessing and transferring technology assets, such as intellectual property databases, technology marketplaces, or innovation hubs. Facilitate technology scouting, matchmaking, and licensing transactions through online platforms, industry networks, or technology transfer offices.

4. **Commercialization and Market Access:**

   a. **Market Validation**: Validate technology concepts, prototypes, or minimum viable products (MVPs) in real-world environments to assess market demand, user feedback, and commercialization potential. Collaborate with industry partners, pilot customers, or early adopters to gather market intelligence, refine product-market fit, and de-risk technology investments.

   b. **Product Development**: Collaborate on product development, design optimization, and manufacturing scale-up activities to translate R&D innovations into market-ready products or solutions. Leverage industry expertise, supply chain networks, and manufacturing capabilities to accelerate product commercialization and time-to-market.

   c. **Go-to-Market Strategies**: Develop go-to-market strategies, distribution channels, and sales partnerships to promote technology adoption, penetration, and market growth. Collaborate with sales channels, distributors, and marketing partners to launch marketing campaigns, customer engagement initiatives, and sales promotions that drive market uptake and revenue generation.

   d. **Regulatory Compliance**: Ensure compliance with regulatory requirements, standards, and certifications necessary for market access and commercialization. Collaborate with regulatory authorities, certification bodies, and compliance experts to navigate regulatory pathways, obtain necessary approvals, and mitigate regulatory risks associated with technology transfer and commercialization.

5. **Monitoring and Evaluation:**

   a. **Performance Metrics**: Define key performance indicators (KPIs), milestones, and success criteria for monitoring and evaluating the progress and outcomes of collaborative technology transfer initiatives. Measure the impact, effectiveness, and return on investment (ROI) of collaboration efforts in terms of technology adoption, market penetration, and economic value creation.

   b. **Feedback Mechanisms**: Establish feedback mechanisms, evaluation surveys, or stakeholder consultations to solicit input, insights, and lessons learned from collaborators, partners, and end-users involved in technology transfer activities. Capture feedback on collaboration effectiveness, process efficiency, and value proposition to inform continuous improvement and future collaboration strategies.

   c. **Post-Transfer Support**: Provide post-transfer support, technical assistance, and ongoing collaboration opportunities to facilitate technology adoption, implementation, and integration by end-users or licensees. Offer training programs, technical support services, and user forums to address implementation challenges, optimize technology utilization, and foster long-term partnerships with collaborators.

Funding and Support:

Funding and support play a crucial role in the development of technology through research and development (R&D) for eventual technology transfer. Adequate funding and support provide the necessary resources, infrastructure, and expertise to drive innovation, accelerate technology development, and facilitate the transfer of technology from R&D to commercialization or practical application. Here's a detailed exploration of funding and support mechanisms in the context of R&D for technology transfer:

1. **Government Grants and Funding Programs:**

   a. **Research Grants**: Government agencies offer research grants, contracts, and funding opportunities to support R&D activities across various scientific disciplines, technological domains, and industry sectors. These grants may be awarded through competitive grant programs, research consortia, or collaborative partnerships to fund basic research, applied research, or technology development projects.

   b. **Innovation Funds**: Government-sponsored innovation funds, technology funds, or venture capital programs provide financial support to startups, entrepreneurs, and innovators to develop and commercialize innovative technologies with commercial potential. These funds may offer seed funding, venture capital investments, or equity financing to early-stage companies or technology ventures.

   c. **Technology Development Grants**: Government agencies administer technology development grants, challenge grants, or innovation prizes to incentivize the development of novel technologies that address specific societal challenges, market needs, or strategic priorities. These grants may support prototype development, proof-of-concept studies, or pilot projects that demonstrate the feasibility and impact of technology solutions.

   d. **Tax Incentives and Credits**: Governments offer tax incentives, research and development tax credits, or tax breaks to encourage private sector investment in R&D activities and technology development. These incentives reduce the cost of R&D

investments, stimulate innovation, and incentivize collaboration between industry, academia, and research institutions.

2. **Industry Partnerships and Corporate Sponsorship:**

    a. **Corporate R&D Funding**: Industry partners, technology companies, and corporations invest in R&D activities, technology development projects, and collaborative research initiatives to drive innovation and gain a competitive edge in the marketplace. Companies may allocate internal R&D budgets, establish corporate venture capital funds, or engage in strategic partnerships with startups, research institutions, or academic centers.

    b. **Industry Consortia**: Industry consortia, technology alliances, or collaborative networks bring together multiple companies, stakeholders, and industry partners to pool resources, share risks, and collaborate on pre-competitive research, technology development, or standardization efforts. Consortia members contribute funding, expertise, and intellectual property to advance shared objectives and address common challenges.

    c. **Technology Transfer Partnerships**: Collaborate with industry partners on technology transfer partnerships, licensing agreements, or joint ventures to commercialize R&D innovations and bring them to market. Industry partners may provide funding, market access, manufacturing capabilities, or distribution channels to facilitate technology transfer and accelerate commercialization.

3. **Academic and Institutional Support:**

    a. **Research Institutions**: Academic institutions, research centers, and universities provide support for R&D activities, technology development projects, and collaborative research initiatives through internal funding mechanisms, research grants, or philanthropic donations. These institutions offer access to state-of-the-art laboratories, research infrastructure, and academic expertise to support technology transfer and innovation.

b. **Technology Transfer Offices (TTOs):** Technology transfer offices within research institutions, universities, or government agencies facilitate technology transfer and commercialization activities by providing expertise, resources, and support for intellectual property management, patent licensing, startup incubation, and industry engagement. TTOs help researchers navigate the technology transfer process, secure funding, and forge collaborations with industry partners.

4. **Venture Capital and Private Equity Investments:**

   a. **Venture Capital Financing**: Venture capital firms, private equity investors, and angel investors provide funding and equity investments to startups, early-stage companies, and technology ventures to support R&D activities, product development, and commercialization efforts. Venture capital funding enables technology startups to scale their operations, expand their market reach, and bring innovative products to market.

   b. **Technology Incubators and Accelerators**: Technology incubators, startup accelerators, and innovation hubs offer funding, mentorship, and support services to early-stage startups and technology ventures to accelerate their growth and development. These programs provide access to funding, mentorship, networking opportunities, and industry connections that help startups navigate the challenges of technology development and commercialization.

5. **Philanthropic Donations and Nonprofit Support:**

   a. **Philanthropic Foundations**: Philanthropic organizations, charitable foundations, and nonprofit entities provide grants, donations, and support for R&D initiatives, technology development projects, and innovation-driven solutions that address societal challenges, promote economic development, or advance scientific knowledge. These organizations fund research in areas such as healthcare, education, environmental sustainability, and social impact.

b. **Nonprofit Incubators and Collaboratives**: Nonprofit incubators, research collaboratives, and social impact organizations offer support for technology development, innovation ecosystems, and community-driven initiatives that create positive social change. These organizations provide funding, mentorship, and capacity-building programs to support technology-driven solutions with social impact.

6. **International Collaboration and Funding:**

a. **Global Partnerships**: Collaborate with international partners, multinational organizations, and global research networks to access funding, expertise, and resources for R&D activities, technology development projects, and collaborative research initiatives. Participate in international consortia, joint research programs, or bilateral agreements that promote cross-border collaboration and knowledge exchange.

b. **International Funding Agencies**: International funding agencies, multilateral organizations, and development banks administer grant programs, research funds, and technical assistance initiatives to support R&D projects, technology transfer activities, and innovation-driven development in developing countries or emerging markets. These agencies provide financial support, capacity-building programs, and institutional partnerships to address global challenges and promote sustainable development.

7. **Crowdfunding and Alternative Financing:**

a. **Crowdfunding Platforms**: Crowdfunding platforms, online marketplaces, and peer-to-peer lending networks enable individuals, entrepreneurs, and startups to raise funds for R&D projects, technology development initiatives, or product prototypes through contributions from a large number of supporters. Crowdfunding campaigns offer a platform for showcasing innovative ideas, generating public interest, and validating market demand for technology solutions.

b. **Alternative Financing Models**: Explore alternative financing models, such as revenue-based financing, income-share agreements, or royalty-based investments, that offer flexible funding options for technology development and commercialization. These models provide capital without equity dilution, repayment obligations, or traditional debt financing requirements, allowing innovators to retain ownership and control over their intellectual property.

8. **Collaborative Research Consortia and Public-Private Partnerships:**

a. **Pre-Competitive Research Consortia**: Collaborate with industry consortia, research networks, or public-private partnerships that focus on pre-competitive research, technology development, or standardization efforts in specific industries or sectors. These consortia bring together multiple stakeholders, including industry partners, academic institutions, and government agencies, to address common challenges, advance shared objectives, and drive collective innovation.

b. **Public-Private Partnerships (PPPs)**: Engage in public-private partnerships, joint ventures, or cooperative agreements with government agencies, industry partners, and research organizations to fund and support R&D initiatives, technology development projects, and infrastructure investments. PPPs leverage public and private sector resources, expertise, and capabilities to address complex challenges, stimulate economic growth, and enhance societal well-being.

TECHNOLOGY TRANSFER FROM R & D TO PRODUCTION

The transfer of technology from Research and Development (R&D) to production is a critical stage in the technology transfer process, where innovative ideas and prototypes are transformed into commercially viable products or processes. This transition involves a series of steps and considerations to ensure the successful scaling, optimization, and integration of new technologies into manufacturing operations. Here's a detailed exploration of technology transfer from R&D to production:

Technology Maturation and Validation:

Technology maturation and validation are critical stages in the process of transferring technology from research and development (R&D) to production. These stages involve refining the technology, optimizing its performance, and validating its suitability for practical application in a production environment. Here's a detailed exploration of technology maturation and validation in the context of technology transfer from R&D to production:

1. **Technology Maturation:**
   a. **Prototype Development**: Build upon the initial prototypes or proof-of-concept models developed during the R&D phase to create more advanced prototypes that closely resemble the final product design. Refine the design, functionality, and performance of the prototypes through iterative testing, evaluation, and optimization.
   b. **Iterative Improvement**: Adopt an iterative approach to technology development, where successive iterations of the prototype are designed, tested, and refined based on feedback, user

requirements, and performance objectives. Incorporate design modifications, feature enhancements, and performance optimizations to mature the technology iteratively.

c. **Scale-Up Process**: Scale up the production process from laboratory-scale or small-scale prototypes to larger-scale production systems or manufacturing facilities. Address scalability challenges, production constraints, and process bottlenecks to ensure that the technology can be manufactured at commercial scale without compromising quality, efficiency, or cost-effectiveness.

d. **Materials Selection and Procurement**: Evaluate and select materials, components, and suppliers for the production of the technology based on factors such as cost, quality, availability, and suitability for the intended application. Establish supply chain relationships, procurement agreements, and quality control measures to ensure reliable access to materials and components.

2. **Performance Validation:**

a. **Functional Testing**: Conduct comprehensive functional testing and validation of the technology to assess its performance, reliability, and functionality under real-world operating conditions. Design test protocols, performance metrics, and acceptance criteria that simulate typical usage scenarios, environmental conditions, and performance requirements.

b. **Quality Assurance**: Implement quality assurance processes, standards, and procedures to ensure that the technology meets specified quality standards, regulatory requirements, and industry best practices. Perform quality control inspections, product testing, and compliance checks to verify conformance to quality standards and regulatory guidelines.

c. **Reliability Testing**: Subject the technology to rigorous reliability testing, stress testing, and durability assessments to evaluate its long-term performance, robustness, and resilience to adverse conditions. Identify potential failure modes, weak points, or reliability issues through accelerated life testing, reliability modeling, and failure analysis techniques.

d. **Compliance Certification**: Obtain regulatory certifications, compliance approvals, or industry certifications necessary for the commercialization and market acceptance of the technology. Ensure that the technology complies with applicable safety standards, product regulations, environmental requirements, and industry-specific certifications relevant to the target market.

3. **User Feedback and Iterative Refinement:**

a. **User Evaluation**: Gather feedback from end-users, stakeholders, and customers through user testing, usability studies, and customer surveys to assess user satisfaction, preferences, and usability issues. Incorporate user feedback, feature requests, and usability enhancements into the design iteration process to improve the user experience and product usability.

b. **Iterative Refinement**: Iterate on the technology design, user interface, and product features based on user feedback, market insights, and usability testing results. Continuously refine the technology through iterative design cycles that prioritize user-centric design, functionality improvements, and feature enhancements.

4. **Pilot Testing and Field Trials:**

a. **Pilot Production Runs**: Conduct pilot production runs or small-scale manufacturing trials to validate the scalability, repeatability, and performance consistency of the production process. Produce limited quantities of the technology under production conditions to identify and resolve manufacturing challenges, process variability, and production bottlenecks.

b. **Field Trials and Deployment:** Deploy the technology in real-world settings, field trials, or pilot projects to evaluate its performance, functionality, and user acceptance in practical applications. Collaborate with pilot customers, early adopters, or industry partners to gather field data, validate performance metrics, and assess the technology's impact in real-world environments.

c. **Performance Monitoring**: Monitor the performance of the technology during field trials or pilot deployments to track key performance indicators, usage patterns, and operational metrics. Collect field data, sensor readings, and performance logs to evaluate the technology's reliability, efficiency, and effectiveness over time.

5. **Documentation and Knowledge Transfer:**

a. **Technical Documentation**: Prepare comprehensive technical documentation, user manuals, and operating instructions that provide guidance on the installation, operation, and maintenance of the technology. Document design specifications, performance characteristics, and troubleshooting procedures to support technology deployment, training, and support activities.

b. **Knowledge Transfer**: Transfer technical knowledge, expertise, and best practices from R&D teams to production personnel, manufacturing engineers, and operational staff responsible for technology implementation. Conduct training sessions, knowledge transfer workshops, and skill development programs to ensure that production teams are equipped with the necessary skills and expertise to manufacture and support the technology effectively.

6. **Continuous Improvement and Feedback Loop:**

   a. **Continuous Monitoring**: Establish a feedback loop for continuous monitoring, evaluation, and improvement of the technology throughout its lifecycle. Collect feedback from end-users, production teams, and stakeholders to identify opportunities for optimization, performance enhancement, and feature updates.

   b. **Continuous Improvement Process**: Implement a continuous improvement process that systematically captures, prioritizes, and addresses feedback, suggestions, and lessons learned from technology users, production teams, and stakeholders. Iterate on the technology design, production process, and support services to drive ongoing innovation and improvement.

Process Development and Optimization:

Process development and optimization are crucial stages in the technology transfer process from research and development (R&D) to production. These stages involve transforming the R&D-developed technology into a scalable, efficient, and reliable production process that can meet quality standards, cost targets, and market demand. Here's a detailed exploration of process development and optimization in the context of technology transfer:

1. **Process Development:**

   a. **Process Mapping**: Begin by mapping out the entire production process, from raw material acquisition to final product assembly, to identify key steps, subprocesses, and dependencies. Document process flows, equipment requirements, material handling procedures, and process parameters to create a comprehensive process map.

   b. **Process Design**: Design the production process based on the requirements of the technology, product specifications, and quality standards. Determine the sequence of operations, equipment layout, workflow optimization, and resource allocation to ensure efficient and effective production.

c. **Technology Adaptation**: Adapt the R&D-developed technology to suit the requirements of the production environment, including scalability, repeatability, and manufacturability. Modify process parameters, equipment configurations, and material specifications as needed to optimize the technology for large-scale production.

d. **Equipment Selection**: Select appropriate manufacturing equipment, machinery, and tools that are capable of handling the production requirements and specifications of the technology. Evaluate factors such as capacity, throughput, precision, reliability, and compatibility with process inputs and outputs.

e. **Automation and Control**: Integrate automation technologies, control systems, and process monitoring tools to enhance process efficiency, consistency, and quality control. Implement sensors, actuators, and programmable logic controllers (PLCs) to automate repetitive tasks, regulate process parameters, and ensure product consistency.

f. **Quality Assurance**: Embed quality assurance measures, in-process controls, and inspection checkpoints into the production process to detect defects, deviations, or non-conformities early in the manufacturing process. Implement statistical process control (SPC) techniques, quality management systems, and error-proofing methods to maintain product quality and consistency.

2. **Process Optimization:**

a. **Continuous Improvement Culture**: Foster a culture of continuous improvement and operational excellence within the production team by encouraging feedback, idea generation, and problem-solving initiatives. Empower employees to identify inefficiencies, bottlenecks, and opportunities for optimization in the production process.

b. **Lean Manufacturing Principles**: Apply lean manufacturing principles, such as value stream mapping, waste reduction, and process standardization, to streamline operations, eliminate non-value-added activities, and optimize resource utilization. Implement lean tools and techniques, such as 5S, kaizen, and Kanban, to optimize workflow, reduce cycle times, and enhance productivity.

c. **Six Sigma Methodology**: Deploy Six Sigma methodology and statistical analysis techniques to identify process variations, defects, and sources of variability that impact product quality and consistency. Conduct root cause analysis, process capability studies, and design of experiments (DOE) to optimize process parameters and reduce defects.

d. **Process Simulation and Modeling**: Utilize process simulation software, computer-aided design (CAD) tools, and mathematical modeling techniques to simulate, analyze, and optimize the production process virtually. Model process flows, material flows, and production scenarios to identify optimization opportunities, validate process changes, and predict performance outcomes.

e. **Supply Chain Integration**: Integrate the production process with upstream and downstream supply chain operations to optimize material flow, inventory management, and logistics. Collaborate with suppliers, vendors, and logistics partners to synchronize production schedules, reduce lead times, and minimize supply chain disruptions.

f. **Energy Efficiency and Sustainability**: Optimize energy consumption, resource utilization, and environmental impact through energy-efficient technologies, sustainable practices, and eco-friendly manufacturing processes. Implement energy management systems, waste reduction initiatives, and green manufacturing practices to minimize environmental footprint and enhance sustainability.

3. **Scale-Up and Commercialization:**
   a. **Pilot Production Runs**: Conduct pilot production runs or small-scale manufacturing trials to validate the scalability, repeatability, and performance consistency of the optimized production process. Produce limited quantities of the technology under production conditions to identify and resolve scale-up challenges, process variability, and production bottlenecks.
   b. **Production Ramp-Up:** Gradually ramp up production volumes and capacities to meet increasing demand and market growth. Monitor production performance, quality metrics, and operational parameters during the ramp-up phase to ensure smooth transition and maintain product quality standards.
   c. **Cost Optimization**: Identify opportunities for cost optimization, value engineering, and cost reduction throughout the production process. Analyze cost drivers, overhead expenses, and production inefficiencies to implement cost-saving measures, supplier negotiations, and process improvements that enhance profitability and competitiveness.
   d. **Regulatory Compliance**: Ensure compliance with regulatory requirements, safety standards, and quality regulations relevant to the production process and end-use applications of the technology. Obtain necessary certifications, permits, and approvals from regulatory authorities to demonstrate compliance with applicable regulations and standards.

4. **Knowledge Transfer and Training:**

   a. **Skill Development**: Provide training, skill development programs, and knowledge transfer initiatives to equip production personnel with the necessary competencies, technical skills, and operational knowledge to execute the optimized production process effectively. Conduct training sessions, workshops, and hands-on exercises to familiarize employees with new equipment, processes, and procedures.

   b. **Documentation and Standard Operating Procedures (SOPs)**: Document standard operating procedures (SOPs), work instructions, and process documentation that outline step-by-step guidelines for executing the optimized production process. Document process parameters, equipment settings, and quality control measures to ensure consistency, repeatability, and compliance with quality standards.

   c. **Continuous Learning**: Promote a culture of continuous learning and knowledge sharing among production teams through regular feedback sessions, performance reviews, and cross-functional collaboration. Encourage employees to share best practices, lessons learned, and insights gained from process optimization initiatives to drive ongoing improvement and innovation.

Scale-Up and Technology Transfer:

Scale-up and technology transfer are critical phases in the process of transferring technology from research and development (R&D) to production. These phases involve transitioning the technology from laboratory-scale or pilot-scale development to full-scale manufacturing, ensuring that the production process is robust, efficient, and capable of meeting market demand and quality standards. Here's a detailed exploration of scale-up and technology transfer in the context of technology transfer from R&D to production:

1. **Scale-Up Process:**
   a. **Definition of Scale-Up Objectives**: Define clear objectives for the scale-up process, including production volume targets, quality specifications, and timeline milestones. Establish performance metrics, scalability criteria, and success criteria to measure progress and ensure alignment with business goals.
   b. **Process Optimization for Scale**: Optimize the production process for scalability, taking into account factors such as equipment capacity, material handling requirements, and process parameters. Identify potential scalability challenges, such as equipment limitations, process bottlenecks, and material compatibility issues, and develop strategies to address them.
   c. **Equipment Selection and Upgrading**: Select or upgrade production equipment and facilities to accommodate increased production volumes and scale-up requirements. Assess equipment performance, capacity, reliability, and maintenance requirements to ensure compatibility with the scaled-up production process.
   d. **Raw Material Sourcing and Procurement**: Identify reliable sources of raw materials, components, and supplies needed for scaled-up production. Establish supply chain relationships, procurement agreements, and quality control measures to ensure consistent and reliable supply of materials to support production scalability.
   e. **Process Validation and Verification**: Validate and verify the scaled-up production process to ensure that it meets quality standards, regulatory requirements, and performance specifications. Conduct process validation studies, equipment qualification tests, and product testing to demonstrate process robustness and consistency.

f. **Risk Assessment and Mitigation**: Conduct risk assessments to identify potential risks, hazards, and vulnerabilities associated with the scale-up process. Develop risk mitigation strategies, contingency plans, and safety protocols to minimize the impact of unforeseen events and ensure continuity of production operations.

2. **Technology Transfer Process:**

   a. **Documentation and Knowledge Transfer**: Document the production process, standard operating procedures (SOPs), and technical specifications to facilitate knowledge transfer from R&D to production teams. Compile comprehensive documentation, training materials, and instructional guides that outline key process steps, equipment requirements, and quality control measures.

   b. **Cross-Functional Collaboration**: Foster collaboration and communication between R&D, engineering, production, quality assurance, and other functional teams involved in the technology transfer process. Establish cross-functional teams, task forces, or working groups to coordinate activities, address challenges, and align objectives across departments.

   c. **Pilot Production Runs**: Conduct pilot production runs or small-scale manufacturing trials to validate the technology transfer process and assess the performance of the scaled-up production process. Monitor key performance indicators, process parameters, and product quality metrics to identify areas for improvement and optimization.

   d. **Training and Skill Development**: Provide training, skill development programs, and hands-on workshops to equip production personnel with the necessary competencies, technical skills, and operational knowledge to execute the scaled-up production process effectively. Offer training sessions on equipment operation, process control, safety protocols, and quality assurance procedures.

e. **Supplier and Vendor Engagement**: Collaborate with suppliers, vendors, and subcontractors to ensure seamless integration of components, materials, and services into the scaled-up production process. Communicate production requirements, quality standards, and delivery schedules to suppliers to minimize supply chain disruptions and ensure timely delivery of materials.

f. **Regulatory Compliance and Certification**: Ensure compliance with regulatory requirements, industry standards, and quality certifications applicable to the production process and end-use applications of the technology. Obtain necessary regulatory approvals, certifications, and permits from regulatory authorities to demonstrate compliance with safety, environmental, and quality standards.

3. **Performance Monitoring and Optimization:**

a. **Continuous Monitoring and Feedback**: Implement systems for continuous monitoring, performance measurement, and feedback collection to track the performance of the scaled-up production process. Monitor key performance indicators (KPIs), production metrics, and quality parameters to identify deviations, trends, and opportunities for improvement.

b. **Root Cause Analysis and Problem-Solving**: Conduct root cause analysis and problem-solving exercises to identify and address production issues, process inefficiencies, and quality deviations. Engage cross-functional teams in problem-solving workshops, brainstorming sessions, and root cause analysis exercises to develop corrective and preventive actions.

c. **Lean Manufacturing Principles**: Apply lean manufacturing principles, such as value stream mapping, waste reduction, and process optimization, to streamline operations, eliminate non-value-added activities, and improve efficiency in the scaled-up production process. Implement lean tools and techniques, such as 5S, kaizen, and visual management, to optimize workflow, reduce lead times, and enhance productivity.

d. **Continuous Improvement Culture**: Foster a culture of continuous improvement and operational excellence within the production team by encouraging employee engagement, empowerment, and participation in improvement initiatives. Recognize and reward employees for their contributions to process optimization, quality improvement, and cost reduction efforts.

4. **Commercialization and Market Entry:**

   a. **Market Validation and Customer Feedback**: Validate the scaled-up production process through market testing, customer feedback, and pilot deployments to ensure market acceptance and demand for the technology. Gather feedback from early adopters, pilot customers, and market stakeholders to refine product features, address user needs, and enhance customer satisfaction.

   b. **Scalability Assessment:** Assess the scalability of the production process to meet market demand and accommodate future growth opportunities. Evaluate production capacity, flexibility, and scalability to ensure that the scaled-up production process can support increased volumes, fluctuating demand, and changing market dynamics.

   c. **Supply Chain Integration and Logistics**: Integrate the scaled-up production process with upstream and downstream supply chain operations to optimize material flow, inventory management, and logistics. Collaborate with suppliers, distributors, and logistics partners to synchronize production schedules, minimize lead times, and reduce supply chain risks.

d. **Go-to-Market Strategy**: Develop a go-to-market strategy, sales plan, and distribution channels to commercialize the technology and enter the market successfully. Define target markets, customer segments, and value propositions that differentiate the technology from competitors and address unmet needs in the marketplace.

e. **Customer Support and Service**: Establish customer support mechanisms, warranty policies, and after-sales service offerings to provide ongoing support to customers and ensure satisfaction with the technology. Offer technical support, troubleshooting assistance, and product training to help customers maximize the value of the technology and address any issues or concerns.

Collaboration and Knowledge Transfer:

Collaboration and knowledge transfer are essential components of successful technology transfer from research and development (R&D) to production. Effective collaboration facilitates the exchange of expertise, resources, and best practices between R&D teams, production teams, and other stakeholders involved in the technology transfer process. Knowledge transfer ensures that valuable insights, technical know-how, and intellectual property developed during R&D are effectively communicated and applied in the production environment. Here's a detailed exploration of collaboration and knowledge transfer in technology transfer:

1. **Cross-Functional Collaboration:**

   a. **Team Integration**: Foster collaboration and teamwork between R&D, engineering, production, quality assurance, and other functional teams involved in the technology transfer process. Establish cross-functional teams or project groups to facilitate communication, coordination, and alignment of objectives across departments.

b. **Collaborative Problem-Solving**: Encourage collaborative problem-solving and decision-making to address challenges, resolve conflicts, and overcome obstacles encountered during the technology transfer process. Engage cross-functional teams in brainstorming sessions, root cause analysis, and problem-solving workshops to develop innovative solutions and drive continuous improvement.

c. **Regular Communication Channels**: Establish regular communication channels, such as meetings, status updates, and progress reports, to keep stakeholders informed about the status of technology transfer activities, milestones achieved, and upcoming tasks. Encourage open dialogue, feedback exchange, and information sharing to promote transparency and collaboration.

2. **Knowledge Transfer Mechanisms:**
   a. **Documentation and Technical Reports**: Document key findings, technical specifications, and research outcomes generated during the R&D phase in comprehensive reports, technical documentation, and research papers. Compile research data, experimental results, and design documentation to create a knowledge repository that can be accessed and utilized by production teams.

   b. **Training and Skill Development**: Provide training, workshops, and hands-on sessions to transfer technical knowledge, skills, and best practices from R&D experts to production personnel. Offer training programs on equipment operation, process control, quality assurance, and safety protocols to ensure that production teams are equipped with the necessary competencies to execute the technology transfer process effectively.

c. **On-the-Job Learning**: Facilitate on-the-job learning and knowledge transfer through mentorship, coaching, and shadowing opportunities where production personnel can learn from experienced R&D professionals. Encourage knowledge sharing, collaboration, and cross-training initiatives to build a culture of continuous learning and skill development within the organization.

d. **Technology Transfer Workshops**: Organize technology transfer workshops, knowledge exchange sessions, or technology showcases where R&D teams can demonstrate and explain the key concepts, principles, and applications of the technology to production teams. Provide hands-on demonstrations, case studies, and real-world examples to illustrate how the technology can be applied in the production environment.

3. **Collaborative Projects and Joint Initiatives:**

   a. **Joint Development Projects**: Collaborate on joint development projects, research initiatives, or collaborative partnerships that bring together R&D expertise with production capabilities to accelerate technology transfer and innovation. Pool resources, share risks, and leverage complementary strengths to address common challenges, explore new opportunities, and drive collective progress.

   b. **Technology Transfer Partnerships**: Form technology transfer partnerships, licensing agreements, or joint ventures between R&D organizations and production facilities to facilitate the transfer of technology and intellectual property rights. Establish clear roles, responsibilities, and agreements governing the terms of technology transfer, intellectual property ownership, and commercialization rights.

c. **Collaborative Problem-Solving**: Collaborate on problem-solving initiatives, process optimization projects, or quality improvement programs that involve joint efforts from R&D and production teams to enhance product quality, optimize production efficiency, and drive operational excellence. Utilize cross-functional teams, root cause analysis techniques, and continuous improvement methodologies to identify and address production challenges collaboratively.

4. **Knowledge Management and Retention:**

   a. **Knowledge Capture and Preservation**: Develop processes and tools for capturing, documenting, and preserving tacit knowledge, expertise, and lessons learned from R&D activities. Implement knowledge management systems, databases, and repositories to store, organize, and retrieve valuable information for future reference and use.

   b. **Succession Planning and Talent Development**: Invest in succession planning and talent development initiatives to ensure continuity of knowledge transfer and retention within the organization. Identify key knowledge holders, subject matter experts, and critical roles involved in technology transfer, and implement strategies to transfer knowledge to successors and future generations of employees.

   c. **Community of Practice**: Establish communities of practice, peer networks, or knowledge sharing forums where employees can exchange ideas, collaborate on projects, and share best practices related to technology transfer and production processes. Encourage participation, knowledge sharing, and cross-functional collaboration to foster a culture of continuous learning and knowledge exchange.

5. **Feedback Mechanisms and Continuous Improvement:**

    a. **Feedback Collection and Evaluation**: Solicit feedback from production teams, end-users, and stakeholders involved in the technology transfer process to assess the effectiveness of knowledge transfer efforts, identify areas for improvement, and address gaps or challenges encountered during the process. Use surveys, focus groups, and feedback mechanisms to gather insights, suggestions, and lessons learned.

    b. **Continuous Improvement Initiatives**: Implement continuous improvement initiatives, feedback loops, and performance evaluation mechanisms to drive ongoing improvement in knowledge transfer processes and collaborative practices. Analyze feedback data, performance metrics, and process outcomes to identify trends, root causes, and improvement opportunities that enhance the effectiveness and efficiency of technology transfer efforts.

    c. **Adaptive Learning and Flexibility**: Embrace adaptive learning approaches and flexibility in knowledge transfer strategies to accommodate diverse learning styles, preferences, and needs of production teams. Tailor knowledge transfer activities, training programs, and communication channels to the specific requirements and capabilities of the target audience, and adjust strategies based on feedback and performance outcomes.

Risk Management and Continual Improvement:

Risk management and continual improvement are integral aspects of technology transfer from research and development (R&D) to production. Effective risk management involves identifying, assessing, and mitigating potential risks and uncertainties associated with the technology transfer process, while continual improvement focuses on ongoing refinement and enhancement of processes, systems, and practices to optimize performance and mitigate future risks. Here's a detailed exploration of risk management and continual improvement in the context of technology transfer:

1. **Risk Management:**

    a. **Risk Identification:** Identify and categorize potential risks and uncertainties that may impact the technology transfer process, including technical risks, operational risks, regulatory risks, and market risks. Conduct risk assessments, brainstorming sessions, and risk workshops to identify and prioritize key risks based on their likelihood and potential impact on project objectives.

    b. **Risk Analysis and Assessment**: Evaluate the severity, likelihood, and consequences of identified risks using qualitative and quantitative risk assessment techniques. Assess the potential impact of risks on project timelines, budget constraints, quality standards, and stakeholder interests to determine risk tolerance levels and risk response strategies.

    c. **Risk Mitigation Strategies**: Develop risk mitigation strategies, contingency plans, and risk response actions to address identified risks and minimize their impact on the technology transfer process. Implement preventive measures, risk controls, and mitigation actions to reduce the likelihood of occurrence or severity of identified risks.

    d. **Risk Monitoring and Control**: Monitor, track, and review risk factors throughout the technology transfer process to ensure that risk mitigation measures are effective and responsive to changing conditions. Establish risk monitoring systems, early warning indicators, and performance metrics to detect emerging risks and trigger corrective actions in a timely manner.

e. **Documentation and Communication**: Document risk management plans, risk registers, and risk assessment findings to provide transparency and accountability in managing project risks. Communicate risk management strategies, mitigation plans, and risk status updates to stakeholders, project teams, and decision-makers to foster awareness, alignment, and buy-in.

2. **Continual Improvement:**

   a. **Performance Measurement and Evaluation**: Establish performance metrics, key performance indicators (KPIs), and performance targets to measure the effectiveness and efficiency of the technology transfer process. Monitor process performance, productivity levels, and quality outcomes to identify areas for improvement and track progress towards project objectives.

   b. **Root Cause Analysis**: Conduct root cause analysis, process audits, and performance reviews to identify underlying factors contributing to process inefficiencies, deviations, or quality issues. Analyze process data, trend analysis, and performance metrics to identify root causes and systemic issues that hinder performance and effectiveness.

   c. **Continuous Learning and Adaptation**: Foster a culture of continuous learning, innovation, and adaptation within the organization by encouraging feedback, experimentation, and knowledge sharing among project teams. Encourage employees to embrace new ideas, adopt best practices, and challenge the status quo to drive continual improvement and innovation in technology transfer processes.

   d. **Kaizen and Lean Practices**: Implement kaizen principles, lean methodologies, and continuous improvement tools to systematically identify, prioritize, and address process inefficiencies, waste, and non-value-added activities. Engage cross-functional teams in kaizen events, process mapping exercises, and improvement projects to streamline workflows, optimize resource utilization, and enhance process efficiency.

e. **Feedback Mechanisms and Lessons Learned**: Solicit feedback from project teams, stakeholders, and end-users involved in the technology transfer process to gather insights, lessons learned, and improvement suggestions. Conduct post-project reviews, lessons learned sessions, and retrospective analyses to capture valuable feedback and identify opportunities for process refinement and enhancement.

3. **Adaptive Management and Flexibility:**

a. **Adaptive Planning and Flexibility**: Embrace adaptive management approaches and flexibility in project planning, execution, and decision-making to respond to changing conditions, unexpected challenges, and evolving stakeholder needs. Anticipate potential disruptions, uncertainties, and external factors that may impact the technology transfer process, and develop contingency plans and alternative strategies to mitigate risks and maintain project momentum.

b. **Agile Methodologies**: Apply agile methodologies, iterative development practices, and agile project management techniques to promote flexibility, adaptability, and responsiveness in technology transfer projects. Break down project tasks into smaller, manageable iterations or sprints, and prioritize deliverables based on stakeholder feedback and changing requirements.

c. **Iterative Learning and Adaptation**: Emphasize iterative learning and adaptation throughout the technology transfer process by conducting regular reviews, retrospectives, and lessons learned sessions to reflect on progress, identify areas for improvement, and adjust strategies as needed. Encourage feedback loops, collaborative decision-making, and experimentation to facilitate continuous adaptation and improvement.

Regulatory Compliance and Certification:

Regulatory compliance and certification play a crucial role in technology transfer from research and development (R&D) to production. Compliance with relevant regulations, standards, and certifications ensures that the transferred technology meets legal requirements, quality standards, and safety regulations, enabling its successful commercialization and market entry. Here's a detailed exploration of regulatory compliance and certification in the context of technology transfer:

1. **Regulatory Landscape Assessment:**
   a. **Regulatory Analysis**: Conduct a comprehensive analysis of regulatory requirements, standards, and guidelines applicable to the technology being transferred and its intended market. Identify relevant regulatory agencies, governing bodies, and industry-specific regulations that impact the production, distribution, and use of the technology.

   b. **Regulatory Requirements Mapping**: Map out the regulatory requirements and compliance obligations relevant to the technology transfer process, including product safety, environmental regulations, quality standards, labeling requirements, and intellectual property rights. Ensure alignment with national and international regulatory frameworks governing the target market.

   c. **Risk-Based Approach**: Adopt a risk-based approach to regulatory compliance, focusing efforts on addressing high-risk areas, critical compliance requirements, and regulatory constraints that have the greatest impact on product safety, quality, and market access. Prioritize regulatory compliance activities based on risk assessment findings and compliance priorities.

2. **Regulatory Strategy Development:**

   a. **Regulatory Planning**: Develop a regulatory strategy and roadmap that outlines the regulatory pathway, submission requirements, and timeline for obtaining regulatory approvals and certifications necessary for commercialization. Define regulatory milestones, submission timelines, and resource requirements to guide regulatory compliance activities throughout the technology transfer process.

   b. **Regulatory Liaison**: Establish communication channels and engage with regulatory authorities, notified bodies, and certification agencies to seek guidance, clarification, and feedback on regulatory compliance requirements and submission processes. Build relationships with regulatory stakeholders and proactively address regulatory concerns or inquiries to expedite the regulatory review process.

   c. **Pre-Submission Consultation**: Seek pre-submission consultations or meetings with regulatory agencies to discuss regulatory strategy, submission plans, and compliance requirements. Present the technology transfer plan, risk management strategy, and quality assurance measures to regulatory authorities to gain early feedback and alignment on regulatory expectations.

3. **Compliance Documentation and Quality Assurance:**

   a. **Documentation Management**: Prepare and maintain comprehensive documentation, records, and technical files that demonstrate compliance with regulatory requirements throughout the technology transfer process. Document design specifications, manufacturing processes, quality control procedures, and validation studies to support regulatory submissions and audits.

b. **Quality Management System (QMS)**: Implement a robust quality management system (QMS) that complies with relevant quality standards, such as ISO 9001, ISO 13485, or Good Manufacturing Practice (GMP) regulations, to ensure consistency, traceability, and compliance with quality requirements. Establish procedures, work instructions, and documentation controls to maintain quality standards and regulatory compliance.

c. **Risk Management**: Integrate risk management principles, such as hazard analysis, risk assessment, and risk mitigation strategies, into the quality management system to identify, assess, and mitigate product risks associated with technology transfer and production processes. Develop risk management plans, risk registers, and risk mitigation strategies to address potential safety, efficacy, and quality risks.

d. **Change Control**: Implement change control procedures and change management processes to manage changes to the technology, production processes, or quality systems throughout the technology transfer lifecycle. Document and evaluate proposed changes, assess their impact on product quality and regulatory compliance, and obtain necessary approvals before implementing changes.

4. **Regulatory Submissions and Approvals:**

   a. **Regulatory Submissions Preparation: Prepare and submit regulatory dossiers, applications, and technical documentation** required for regulatory approvals and certifications. Compile comprehensive submission packages that include product specifications, manufacturing data, quality assurance records, and validation reports to support regulatory review and approval.

b. **Regulatory Audits and Inspections**: Prepare for regulatory audits, inspections, and assessments conducted by regulatory authorities or notified bodies to evaluate compliance with regulatory requirements and quality standards. Conduct internal audits, mock inspections, and compliance assessments to identify and address potential non-compliance issues proactively.

c. **Post-Market Surveillance:** Implement post-market surveillance systems and vigilance procedures to monitor the safety, performance, and quality of the technology following commercialization. Collect and analyze post-market data, adverse event reports, and customer feedback to identify emerging risks, product issues, and regulatory compliance concerns, and take appropriate corrective actions as needed.

5. **Certification and Market Access:**

a. **Product Certification**: Obtain necessary certifications, approvals, and regulatory clearances required for market entry and commercialization of the technology. Seek product certification marks, conformity assessments, and regulatory approvals from recognized certification bodies, notified bodies, or regulatory agencies to demonstrate compliance with applicable standards and regulations.

b. **Market Access Strategy**: Develop a market access strategy that aligns regulatory compliance efforts with commercialization objectives, market entry timelines, and target market requirements. Identify market entry barriers, import regulations, and product registration requirements in the target markets and develop strategies to address them effectively.

c. **Global Harmonization**: Leverage global harmonization initiatives, mutual recognition agreements, and harmonized standards to streamline regulatory compliance efforts and facilitate market access in multiple jurisdictions. Align regulatory submissions and compliance strategies with international standards and regulatory frameworks to expedite market entry and reduce regulatory barriers.

OPTIMIZATION OF TECHNOLOGY TRANSFER

Optimizing technology transfer is crucial for ensuring the efficient and effective dissemination of innovative technologies from research and development (R&D) to commercialization or practical application. Optimization involves streamlining processes, enhancing collaboration, and leveraging resources to maximize the impact and value of technology transfer initiatives. Here's a detailed exploration of how optimization can be achieved in technology transfer:

1. **Clear Objectives and Strategic Planning:**

   a. **Define Goals and Priorities**: Clearly articulate the objectives and desired outcomes of technology transfer initiatives, such as commercialization, innovation diffusion, or societal impact. Establishing clear goals helps focus efforts and resources on activities that align with organizational priorities and strategic objectives.

   b. **Develop Strategic Roadmaps**: Develop comprehensive technology transfer roadmaps that outline the steps, milestones, and timelines for transferring technologies from R&D to commercialization. Strategic planning enables proactive decision-making, resource allocation, and risk management throughout the technology transfer process.

2. **Streamlined Processes and Workflows:**
   a. **Standardized Procedures**: Standardize technology transfer processes, workflows, and documentation to ensure consistency, efficiency, and transparency. Establishing clear protocols for intellectual property management, licensing negotiations, and project management minimizes delays, confusion, and errors during technology transfer activities.
   b. **Automation and Digital Tools**: Leverage automation and digital tools to streamline administrative tasks, facilitate information sharing, and improve collaboration among stakeholders. Electronic document management systems, project management platforms, and licensing software can enhance productivity and communication in technology transfer operations.

3. **Effective Communication and Collaboration:**
   a. **Cross-Functional Teams**: Foster collaboration and interdisciplinary teamwork among researchers, technology transfer professionals, industry partners, and other stakeholders involved in technology transfer activities. Cross-functional teams bring together diverse perspectives, expertise, and resources to address complex challenges and accelerate innovation.
   b. **Stakeholder Engagement**: Engage stakeholders early and often throughout the technology transfer process to solicit feedback, address concerns, and build consensus. Regular communication and transparent decision-making foster trust, commitment, and alignment among all parties involved in technology transfer initiatives.

4. **Strategic Partnerships and Networking:**
   a. **Industry Engagement**: Cultivate strategic partnerships and collaborations with industry partners, investors, accelerators, and

technology transfer offices to facilitate technology commercialization and market access. Industry engagement provides valuable market insights, access to resources, and opportunities for technology validation and co-development.

b. **International Collaboration**: Explore opportunities for international collaboration and technology transfer partnerships to expand market reach, access new technologies, and leverage global expertise. International collaboration enhances innovation capacity, fosters cultural exchange, and accelerates the adoption of best practices in technology transfer.

5. **Resource Optimization and Capacity Building:**

   a. **Resource Allocation**: Optimize resource allocation and utilization to maximize the efficiency and effectiveness of technology transfer initiatives. Allocate funding, personnel, and infrastructure based on strategic priorities, market potential, and risk considerations to ensure the successful execution of technology transfer projects.

   b. **Capacity Building**: Invest in capacity building initiatives, training programs, and professional development opportunities to enhance the skills, knowledge, and capabilities of technology transfer professionals and stakeholders. Building a skilled workforce and supportive ecosystem strengthens the foundation for successful technology transfer and innovation-driven growth.

6. **Performance Monitoring and Evaluation:**

   a. **Key Performance Indicators (KPIs)**: Define and track key performance indicators (KPIs) to measure the progress, impact, and outcomes of technology transfer activities. KPIs may include metrics related to technology commercialization, intellectual property licensing, industry partnerships, and economic impact.

b. **Continuous Improvement**: Continuously evaluate and refine technology transfer processes based on performance feedback, lessons learned, and best practices. Adopt a culture of continuous improvement that encourages innovation, experimentation, and adaptation to changing market dynamics and stakeholder needs.

PRODUCTION OF TECHNOLOGY TRANSFER

The production phase in technology transfer marks the transition from the development and validation of innovative technologies to their actual manufacturing or implementation. This stage is crucial for ensuring that the transferred technology can be effectively scaled up, produced, and deployed in real-world settings. Here's a detailed exploration of the production phase in technology transfer:

1. **Scale-Up and Manufacturing Process Design:**
   a. **Scaling Strategies**: Determine the appropriate scaling strategy for the technology, considering factors such as production volume, manufacturing complexity, and resource availability. Common scaling approaches include batch processing, continuous manufacturing, or modular expansion.
   b. **Process Optimization**: Optimize manufacturing processes to improve efficiency, quality, and cost-effectiveness. Conduct thorough process characterization, optimization studies, and risk assessments to identify critical process parameters and ensure consistent performance at scale.
   c. **Equipment Selection**: Select suitable equipment, machinery, and production facilities to support the scaled-up manufacturing process. Evaluate equipment specifications, capabilities, and compatibility with the technology requirements to minimize bottlenecks and ensure smooth production operations.

2. **Quality Control and Assurance:**

a. **Quality Management Systems**: Implement robust quality management systems to maintain product quality, compliance, and consistency throughout the production process. Establish standard operating procedures (SOPs), quality control protocols, and documentation practices to monitor, verify, and document product specifications and performance.

b. **Quality Testing and Inspection**: Conduct rigorous testing, inspection, and validation activities to ensure that manufactured products meet regulatory standards, customer requirements, and performance expectations. Utilize analytical techniques, sampling plans, and statistical methods to assess product quality and identify opportunities for improvement.

3. **Supply Chain Management:**

a. **Raw Material Sourcing**: Identify reliable suppliers and sources of raw materials, components, and resources required for manufacturing the technology. Establish procurement processes, supplier agreements, and quality assurance measures to ensure the availability and quality of inputs for production.

b. **Logistics and Inventory Management**: Develop efficient logistics and inventory management systems to optimize the flow of materials, components, and finished products within the supply chain. Implement inventory tracking, just-in-time (JIT) delivery, and demand forecasting strategies to minimize lead times, reduce costs, and mitigate risks.

4. **Regulatory Compliance and Certification:**

a. **Regulatory Requirements**: Ensure compliance with regulatory standards, industry regulations, and certification requirements applicable to the technology and target markets. Engage regulatory experts, consultants, and authorities early in the production process to navigate regulatory pathways, obtain necessary approvals, and address compliance issues.

b. **Certification and Validation**: Obtain relevant certifications, approvals, and validations from regulatory agencies, standards organizations, or certifying bodies to demonstrate product safety, efficacy, and quality. Conduct validation studies, performance testing, and documentation reviews to meet regulatory requirements and gain market acceptance.

5. **Capacity Building and Training:**

a. **Workforce Development**: Invest in workforce training and development programs to build technical skills, knowledge, and expertise among production personnel. Provide training on equipment operation, process protocols, safety procedures, and quality standards to ensure competency and compliance in manufacturing operations.

b. **Technology Transfer Support**: Offer ongoing support, guidance, and assistance to production teams during the technology transfer process. Provide access to technical resources, troubleshooting assistance, and knowledge transfer activities to facilitate the successful implementation and adoption of the transferred technology.

6. **Continuous Improvement and Optimization:**

a. **Continuous Monitoring and Feedback**: Monitor production performance, collect feedback, and analyze data to identify opportunities for optimization and improvement. Implement performance metrics, key performance indicators (KPIs), and quality control measures to track progress and drive continuous improvement initiatives.

b. **Process Optimization**: Continuously evaluate and optimize manufacturing processes, equipment configurations, and supply chain operations to enhance efficiency, reliability, and cost-effectiveness. Embrace lean manufacturing principles, Six Sigma methodologies, and Kaizen practices to streamline workflows, reduce waste, and maximize value creation.

QUALITATIVE AND QUANTITATIVE TECHNOLOGY MODELS

In technology transfer, both qualitative and quantitative models play crucial roles in understanding, assessing, and facilitating the transfer of technologies from research and development (R&D) to practical application or commercialization. These models help evaluate the potential impact, feasibility, and value of transferring technologies, as well as guide decision-making and resource allocation throughout the technology transfer process. Here's a detailed exploration of qualitative and quantitative technology models in technology transfer:

1. **Qualitative Technology Models:**
   a. **Technology Readiness Levels (TRL):** TRL is a qualitative scale used to assess the maturity of a technology based on its development stage and readiness for deployment. The scale ranges from TRL 1 (basic principles observed) to TRL 9 (technology proven through successful operational deployment). TRL models help stakeholders evaluate the progress, risks, and investment needs associated with technology transfer projects.

   b. **Technology Capability Assessments**: Qualitative assessments of a technology's capabilities, features, and potential applications help stakeholders understand its strengths, limitations, and competitive advantages. Capability assessments consider factors such as technical complexity, performance metrics, intellectual property protection, and market fit to determine the suitability of the technology for transfer and commercialization.

c. **SWOT Analysis (Strengths, Weaknesses, Opportunities, Threats):** SWOT analysis is a strategic planning tool used to assess the internal strengths and weaknesses of a technology, as well as the external opportunities and threats in its target market or industry. SWOT analysis helps identify critical success factors, risks, and challenges that may impact the technology transfer process and guide decision-making.

d. **Technology Readiness Assessments**: Qualitative assessments of technology readiness consider factors such as technical feasibility, scalability, and alignment with organizational goals and priorities. Technology readiness assessments help stakeholders evaluate the readiness of a technology for transfer and identify potential barriers, gaps, or areas for improvement.

2. **Quantitative Technology Models:**

a. **Cost-Benefit Analysis (CBA)**: CBA is a quantitative method used to evaluate the economic feasibility and financial returns of technology transfer projects. CBA compares the costs associated with technology development, transfer, and commercialization against the expected benefits, such as increased revenues, cost savings, or societal impact. CBA helps stakeholders assess the value proposition and investment potential of transferring a technology.

b. **Return on Investment (ROI) Analysis**: ROI analysis quantifies the financial returns and benefits generated from investing in technology transfer initiatives. ROI considers factors such as revenue generation, cost savings, market share expansion, and intangible benefits (e.g., brand reputation, societal value) to assess the profitability and efficiency of technology transfer projects. ROI analysis helps prioritize investment decisions and allocate resources effectively.

c. **Market Forecasting and Demand Analysis**: Quantitative models for market forecasting and demand analysis help stakeholders assess the market potential, size, and growth prospects for a transferred technology. Market forecasting considers factors such as market trends, customer preferences, competitive landscape, and regulatory dynamics to estimate future demand and revenue opportunities. Market analysis guides market entry strategies, pricing decisions, and resource allocation for technology commercialization.

d. **Risk Assessment and Mitigation Models**: Quantitative risk assessment models help stakeholders identify, quantify, and mitigate risks associated with technology transfer projects. Risk assessment considers factors such as technical, financial, regulatory, and market risks to evaluate their likelihood and potential impact on project outcomes. Quantitative risk models facilitate risk prioritization, mitigation planning, and decision-making to minimize project uncertainties and maximize success.

DOCUMENTATION IN TECHNOLOGY TRANSFER

Documentation plays a vital role in technology transfer by capturing, organizing, and disseminating essential information and knowledge throughout the transfer process. Effective documentation facilitates communication, collaboration, and decision-making among stakeholders, ensuring that critical details, requirements, and responsibilities are documented and accessible. Here's a detailed exploration of documentation in technology transfer:

1. **Intellectual Property Documentation:**

a. **Patent Filings and Applications**: Documenting inventions, innovations, and discoveries through patent filings and applications is essential for protecting intellectual property rights and establishing ownership. Patent documentation includes detailed descriptions, claims, drawings, and specifications that provide a legal basis for protecting and licensing the technology.

b. **Technology Disclosure Statements**: Technology disclosure statements document the key features, applications, and potential commercial value of a technology. They provide a comprehensive overview of the technology's technical specifications, novelty, and market relevance, facilitating technology evaluation, licensing negotiations, and commercialization efforts.

2. **Technology Transfer Agreements:**

a. **Licensing Agreements**: Licensing agreements document the terms, conditions, and rights associated with the transfer of intellectual property from a technology owner (licensor) to a recipient (licensee). These agreements outline licensing fees, royalties, exclusivity clauses, sublicensing rights, and other contractual obligations to govern the use, development, and commercialization of the licensed technology.

b. **Collaborative Research and Development Agreements**: Collaborative research and development agreements document the terms, scope, and objectives of collaborative efforts between technology providers and recipients. These agreements define project milestones, deliverables, funding arrangements, and intellectual property ownership to ensure transparency, accountability, and alignment of interests among collaborators.

3. **Technical Documentation:**

a. **Technical Reports and Documentation**: Technical reports document the research findings, experimental data, methodologies, and results generated during technology development and validation. These reports provide detailed insights into the technology's performance, feasibility, and potential applications, serving as valuable reference materials for technology transfer stakeholders.

b. **Design Specifications and Protocols**: Design specifications and protocols document the technical requirements, specifications, and operating procedures for manufacturing, testing, and using the transferred technology. These documents provide guidelines for quality control, process optimization, and troubleshooting to ensure consistency, reliability, and compliance in technology transfer operations.

4. **Regulatory Documentation:**

   a. **Regulatory Filings and Submissions**: Regulatory documentation includes filings, submissions, and approvals required to comply with regulatory requirements and standards governing the development, testing, and commercialization of the transferred technology. Regulatory documentation may include applications for FDA approval, CE marking, ISO certification, or other regulatory clearances necessary for market entry.

   b. **Quality Management Documents**: Quality management documents, such as quality manuals, standard operating procedures (SOPs), and validation reports, document the quality assurance and control processes implemented throughout the technology transfer lifecycle. These documents ensure that manufacturing operations comply with regulatory standards, industry best practices, and quality management systems.

5. **Project Management Documentation:**

   a. **Project Plans and Timelines**: Project plans and timelines document the objectives, scope, milestones, and timelines for technology transfer projects. These documents outline the project's organizational structure, resource requirements, risk management strategies, and communication protocols to ensure project success and accountability.

   b. **Meeting Minutes and Progress Reports**: Meeting minutes and progress reports document the discussions, decisions, and actions taken during project meetings and milestone reviews. These documents provide a record of project status, updates, issues, and resolutions, enabling stakeholders to track progress, address challenges, and maintain project momentum.

6. **Training and Knowledge Transfer Documentation:**

   a. **Training Materials and Manuals**: Training materials and manuals document the training content, materials, and resources provided to technology transfer stakeholders, including production personnel, researchers, and collaborators. These documents support capacity building, skill development, and knowledge transfer initiatives to ensure effective implementation and adoption of transferred technologies.

   b. **Knowledge Repositories and Databases:** Knowledge repositories and databases centralize and organize relevant information, documents, and resources related to technology transfer projects. These repositories serve as repositories of institutional knowledge, lessons learned, best practices, and reference materials for future technology transfer initiatives.

Development report

A development report is a crucial component of documentation in technology transfer, providing a comprehensive overview of the research, development, and validation activities undertaken to advance a technology from its conceptual stage to a stage where it is ready for transfer and commercialization. This report serves as a formal record of the progress, findings, challenges, and outcomes of the technology development process, facilitating communication, decision-making, and knowledge transfer among stakeholders involved in the technology transfer initiative. Here's a detailed exploration of the development report in technology transfer:

1. **Purpose and Objectives:**

    a. **Define Objectives**: The development report begins by clearly defining the objectives and scope of the technology development effort. This includes outlining the intended applications, target markets, performance criteria, and key deliverables of the technology being developed.

    b. **State Purpose**: The report articulates the purpose of the development activities, whether it's to address a specific market need, solve a technical problem, or capitalize on a scientific discovery. By stating the purpose, stakeholders understand the rationale behind the development efforts and the expected benefits of the technology.

2. **Methodology and Approach:**

    a. **Describe Methodologies**: The report describes the methodologies, techniques, and approaches used in the development process. This includes outlining the experimental procedures, research methodologies, data collection methods, and analytical techniques employed to advance the technology.

    b. **Explain Iterative Processes**: Many technology development efforts involve iterative processes, where prototypes are designed, tested, and refined based on feedback and evaluation. The report explains how iterations were conducted, what changes were made, and the rationale behind those **modifications.**

3. **Research Findings and Results:**
   a. **Present Findings**: The development report presents the findings, results, and outcomes of the research and experimentation conducted during the development process. This includes summarizing experimental data, analysis results, performance metrics, and any significant discoveries or insights.
   b. **Discuss Challenges and Solutions**: Challenges encountered during the development process are also documented, along with the strategies and solutions employed to address them. This may include technical hurdles, resource constraints, regulatory issues, or unexpected outcomes that needed to be overcome.

4. **Technical Specifications and Design Details:**
   a. **Document Specifications**: Technical specifications and design details of the technology are documented in the report. This includes describing the architecture, components, functionality, and performance characteristics of the technology, as well as any design considerations or trade-offs that were made.
   b. **Provide Diagrams and Visual**s: Diagrams, schematics, flowcharts, and visual representations of the technology design are included to enhance understanding and clarity. These visuals help stakeholders visualize the technology and its components, facilitating discussions and decision-making.

5. **Validation and Testing:**
   a. **Detail Validation Activities**: The report details the validation and testing activities conducted to assess the performance, reliability, and safety of the technology. This includes describing the test

protocols, experimental setups, test results, and validation criteria used to evaluate the technology's suitability for transfer and commercialization.

   b. **Summarize Results:** The results of validation and testing efforts are summarized, highlighting any deviations from expected outcomes, areas of improvement, or validation successes. This information helps stakeholders assess the readiness and maturity of the technology for transfer.

6. **Conclusion and Recommendations:**

   a. **Provide Conclusion**: The development report concludes by summarizing the key findings, achievements, and implications of the technology development process. It highlights the significance of the research outcomes, their potential impact, and the next steps in the technology transfer journey.

   b. **Offer Recommendations**: Recommendations for future actions, investments, or refinements may be provided based on the findings and insights gleaned from the development activities. These recommendations guide decision-making and resource allocation for subsequent stages of technology transfer, such as commercialization planning or further research.

7. **References and Appendices:**

   a. **Cite References**: Any references, citations, or sources of information used in the development report are cited accurately according to a standard citation format. This allows stakeholders to verify information, access additional resources, and trace the origins of key findings or insights.

   b. **Include Appendices**: Supplementary materials, data, or documentation that support the findings and conclusions of the development report are included in the appendices. This may include raw data, experimental protocols, technical drawings, or additional analyses that provide further context or detail.

Technology transfer plan and Exhibit

In technology transfer, a technology transfer plan and exhibit are essential components of documentation that outline the strategies, processes, and activities involved in transferring a technology from research and development (R&D) to commercialization or practical application. These documents provide a roadmap for stakeholders involved in the technology transfer initiative, guiding decision-making, resource allocation, and implementation efforts. Here's a detailed exploration of the technology transfer plan and exhibit in technology transfer documentation:

1. **Technology Transfer Plan:**

    a. **Overview and Objectives**: The technology transfer plan begins with an overview of the technology being transferred and the objectives of the technology transfer initiative. This includes defining the technology's scope, intended applications, target markets, and desired outcomes.

    b. **Stakeholder Identification**: Identify key stakeholders involved in the technology transfer process, including technology owners, recipients, collaborators, funding agencies, regulatory authorities, and other relevant parties. Understand their roles, responsibilities, interests, and expectations in the technology transfer initiative.

    c. **Timeline and Milestones**: Develop a timeline that outlines the major milestones, activities, and deliverables associated with the technology transfer project. Establish realistic timelines for each phase of the transfer process, including technology assessment, negotiation, validation, commercialization, and post-transfer support.

d. **Resource Allocation and Budget**: Define the resources, funding, and budget required to support the technology transfer activities. This includes identifying personnel, equipment, facilities, funding sources, and other resources needed to execute the transfer plan effectively. Allocate resources based on project priorities, risks, and constraints.

e. **Technology Assessment and Due Diligence**: Conduct a comprehensive assessment and due diligence of the technology to evaluate its readiness, feasibility, and potential for transfer. Assess technical feasibility, market demand, intellectual property rights, regulatory compliance, and commercialization potential to identify opportunities and risks.

f. **Risk Management and Mitigation**: Identify potential risks, challenges, and barriers that may impact the success of the technology transfer project. Develop risk mitigation strategies, contingency plans, and risk management protocols to address technical, financial, regulatory, and market risks effectively.

g. **Communication and Collaboration**: Establish communication channels, protocols, and mechanisms for facilitating collaboration and information exchange among stakeholders. Define roles, responsibilities, and communication pathways to ensure transparency, accountability, and alignment of interests throughout the technology transfer process.

h. **Monitoring and Evaluation**: Define key performance indicators (KPIs), metrics, and benchmarks for monitoring and evaluating the progress and outcomes of the technology transfer initiative. Establish mechanisms for regular progress reporting, milestone reviews, and performance assessment to track project success and identify areas for improvement.

2. **Exhibit:**

   a. **Visual Representation**: The exhibit complements the technology transfer plan by providing a visual representation of key elements, relationships, and processes outlined in the plan. This may include flowcharts, diagrams, graphs, tables, or other visual aids that help stakeholders understand complex concepts, workflows, and interdependencies.

   b. **Technology Roadmap**: Present a technology roadmap that illustrates the progression of the technology transfer project over time, from initial assessment to final commercialization. The roadmap highlights major milestones, activities, dependencies, and timelines associated with each phase of the transfer process.

   c. **Organizational Structure:** Illustrate the organizational structure and roles of stakeholders involved in the technology transfer initiative. This may include depicting reporting relationships, decision-making processes, and communication channels within the project team, as well as external collaborators and partners.

   d. **Resource Allocation:** Visualize resource allocation, budget allocation, and resource dependencies associated with the technology transfer project. Use charts, graphs, or diagrams to show how resources are allocated across different activities, phases, or stakeholders, and highlight areas of resource constraints or optimization.

   e. **Risk Management Matrix**: Present a risk management matrix that categorizes and prioritizes potential risks, along with corresponding mitigation strategies and action plans. The exhibit visually represents the likelihood and impact of each risk, as well as the effectiveness of mitigation measures in reducing risk exposure.

f. **Progress Tracking**: Include visual indicators or progress trackers that show the status, completion, and performance of key activities and milestones in the technology transfer plan. This allows stakeholders to easily monitor progress, identify bottlenecks, and track project outcomes in real time.

g. **Decision Points and Gates**: Highlight decision points, review gates, and critical milestones in the technology transfer process where key decisions need to be made or progress needs to be assessed. Visualize decision criteria, approval workflows, and escalation paths to ensure timely and informed decision-making throughout the project lifecycle.

Multiple-Choice Questions (MCQs)

1. What does technology transfer primarily involve?

    A) The movement of people between companies

    B) Transferring funds from one department to another

    C) The transfer of knowledge, technologies, skills, or innovations

    D) Purchasing new technologies from vendors

2. Which of the following is NOT a type of technology transfer?

    A) Intra-organizational Transfer

    B) Inter-organizational Transfer

    C) International Transfer

    D) Intergalactic Transfer

3. What is a common challenge in technology transfer?

    A) Simplified communication processes

    B) Intellectual Property Rights

    C) Decreased market demand

    D) Overabundance of resources

4. Which stakeholder is typically not directly involved in technology transfer?

A) Technology Owners

B) Recipients or Licensees

C) Customers

D) Intermediaries

5. What is the main motivation behind commercialization and market access in technology transfer?

A) Decreasing the organization's revenue

B) Reducing the number of employees

C) Expanding market reach and revenue generation

D) Limiting knowledge dissemination

6. Which method is not a best practice in technology transfer?

A) Developing Clear Policies and Procedures

B) Ignoring partnership opportunities

C) Building Strategic Partnerships

D) Promoting Open Innovation

7. What type of technology transfer includes academia-industry collaborations?

A) Intra-organizational Transfer

B) Inter-organizational Transfer

C) International Transfer

D) Informal Transfer

8. Which is a key component of the R&D process in technology development?

A) Avoiding stakeholder engagement

B) Skipping the prototyping stage

C) Data Analysis and Interpretation

D) Limiting communication with partners

9. What is crucial to the commercialization phase of technology transfer?

A) Reducing market analysis

B) Ignoring customer feedback

C) Intellectual Property Management

D) Decreasing product quality

10. What represents the final stage of technology readiness levels (TRL)?

    A) TRL 1

    B) TRL 5

    C) TRL 7

    D) TRL 9

11. In the context of technology transfer, what is an important aspect of regulatory compliance?

    A) Avoiding standard procedures

    B) Failing to meet industry standards

    C) Documentation Management

    D) Reducing quality management

12. What is not a method used for optimizing technology transfer?

    A) Standardizing procedures

    B) Automating processes

    C) Limiting stakeholder engagement

    D) Defining goals and priorities

13. Which is not considered a quantitative model in technology transfer?

    A) Cost-Benefit Analysis (CBA)

    B) Return on Investment (ROI) Analysis

    C) Market Forecasting and Demand Analysis

    D) Technology Readiness Levels (TRL)

14. What role do Technology Transfer Offices (TTOs) play in technology transfer?

    A) Managing food services

    B) Facilitating technology transfer activities

    C) Reducing product development

    D) Overseeing recreational activities

15. What does a SWOT analysis in technology transfer help identify?

A) Only strengths

B) Only weaknesses

C) Only opportunities

D) Strengths, Weaknesses, Opportunities, Threats

16. What is critical during the 'Scale-Up and Technology Transfer' phase?

A) Reducing production

B) Ignoring market demand

C) Equipment Selection and Upgrading

D) Decreasing quality standards

17. Which of the following is not typically involved in the production phase of technology transfer?

A) Quality Control and Assurance

B) Supply Chain Management

C) Reducing regulatory compliance

D) Capacity Building and Training

18. In the development of technology through R&D, what does 'Iterative Design' involve?

A) Finalizing designs in the first attempt

B) Repeatedly refining and testing designs

C) Using a single prototype without modifications

D) Avoiding feedback from users

19. What is the role of 'Documentation' in technology transfer?

A) To complicate communication

B) To track progress and facilitate decision-making

C) To avoid recording any processes or results

D) To limit knowledge sharing among stakeholders

20. What is not a focus of 'Funding and Support' in technology transfer?

A) Seeking government grants

B) Developing partnerships

C) Ignoring financial planning

D) Engaging venture capital

Short Answer Type Questions

1. Define technology transfer and its importance in modern industry.

2. What is a technology transfer agreement and what does it typically include?

3. Explain the role of intellectual property in technology transfer.

4. What is the difference between intra-organizational and inter-organizational technology transfer?

5. List three key stakeholders involved in the technology transfer process and their roles.

6. How does technology readiness level (TRL) impact technology transfer?

7. Describe two challenges commonly faced during technology transfer.

8. What are technology transfer offices (TTOs) and what functions do they serve?

9. Explain the significance of collaboration in technology transfer.

10. What is a licensing agreement in the context of technology transfer?

11. How can market analysis benefit technology transfer processes?

12. Identify and explain one method for managing intellectual property during technology transfer.

13. What role do regulatory standards play in technology transfer?

14. How does risk management integrate into the technology transfer process?

15. What is the purpose of a pilot production run in technology transfer?

16. Discuss the impact of digital tools on technology transfer.

17. What is meant by 'commercialization' in technology transfer?

18. Explain the concept of 'scale-up' in manufacturing related to technology transfer.

19.Describe the role of quality assurance in the technology transfer process.

20.What factors should be considered when selecting equipment for producing a transferred technology?

Long Answer Type Questions

1. Discuss the process of developing a technology transfer plan and what key elements it should contain.

2. Describe the typical steps involved in the technology assessment phase of technology transfer and explain their importance.

3. Explain how technology transfer contributes to innovation within an industry and give examples of possible outcomes.

4. Detail the process and importance of stakeholder engagement in successful technology transfer.

5. Describe the role and impact of international collaboration in technology transfer, including any challenges and benefits.

6. Explain the process of regulatory compliance in technology transfer and why it is critical for the successful commercialization of technology.

7. Discuss the various types of documentation required in technology transfer and their purposes.

8. Outline the role of continuous improvement in the technology transfer process and how it can be achieved.

9. Describe how intellectual property management is handled in multinational technology transfer projects.

10.Discuss the importance of resource optimization during technology transfer and strategies to effectively manage resources.

Answer Key

1. (C) The transfer of knowledge, technologies, skills, or innovations

2. (D) Intergalactic Transfer

3. (B) Intellectual Property Rights

4. (C) Customers

5. (C) Expanding market reach and revenue generation

6. (B) Ignoring partnership opportunities

7. (B) Inter-organizational Transfer

8. (C) Data Analysis and Interpretation

9. (C) Intellectual Property Management

10.(D) TRL 9

11.(C) Documentation Management

12.(C) Limiting stakeholder engagement

13.(D) Technology Readiness Levels (TRL)

14.(B) Facilitating technology transfer activities

15.(D) Strengths, Weaknesses, Opportunities, Threats

16.(C) Equipment Selection and Upgrading

17.(C) Reducing regulatory compliance

18.(B) Repeatedly refining and testing designs

19.(B) To track progress and facilitate decision-making

20.(C) Ignoring financial planning